Virtual Teams

by Tara Powers, MS

for **dummies**®

A Wiley Brand

Virtual Teams For Dummies®

Published by: **John Wiley & Sons, Inc.,** 111 River Street, Hoboken, NJ 07030-5774, www.wiley.com

Copyright © 2018 by John Wiley & Sons, Inc., Hoboken, New Jersey

Published simultaneously in Canada

For general information on our other products and services, please contact our Customer Care Department within the U.S. at 877-762-2974, outside the U.S. at 317-572-3993, or fax 317-572-4002. For technical support, please visit https://hub.wiley.com/community/support/dummies

Wiley publishes in a variety of print and electronic formats and by print-on-demand. Some material included with standard print versions of this book may not be included in e-books or in print-on-demand. If this book refers to media such as a CD or DVD that is not included in the version you purchased, you may download this material at http://booksupport.wiley.com. For more information about Wiley products, visit www.wiley.com.

Library of Congress Control Number: 2018946893

ISBN 978-1-119-45380-2 (pbk); ISBN 978-1-119-453789-6 (ebk); 978-1-119-45378-9 (ebk)

Manufactured in the United States of America

C10002111_070218

Contents at a Glance

Introduction 1

Part 1: Getting Started with Virtual Teams 5

CHAPTER 1: The Big Picture of Virtual Teams 7

CHAPTER 2: Envisioning Virtual Teams in Your Business............. 23

CHAPTER 3: Preparing for Your Career as a Virtual Team Member............. 45

Part 2: Building a Strong Virtual Team...................... 73

CHAPTER 4: Planning Ahead for Your Team's Success................. 75

CHAPTER 5: Finding and Hiring the Right People 93

CHAPTER 6: Contracting with Contract Workers.................... 113

CHAPTER 7: Structuring and Assembling Your Team................. 123

Part 3: Creating and Nurturing a Productive Team Culture.................................... 143

CHAPTER 8: Making Work Culture Considerations................... 145

CHAPTER 9: Managing Differences in Gender, Generation, and Culture 161

CHAPTER 10: Transitioning from Old-School Manager to Virtual Team Leader 175

Part 4: Getting Your Team Rolling 189

CHAPTER 11: Establishing Best Practices of Engagement 191

CHAPTER 12: Building Trust and Rapport.......................... 207

CHAPTER 13: Adopting Best Practices in Communication....................... 225

CHAPTER 14: Measuring Virtual Team and Team Member Success 245

CHAPTER 15: Training Your Virtual Team 253

CHAPTER 16: Checking All Things Technology: What You Need to Know 265

CHAPTER 17: Rolling with the Changes............................ 281

Part 5: Best Practices in Managing Your Virtual Team 293

CHAPTER 18: Leading by Example 295

CHAPTER 19: Understanding What Drives Motivation 305

CHAPTER 20: Managing Workflow and Execution........................... 319

Part 6: The Part of Tens.................................. 327

CHAPTER 21: Ten Predictors of Virtual Team Success 329

CHAPTER 22: Ten Signs Your Organization Is Ready for Virtual Teams........... 335

Index 341

Table of Contents

INTRODUCTION 1

About This Book. 1

Foolish Assumptions. 3

Icons Used in This Book 4

Where to Go from Here 4

PART 1: GETTING STARTED WITH VIRTUAL TEAMS 5

CHAPTER 1: **The Big Picture of Virtual Teams**. 7

Embracing the New Virtual Team Reality. 8

Why virtual teams are rapidly growing. .8

Globalization effect 9

Generational worker shift 11

Sorting Out Virtual Team Concepts 11

Understanding the Benefits and Challenges. 12

Noting virtual benefits 13

Considering virtual drawbacks 14

Jumping into the Virtual Workforce 16

Having the right environment 16

Maintaining balance and focus 16

Building community 16

Connecting using collaborative technology. 17

Appreciating team culture 18

Practicing emotional intelligence 18

Assembling a Virtual Team. 18

Managing a Virtual Team 19

CHAPTER 2: **Envisioning Virtual Teams in Your Business** 23

Contemplating Using Virtual Teams 24

Thinking about these key factors 25

Embracing the challenges: The five flaws of virtual teams 27

Deciding Whether Virtual Teams Make Good Business Sense. 29

Finding a place for virtual teams. 30

Counting the real ROI savings 31

Winning the recruitment and retention war 32

Impacting the environment 33

Deciding on Your Plan. 34

Defining purpose and goals. 34

Figuring out the roles to fill 35

Communicating about virtual team adoption. 37

Setting Up Your Virtual Team for Success 38
        Having the right resources in place 38
        Arranging your remote office 39
        Establishing communication expectations 39
    Paying Attention to What You Need. 40
        Size matters: small versus large teams 40
        Choosing the right technology. 41
    Creating Connection and Community 41
        Connecting your virtual team to the larger organization 42
        Connecting virtual team members to each other. 42
        Fighting isolationism on your virtual team 43

CHAPTER 3: **Preparing for Your Career as a Virtual
            Team Member**. 45
    Deciding If Working Virtually Is Right for You .46
        Eyeing why virtual work is so attractive 46
        Recognizing the personal impacts of working virtually 48
        Predicting whether you'll excel as a virtual team member 50
        Assessing your skills for virtual freelance work 52
    Proposing Virtual Work to Your Boss and Teammates 52
        Preparing your proposal 52
        Focusing on the benefits 56
        Addressing key concerns 58
    Determining Whether You Have a Workspace That Works. 60
        Working from home 61
        Considering hoteling. 62
        Becoming a globe-trotter 65
    Creating Your Remote Worker Brand. 66
        Reworking your resume 66
        Building your portfolio 67
        Establishing your online presence 68
        Keeping current on the latest communication
        and collaboration tools. 69
        Shopping for virtual worker–friendly clientele 70
        Focusing on healthy work-life balance 71

PART 2: BUILDING A STRONG VIRTUAL TEAM. 73

CHAPTER 4: **Planning Ahead for Your Team's Success** 75
    Defining Your Team Purpose. 76
        Aligning with company vision and values 76
        Communicating why your team exists. 78
        Having clarity around team priorities. 80
        Considering what you want your team to be known for. 81

Choosing a Team Framework 82
    Using a framework that builds trust and mutual respect 82
    Letting your team decide 85
Establishing Team Goals: What Does Success Look Like? 85
    Aligning virtual team goals with company goals 86
    Setting goals that are motivating, inspiring, and purposeful 87
    Understanding what resources are needed
    to achieve team goals 88
Determining Team Member Roles 89
    Ensuring team members understand their roles
    and why they're important 90
    Incorporating systems thinking to support how
    your team works together 91

CHAPTER 5: Finding and Hiring the Right People 93
Attracting Your Virtual Team Talent 94
    Making your business attractive to teleworkers 95
    Composing virtual worker–friendly job ads .95
    Recruiting Online 96
Hiring Based on Skill, Behavior, and Fit 97
    Hiring for skill 98
    Hiring for behavioral competencies and interests 98
    Hiring for cultural fit 100
Seeking Out the Right Qualities in Virtual Team Members 101
    Determine whether they're self-directed 102
    Be on the lookout for strong communication skills 102
    Specify the importance of engagement 103
Holding the Candidate Interview 105
    Preparing for the interview 105
    Knowing what and what not to ask 105
    Discussing your expectations and theirs up front 107
    Evaluating responses 108
Checking Out the Past 109
    Reviewing work samples 109
    Contacting references 109
Making an Offer 110

CHAPTER 6: Contracting with Contract Workers 113
Deciding Whether You Need a Contract 114
    Differentiating between an employee and
    independent contractor 114
    Figuring out a worker's status if you still aren't sure 116

Choosing to Work with an IC: What You Need to Do 116
    Checking credentials. 117
    Keeping records. 117
    Knowing what to include in a contract. 118
    Specifying compensation 119
    Understanding insurance requirements for ICs 120
    Clarifying contractor status 120
Requiring a Nondisclosure Agreement (NDA) or Not. 121
Navigating the Legalities of Noncompete Agreements 122

CHAPTER 7: **Structuring and Assembling Your Team**. 123
Organizing Your Team the Smart Way. 124
    How teams are structured. 124
    The importance of frameworks. 125
Focusing on the Onboarding Process. 125
    Creating an onboarding process that works for your team 126
    Using the buddy system. 128
    Focusing on the first 90 days. 130
Establishing Team Values As Your Bumper Rails 132
    Defining your team values. 132
    Living your team values. 135
Identifying Team Traits That Build Cohesiveness. 137
    Having clear expectations for success 137
    Getting real with feedback and accountability 138
    Rotating leadership. 140

**PART 3: CREATING AND NURTURING
A PRODUCTIVE TEAM CULTURE** 143
CHAPTER 8: **Making Work Culture Considerations** 145
Grasping Why Company Culture Is Key 146
    Recognizing toxic cultures and the mess they create 147
    Identifying a healthy culture and how to build
    one that thrives 149
Taking Note of Your Existing Organizational Culture. 150
    Commanding culture 151
    Energizing culture 152
    Supportive culture. 152
    Analytical culture. 152
Deciding What You Want Your Culture to Be 153
Building and Maintaining the Culture You Want 155
    Establishing principles to guide mindset and behavior. 155
    Putting the right HR policies in place 156
    Pinpointing culture champions. 157

Noting the Benefits and Challenges of a Cross-Cultural Team......158
    Benefits of a cross-cultural team 159
    Challenges of a cross-cultural team 160

CHAPTER 9: **Managing Differences in Gender, Generation, and Culture** 161
Managing Gender Differences................................162
    Recognizing gender benefits 162
    Eradicating gender bias 163
Connecting with the Generations on Your Team 165
    Working with all generations...............................165
    Tapping the power of baby boomers.........................166
    Redirecting Generation X 166
    Tuning in to the high-tech Millennial 167
    Meeting the new kids on the block: Generation Z 168
Building Your Cultural Intelligence 168
    Getting to know your team members 169
    Sharing culture norms 170
    Practicing cultural sensitivity 171
    Offering cross-cultural training 173

CHAPTER 10: **Transitioning from Old-School Manager to Virtual Team Leader** 175
Recognizing Which Leadership Style Works Best 176
    Examining what makes virtual team leaders succeed 176
    Determining if you're a micromanager, coach, or hands-off manager....................................179
    Comparing control-based and trust-based leadership 181
Playing in Your Sandbox.....................................183
    Pushing the boundaries of culture and C-level expectations 183
    Knowing when to manage up 184
Recognizing Common Virtual Team Issues 185
    Poor communication......................................186
    Lack of clarity, direction, and priorities 186
    Loss of team spirit and morale 187
    Lack of trust 187
    Lack of social interaction 187
    Tech issues...188
    Cultural clashes 188

PART 4: GETTING YOUR TEAM ROLLING....................189

CHAPTER 11: **Establishing Best Practices of Engagement**........191

Addressing Personal Disengagement.........................192
Having a Meaningful Team Purpose.........................193
Clarifying the why and how team members contribute 194
Identifying values on your virtual team 195
Recognizing virtual values 196
Using Clear Goals and Expectations to Build Engagement........197
Building Your Road Map Together with Team Agreements 198
Understanding the top areas to cover in your
team agreements 198
Building your agreement virtually........................199
Conducting Virtual Meetings That Have an Impact 201
Ensuring full participation and engagement.................202
Managing tech issues 203
Practicing Virtual Meeting Etiquette 205

CHAPTER 12: **Building Trust and Rapport**.........................207

Getting Started: What You Can Do to Build (or Repair) Trust.......208
Tallying the Leadership Trust Scorecard 210
Setting the stage for trust to exist.......................211
Practicing behaviors that build cohesiveness.................212
Leveraging Team Member Strengths.......................215
Discover your own strengths first.......................216
Recognize the strengths of team members 216
Create opportunity for people to work on a project together... 216
Making Respect a Nonnegotiable 217
Act as if you're all virtual...........................217
Gain understanding from each other......................217
Discourage cliques 217
Address mistakes together 218
Practicing Cultural Appreciation on Global Teams................218
Giving Team Members Face Time.........................219
Recognizing the importance of "in real life" (IRL) meetings......220
Getting up to speed on IRL best practices...................221
Creating a Connection Culture That Transforms Trust 223

CHAPTER 13: **Adopting Best Practices in Communication**.......225

Identifying Four Components to Transform
Your Communications 226
Looking Closer at Text-Only Communication 228
Examining the pros 228
Considering the cons 229
Using text-only communication effectively 230

Providing Consistent and Frequent Feedback 231
    Establishing clear expectations 231
    Recognizing the importance of two-way feedback
    and performance discussions 232
    Giving feedback: The how-to 233
    Shifting focus from individual accountability to
    team accountability. 234
Establishing Best Practices with Communication Agreements 235
    Choosing appropriate communication methods 235
    Agreeing on expected response times. 235
    Setting the rules for handling conflicts. 238
    Choosing a problem-solving model 238
    Agreeing on a process for communicating outside the team. . . .239
    Putting together your plan. 240
    Establishing standards for meeting participation. 241
Utilizing the DISC Assessment Tool 242

CHAPTER 14: **Measuring Virtual Team and Team Member
Success** 245
Tracking Virtual Team Success 246
    Knowing what to track 247
    Recognizing the importance of tools when tracking 247
    Using data to coach your team members .248
Measuring Data That Matters 249
    Looking at the results from an executive point of view. 249
    Interpreting performance from a virtual team
    leader perspective. 249
    Evaluating performance as a virtual team member. 250
Recognizing the Engagement Levels of Your Team Members 251

CHAPTER 15: **Training Your Virtual Team** 253
Training during the First 90 Days 254
    Assigning a mentor to instill culture 255
    Utilizing communication tools for training 255
    Sharing information about your company .256
    Being organized and following up. 256
Keeping Your Team Members on Top of Their Game
with Ongoing Training 257
    Using online training. 258
    Paying attention to trends and practicing innovation:
    VR and AR 259
    Using teach-backs to build cohesion and
    advance understanding and mastery. 260
    Evaluating training effectiveness. 260
    Supporting team members who are struggling 262
    Tackling technology issues. 263
Training Your Veteran Team Members 263

CHAPTER 16: **Checking All Things Technology: What You Need to Know** 265

Assessing the Right Fit for Your Team 266
Focus on the problem, not the technology 266
Avoid jumping on the latest trendy tool. 267
Make a checklist of features 268
Go with tools that your team loves. 269
Include your IT department or tech guru in your decision 269
Choosing Only the Essential Tools Your Team Needs 271
Collaboration suites 272
Project management tracking 272
Workflow management and time tracking 273
Shared calendars 273
Meeting tools 274
Flash polling 274
Brainstorming 274
Social media 275
File sharing 275
Cloud collaboration 275
Mobile options 276
Videoconferencing 276
Chat and instant messaging 276
Training Team Members for Success 276
Using mentoring to help virtual team members
get up to speed 277
Introducing tools strategically 277

CHAPTER 17: **Rolling with the Changes** 281

Adjusting to Shifts in Team Membership 281
Boosting emotional resilience 282
Using consistent communication to get on track quickly 283
Regrouping around team goals, values, and priorities 284
Building Relationships as a New Leader 284
Onboarding strategies for a new leader 285
Sharing cultural norms and styles 285
Getting on Board with a New Team Goal 286
Discussing the why 286
Acknowledging successes and letting go 287
Grounding Your Team after a Reorganization 287
Recognizing the stages of change 288
Practicing empathy and understanding 288

PART 5: BEST PRACTICES IN MANAGING YOUR VIRTUAL TEAM 293

CHAPTER 18: Leading by Example 295

Building a Connection Culture............................295
    Being a leader your team wants to follow..................296
    Getting to know your team members 296
    Reaching out and building rapport.......................298
Focusing On a Healthy Lifestyle 300
    Staying healthy when working virtually 300
    Starting your team wellness 301
    Maintaining boundaries 302
Discovering Your Legacy...............................303
    Figuring out your legacy..............................303
    Leading authentically: The how-to.....................304

CHAPTER 19: Understanding What Drives Motivation 305

Differentiating between Engaged and Passionate Team Members ..306
Creating a Passionate Team 307
    The need to be respected 307
    The need to learn and grow...........................308
    The need to be an insider.............................309
    The need to do meaningful work 310
    The need to be on a winning team......................310
Using Positive Psychology to Create a Motivational Team Environment...312
    Understanding what really motivates people 312
    Using recognition as a powerful motivational technique 314

CHAPTER 20: Managing Workflow and Execution 319

Starting Off on the Right Foot 319
Clarifying How Work Flows through the Team 320
    Deciding on meeting formats to stay up-to-date 321
    Establishing communication guidelines.....................322
    Choosing the right collaborative tracking tools for your team....322
Delegating Effectively to Your Virtual Team 322
    Eyeing the benefits to letting go 323
    Understanding why delegation fails: Leaders don't let go 323
    Trusting in the process...............................324
    Holding team members accountable for deliverables.........325
Knowing How to Communicate Externally Regarding Team Progress 325

PART 6: THE PART OF TENS..............................327

CHAPTER 21: **Ten Predictors of Virtual Team Success** 329
Having the Right Technology....................................329
Hiring the Right Team Leader 330
Hiring the Right Team Members.............................330
Establishing Clear Team Vision and Values.................331
Aligning Team Goals with Company Goals 331
Having a Solid Team Agreement in Place 332
Using a Communication Strategy 332
Agreeing on a Process for Team Workflow 333
Using an Onboarding Strategy for New Team Members 333
Actively Managing Executive Perceptions 333

CHAPTER 22: **Ten Signs Your Organization Is Ready
for Virtual Teams** 335
Having Champions on the Executive Team.....................336
Having Empowered Leaders 336
Leveraging a Supportive Culture............................336
Willing to Invest in Technology 337
Addressing Issues Early 337
Being Prepared for the Logistical Set Up 337
Keeping the Team Focused 338
Using an Onboarding Process...............................338
Training Virtual Team Leaders..............................338
Having a Clear Idea of Roles and Responsibilities 339

INDEX 341

Introduction

Remote work options are driving workplace transformation, and what's known about the office, teamwork, and management will never be the same. In fact, over the next few years, some sources estimate that more than a billion people will work virtually.

New technologies are released everyday to keep people connected across cities, countries, and oceans. Collaborative software, videoconferencing, and online project management are designed to help remote teams of people work effectively together. But not just technology is fueling this trend — rising operational costs, growing commercial real estate expenses, and increasing globalization are other contributors, as well as the promise of higher productivity. Plus, as most hiring managers would probably tell you, the competition for finding and keeping skilled employees is fierce, so extending the geographic reach of your labor force is a huge benefit.

I wrote *Virtual Teams For Dummies* to help you discover everything you need to know about virtual teams and how to make them work. This book represents findings from my own research on virtual teams, my consulting work with virtual teams, and my experiences leading a virtual team for close to ten years. As a result, this book is chockfull with extensive tips, tools, frameworks, lessons learned, models, and checklists to help make your venture into the virtual team world successful.

Companies around the globe are launching headfirst into establishing virtual teams with barely a backward glance at the unique challenges for executives, leaders, and team members. *Virtual Teams For Dummies* provides you best practices, helps you overcome the unique challenges, and allows you to experience all the positive impacts that virtual teams have to offer.

About This Book

New books and information about working on and leading virtual teams are readily available, mostly because virtual teams are quickly becoming one of the most common ways people work together on short-term projects or as intact teams for national or global companies. What makes this book unique is that I look at the world of virtual teams from a holistic perspective; I walk you through the steps of considering virtual teams as a business strategy, understanding why they're good for the planet and people, starting your career as a remote worker, making technology decisions that align with your team values, setting up and leading your global virtual team, and more.

This handy guide answers many questions and concerns that are unique to virtual teams such as:

>> How do you interview candidates properly when you aren't face-to-face?

>> How do you instill a sense of team when working globally?

>> How do you build cross-cultural IQ and appreciation?

>> How do you ensure team members feel like part of the company and fit into the corporate culture?

>> How do you implement training across oceans, cultures, and languages?

>> How do you prepare managers to supervise and lead a team they've never met face-to-face?

>> How do you position yourself and your skills to get hired for a remote opportunity?

When reading this book, keep an open mind for the subtle, yet unique challenges that virtual teams create. Of course, some common practices build trust and cohesion on teams regardless if they work in the same office or on a virtual team, but some of those common practices need more focus, priority, and time when working virtually. A few of the top virtual team nuances that I cover in this book include:

>> **Communication:** Although communication and engagement are common challenges for any team, differences in time zones and lack of face-to-face interactions contribute to the unique challenges of working virtually.

>> **Face-to-face meetings:** Virtual teams who get together in person regularly are able to realize peak effectiveness. However, for teams who are unable to do so because of budgetary or geographic restrictions, technology offers strategies for bringing teams together face-to-face.

>> **Accountability:** Creating accountability, even for a virtual team, is critical for team success. A variety of feedback tools can help team members with continuous feedback on responsiveness, communication, workload, participation level, and engagement.

- >> **Training on technology:** Virtual teams need extensive training on the tech tools that keep them connected. They need full mastery of the technology in order to realize the benefits of virtual team effectiveness and productivity.

- >> **Agreements:** Virtual teams that set standards for how they work together and have strong levels of trust are more likely to be effective.

- >> **Connection:** Establishing connection and building trust virtually takes a commitment of time and attention by the team leader and all team members.

- >> **Cultural IQ:** Virtual teams need expert guidance and training on an ongoing basis and *during every step of their development* from start-up to maturity in order to establish sensitivity and understanding around language and cultural differences.

Finally, throughout this book, I include interviews with companies and people who are doing remarkable work with virtual teams, so be sure to read the sidebar interviews for some juicy thought leadership.

Foolish Assumptions

I make some assumptions about you, the reader, and the help you're looking for. I assumed that you are either:

- >> An executive interested in discovering the pros and cons about virtual teams and making a decision about using them in your business.

- >> A virtual team leader already in the role or moving toward managing a virtual team for the first time and looking for support and coaching on how to do it successfully.

- >> A virtual team member or wannabe remote worker who:

  - Desperately wants to create a virtual work arrangement with your current employer, but you're afraid it will never happen

  - Is searching for your next virtual gig and need tips for improving your online presence

  - Has specialized skills and is looking for work on a global project team

  - Is interested in how to bring ideas to your team to build more trust and cohesion

If you fit any of these descriptions, then the practical and applicable tips, tools, and resources in this book will be immediately helpful.

Icons Used in This Book

Like any *For Dummies* book, I place helpful icons that alert you to something you don't want to miss. Here is what the icons mean:

TIP

These are best practices or steps that you want to consider using and implementing to have a successful virtual work experience.

REMEMBER

This icon marks essential information that you don't want to forget.

WARNING

Be aware of and avoid these common pitfalls.

Where to Go from Here

If you've read a *For Dummies* book before, you know that it's written in a modular format, which means that you can read any chapter that meets your need at the time and get valuable information that can help you, rather than reading the book cover to cover. If you're unsure of where to start, I suggest you start reading from the beginning to discover all the aspects, benefits, and challenges of virtual teams regardless of your position, issue, or situation.

If you're unsure, allow me to offer some suggestions. Depending on your interest in virtual teams, you may find that different chapters benefit you more than others. For example, if you're considering virtual teams for your business or starting your career as a remote worker, then Part 1 on getting started is exactly what you need. If you're launching your first virtual team, reading Part 2 on building a strong team is essential. Everything you need to know about building a strong team culture is in Part 3. If you're interested in the best ideas for building engagement, trust, and collaboration on your virtual team, then Part 4 is the place to go. Don't miss best practices for managing your virtual team in Part 5.

You don't have to read every chapter in the book to get value. Rather, use the table of contents and index as your guides for where to go next. I hope that this book provides you with the tools and techniques you need to make virtual teams and virtual work an important part of your life and your company.

You can also check out the book's Cheat Sheet at www.dummies.com. Just search "virtual teams" for more information to help you in your future endeavors with virtual teams.

1
Getting Started with Virtual Teams

Explore the reasons for the phenomenal rise of virtual teams and remote work around the world.

Consider the pros and cons of using remote workers and virtual teams in your company.

Discover how to set up your virtual team business strategy and prepare your leaders and teams for this new way of work.

Get tips on how to dive into a career as a remote employee, including setting up your virtual office and building your personal brand.

Understand the big picture of what it takes to set up your virtual teams for success.

» Defining virtual teams

» Weighing the pros and cons of going virtual

» Considering going virtual as a career move

» Putting together a virtual team

» Leading a virtual team

Chapter **1**

The Big Picture of Virtual Teams

Companies around the world are currently experiencing one of the greatest shifts in how work gets done around the world. It impacts the way people connect, the way teams communicate, the way leaders build relationships, and the way organizations accomplish results. It can be a positive change for people, the planet, and company profits if approached mindfully and designed to embrace technology, prioritize communication and relationships, and support a strong appreciation of culture and diversity. This transformation is the rise of the virtual team.

In the global marketplace, people can work practically anywhere and anytime. Virtual teams cut across the boundaries of time, space, culture, and sometimes organizations. In fact, every single day more companies are relying on virtual teams to achieve significant business results. Rising costs, global locations, and advances in technology are top reasons why virtual teams have increased by 800 percent worldwide over the past five years alone. Some sources now estimate that more than a billion people will work virtually in the next few years. According to the World Economic Forum, virtual work is one of the biggest drivers of transformation in the workplace, and everyday new collaborative software, videoconferencing, and online project management software is being released for you and I to consume. Remarkably, the majority of virtual team leaders and team members have been given little to no preparation to work in this complex and diverse environment that creates a vast opportunity for supporting companies, leaders, and teams who are moving toward this diverse reality.

This chapter gives you a broad overview of virtual teams, including the variety of ways they are defined as well as emerging technology that is having an impact. I take a high-level look at the pros and cons of virtual teams and help you to think about whether or not working on a virtual team is a career option you want to consider. If you're a company or leader preparing to lead a virtual team, this chapter can provide a head start into the virtual world.

Embracing the New Virtual Team Reality

All aboard! The proverbial virtual team train has left the station and there's no going back. Many organizations are using virtual or dispersed teams to reduce costs, connect talent across geographical boundaries, manage global projects, and improve productivity and collaboration. Not to mention that going virtual is a huge boon for corporate sustainability efforts — reducing greenhouse gases, gasoline consumption, and pollution. Virtual work also means that people can work from anywhere, anytime, which can help unemployment rates among the disabled, military families, people with special needs, and people living in places where a once-booming industry has disappeared, such as coal mining, auto manufacturing, steel, textiles, and more.

The use of virtual teams is continuing to grow and companies around the world must recognize the unique challenges of virtual teams and invest in ongoing training and support to realize the benefits. If managed well, you can expect virtual teams to be highly engaged, accountable, successful at collaborative brainstorming, goal setting, problem solving, and planning. These sections explain the reasons for virtual team growth and the global impacts that they have on the workplace.

Why virtual teams are rapidly growing

What's really happening that is causing virtual teams to quickly become such a natural part of the workplace today? The following looks at it from a couple different viewpoints:

REMEMBER

>> **Employer:** Virtual workers will save your company a whole lot of money, on everything from reduced sick time and absenteeism due to weather to office maintenance expenses. Refer to Chapter 2 for more discussion on the wide array of savings.

Access to talent is another reason many employers are going the virtual route. When you need specialized knowledge or experience that you can't find in your local talent pool, virtual work opportunities allow you to recruit anywhere in the world. Talk about competitive advantage!

>> **Employee:** Many employees have demands that require them to spend hours commuting to work. They end up missing their kids' activities and don't have time for self-care or work-life balance. As a result, they have high levels of stress, sickness, and burnout, which is why more than 85 percent of employees have reported they want to work remotely even if it's part time. Virtual workers can get more done in less time because they can focus with limited interruptions during the workday. In return, they feel a sense of accomplishment, satisfaction, and happiness at the end each day. See Chapter 3 for more information on the benefits of working virtually.

Furthermore, recessions, layoffs, outsourcing, and downsizing prompt employees to hang out their shingle and start their own business to avoid bankruptcy and pay their bills. Many quickly find that they enjoy the benefits of being on their own — when they work, how they work, with whom they work, and what they work on. Many never go back to the traditional workplace; rather, they become teleworkers or flexible workers who can perform their jobs from anywhere in the world.

>> **Technology:** Advances in technology and the ability to connect with people from around the world in an instant are important reasons why virtual work is thriving. Collaborative technology enables you to reach out and connect with your team in a variety of different ways, in any given moment, for any reason. Chapter 16 discusses advances in technology and what technology you need on your team.

Globalization effect

Globalization enables companies to expand their operations internationally. Globalization benefits companies in a variety of ways. Globalization:

>> Expands their customer base around the world

>> Lengthens the popularity of a trend or product (what's hot in the UK may already be an established product in Asia)

>> Spreads out economic risk

- » Helps companies to test and expand in new markets

- » Provides access to international talent

- » Makes distribution less expensive

- » Helps companies manage seasonal fluctuations

VIRTUAL TEAMS — AN HISTORICAL PERSPECTIVE

You may think that the concept of virtual teams is relatively new, but you'd only be partly right. Sure, technological advances, the Internet, and the global workforce created conditions for virtual teams to explode in recent years, but virtual teams have been around for centuries.

Think of it this way: Basically any team that worked together to accomplish anything from separate locations has operated virtually. From the complex multicultural expanse of the Roman Empire to the critical transportation of the Wells Fargo stagecoaches, teams have been geographically dispersed and highly effective for a long time.

Even the concept of working from home isn't new. Farmers, bakers, seamstresses, shoemakers, potters, weavers, and blacksmiths have always worked from their homes. The Industrial Revolution pulled many workers out of their homes and into factories. In the early 20th century, widespread electricity and public transportation drove workers into offices equipped with telephones, telegraphs, and typewriters.

In the 1970s, the OPEC oil crisis and rising fuel costs led Jack Niles (sometimes called The Father of Teleworking) to look for ways to reduce the cost of commuting. He conducted the first formal tests of telecommuting and coined the term *telecommuting* in his book *The Telecommunications-Transportation Tradeoff*. Telecommuting grew rapidly from there. In the 1980s, J.C. Penney began hiring home-based call center agents. The Clean Air Act of 1990 led many large businesses to offer telecommuting, and the National Telecommuting Initiative was created in 1996 with the federal government confirming its support for telecommuting.

Throughout the 20th century, new technologies have fueled the rise in telework and virtual teams. It began with surging sales of PCs, followed by cellular phones, voice mail, and of course that whole Internet thing. All of these factors paved the way for the virtual workplace known today. By the early 21st century, people who worked at least one day at home per week increased by more than 4 million, and today nearly half of working Americans say they spend at least some time working remotely. All signs indicate virtual work will continue to grow.

Today companies have personal and professional relationships that span the globe and are necessary for economic well-being and growth. In order to meet customer needs and demands and access specialized talent, products, and materials, building global teams that work together to accomplish results just makes smart business sense.

WARNING

However, having team members located in different time zones using different languages and living in different cultures, creates unique challenges and opportunities. See Chapter 9 for more information.

Generational worker shift

The workforce is changing. Baby boomers are retiring in droves, and Generation X isn't far behind. By 2025, Millennials who are comfortable working, communicating, socializing, and developing relationships with people located on the other side of the planet, will comprise 75 percent of the global workforce, and members of Generation Z are just beginning to start their careers. It's important to understand that both Millennials and Gen Zers are used to collaborating, getting answers, and solving problems alone or in groups over the Internet. So, it shouldn't come as a surprise then that working in a remote and virtual environment is a no-brainer for these generations and will cause this trend to continue upward for years into the future. Check out Chapter 9 where I discuss in more detail how different generations feel about and work on virtual teams.

Sorting Out Virtual Team Concepts

All this talk of virtual teams can be confusing, especially when people use different terms to describe virtual working arrangements. The following sections preview the different ways that virtual teams or remote work can be defined and provide some basic insight into each term:

» **Geographically dispersed team:** A virtual team employs people who are usually dispersed or distributed around a city, a country, or the world. These dispersed teams work together from different locations and then rely on technology to connect them. They're also referred to as *dispersed teams* or *distributed teams*.

» **Global versus local virtual team:** If you have a global virtual team, members are located in different countries and cities all over the world. If your virtual team is local, most likely your team is located in a similar area perhaps in the United States, or local to your own city such as Boulder, Colorado.

- >> **Telecommuting:** Some virtual team members acknowledge themselves as telecommuters or say that they telecommute for their job. This basically means they're working from home or a location close to their home. *Telecommuting* defines a working arrangement in which the employee doesn't work in the office 100 percent of the time. For example, he can work from a home office, co-working space, coffee shop, or library, and he commutes via technology.

- >> **Hoteling:** Another common remote work term that has been around for close to 20 years is *hoteling*. This describes the practice of providing as-needed, reservation-based office space that is unassigned rather than a permanent workspace. Companies that have outgrown their office space and don't want to purchase or rent more property use hoteling as a way to make more efficient use of their office space and keep costs to a minimum. Hoteling is also a helpful remote working arrangement if you have employees who travel frequently and only need to come into the office occasionally.

- >> **Global outsourcing:** If your team needs a quick turnaround by someone who is an expert in design, transcription, development, marketing, e-learning, websites, SEO, and other easily outsourced tasks, global outsourcing can be a great fit. This is yet another form of virtual work and companies like Upwork, Fiverr, and Freelancer continue to grow as popular options for teams that need to supplement skill sets quickly.

REMEMBER

  Global outsourcing isn't just for quick turnaround jobs. Companies may outsource longer-term assignments to workers in other countries to assist on a particular project that requires skills, language proficiency, or education that may be too difficult or too expensive to find locally.

- >> **Flex jobs:** Many websites are dedicated to remote workers looking for a flexible type of job arrangement or a short-term, contract opportunity with a company. These remote workers may only want part-time work or work for a few months. They also may desire a flexible job arrangement where they're telecommuting occasionally, on call certain days of the week, or working remotely 100 percent of the time.

Understanding the Benefits and Challenges

In 2016, I launched a research study to validate and test the theory that the pros of having a virtual team and business outweigh the cons. This study included input from close to 200 executives, virtual team leaders, and team members from a mix of industries in Fortune 500 companies, government agencies, and small business. The study gathered insights about what makes a virtual team effective and challenges that virtual teams face. I highlight a few of the key findings here.

Noting virtual benefits

Based on my research, virtual team members, leaders, and executives all agree that a main benefit of virtual teams is to promote work-life balance as illustrated in Figure 1-1. Team members and team leaders also see virtual teams as a way to increase productivity, whereas executives view virtual teams as a cost-saving measure and a good way to get the right people to work together regardless of location.

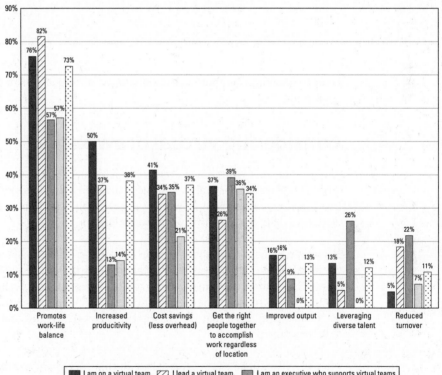

FIGURE 1-1:
Greatest benefits of virtual teams.

Two-thirds of team leaders and half of all executives surveyed said that they estimate virtual teams are currently saving them costs equivalent to 16 to 25 percent of their revenue as Table 1-1 highlights. In a large company, that can equate to millions even billions of dollars in cost savings.

TABLE 1-1   **Cost Savings as a Percentage of Revenue**

Cost savings as a percentage of revenue	Team leader estimate of cost savings	Executive estimate of cost savings
0%	6%	7%
1-5%	17%	7%
6-15%	11%	27%
16-25%	67%	53%
26-50%	0%	4.3%

Refer to Chapter 2 for more discussion on the different pros to going the virtual-team route.

Considering virtual drawbacks

The trust factor is certainly a drawback for virtual team leaders. Blindly trusting virtual employee to do what they say they'll do, in a timely fashion, with an attention to quality, all without being able to personally check in and watch over their work on a daily basis is difficult for some leaders.

My research uncovered other common challenges. These challenges differed if the team was newly formed versus an established virtual team as Figures 1-2 and 1-3 show. The greatest challenge for newly formed virtual teams was figuring out how to effectively use technology and defining how best to communicate. Virtual team leaders also indicated that they struggled with getting the resources they needed to support the team.

After the virtual teams are established, keeping the team engaged and motivated is by far the greatest challenge, along with how to communicate effectively and unlock the team's creativity.

You have to think about several others things when deciding to go virtual in your business, including cybersecurity issues, Internet accessibility, connectivity speeds, confidentiality, and more. Chapter 2 covers these cons in greater detail.

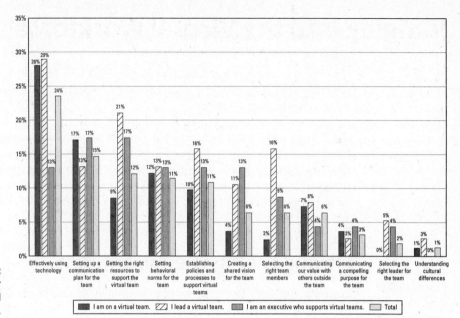

FIGURE 1-2:
Challenges for
newly formed
virtual teams.

Legend: ■ I am on a virtual team. ▨ I lead a virtual team. ▨ I am an executive who supports virtual teams. ▢ Total

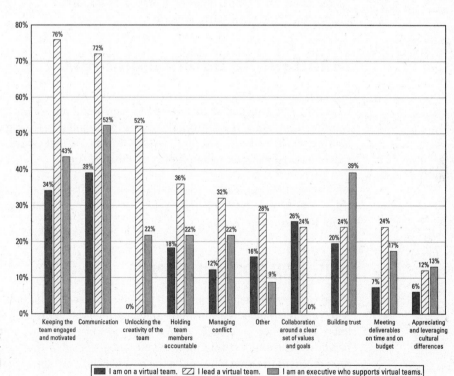

FIGURE 1-3:
Challenges for
established
virtual teams.

Legend: ■ I am on a virtual team. ▨ I lead a virtual team. ▨ I am an executive who supports virtual teams.

Jumping into the Virtual Workforce

If you're considering virtual work or proposing a telecommuting arrangement to your manager, then take into account several important considerations. Many of these considerations require a shift in your mindset and habits, a focus on emotional and social intelligence, and strong communication skills. Be mindful about these areas if you truly want to have success as a virtual team member.

Working virtually has been an empowering life-changing experience for me. However, I wish someone would have shared some of the following advice about virtual work before I made this career leap so I could have been better prepared and set up for success.

Having the right environment

Ensuring you have the right work environment if you're planning on working from home is extremely important to ponder. If your workspace isn't set up for you to be successful, you'll quickly become frustrated and potentially disconnected from your team. Chapter 3 discusses important questions to ask before making the jump to the virtual world.

Maintaining balance and focus

Working virtually takes a heavy dose of discipline and organization to balance work with the constant demands of life happening all around you when you're working from home. If you struggle with self-discipline, working virtually may be an area of difficulty for you as a virtual worker, so make sure you set up clear guidelines and expectations for yourself ahead of time.

Even more important than considering how you'll get work done and maintain balance is how well you'll build relationships in a virtual environment. Think about the following sections.

Building community

When working virtually, be prepared to build a sense of community by connecting with your team members and your manager regularly both for work and to get to know each other personally. If working side-by-side with your coworkers in person is extremely fulfilling for you, then consider that working remotely 100 percent of the time may not be the best idea for you. You may want to consider a part-time telecommuting arrangement or perhaps a flex job where you work remotely a few days a week and a part-time job in an office a few days per week.

Connecting using collaborative technology

As a virtual team member, you generally lose face-to-face, in-person interaction, and I've found that people working remotely have different levels of comfort and acceptance using collaborative technology such as Skype or Zoom to personally connect. Many companies that I work with don't require virtual teams to turn on video when communicating or having a meeting, which is a mistake. If you desire to work virtually, it's up to you to build relationships and trust, which you rarely can achieve over the phone or via text. Turning on your camera so you can connect personally with your team members is an important part of building connection. Flip to Chapter 12 for more strategies and tips to connect.

CREATING A BUSINESS MODEL WITH VIRTUAL TEAMS

You don't need to reinvent the wheel to create virtual teams that work for your business. Model companies who have paved the way and are having great success. Here are three companies that are experiencing success:

- Trello is a free online software tool for managing projects and personal tasks in a flexible and highly visual way. It has a 50-50 operation with remote and on-site employees. Trello's marketing department is 100 percent virtual, and employees credit the company's success with running regular video meetings (three times a week) and encouraging heavy use of chat tools to mimic casual office chatter, especially on nonwork topics. Trello also uses a variety of collaboration tools to stay updated on projects, including (not surprisingly) Trello boards, but the company also uses Slack, Google Docs, Sunrise Calendar, and Appear.

- Zapier focuses on getting all your apps to work together, and it has a 100 percent distributed workforce with more than 100 employees working in more than 15 countries. The company believes in the fast, nimble power of small teams, which means less bureaucracy, less management, and more productivity. Zapier also believes in using a variety of tools to keep its small teams on task like Slack, Async, Trello, Github, and more.

- Intel Corporation, a multinational corporation and technology company best known for building microprocessors, is also a trendsetter in global collaboration systems. More than two-thirds of Intel's teams have members working virtually. The company credits its success to two core functions: personal productivity (using IM or Google Docs to allow employees to connect quickly one-to-one with people all around the world) and team collaboration (collaborative environments in the virtual sphere to share ideas, provide updates, delegate tasks, and more, such as videoconferencing, collaboration platforms, data-sharing tools, and chatroom).

Appreciating team culture

Your virtual team can include people from other towns in your city, your country, or the world. Maybe your team members don't have English as their first language, or maybe their culture and way of life is completely foreign to you. Make sure you consider who is going to be on your team and ideally meet team members as part of the interviewing process. See Chapter 8 for more discussion about how you can build team culture for your virtual team.

Practicing emotional intelligence

Being a virtual team member requires a willingness to go the extra mile to develop strong team relationships by being emotional aware and tuned in to what is happening with other team members. The key to emotional intelligence is recognizing what you and other team members are feeling and then knowing what to do to manage those emotions or reactions. Doing so requires a level of attention, savviness, and vulnerability from you.

Virtual teamwork can be one of the most rewarding and fulfilling roles you'll have in your career. You have to consider several nuances and changes to your own mindset and behaviors. Be sure to check out Chapter 3 where I help you prepare for your next career move as a virtual team member.

Assembling a Virtual Team

When putting your virtual team together, be clear and thoughtful about what you need and whether the job tasks required fit well with doing virtual work. Some job roles across the globe are best suited for virtual work, such as sales, project management, marketing, customer service, developers, researchers, writers, accounting, copywriting, editors, book writing, graphic designers, virtual assistants, web designers, instructional designers, video editors, and e-learning specialists, to name a few. The key is to analyze what gaps you need to fill and ask yourself if someone working remotely can fill that gap.

Hiring remote employees who end up overlapping in terms of their job responsibilities and deliverables, especially when expectations, goals, and deliverables aren't clear is easy. Be sure to assemble your team in a strategic, thoughtful way. You can do it through a simple gap analysis of assessing what you need, what you have, and what gaps exist. Frequently, you can fill the gap with your current team members with training or by encouraging your go-getters to master something new and then give them the time to do their own research or attend online classes.

TIP

To discover is if someone is going to succeed on your virtual team, bring him on for a team project or short-term assignment as a contractor. Have him work with your team for 30 to 60 days to test out if he's a good fit culturally, if he's self-directed and can manage his time and deadlines, and most importantly if he can demonstrate the right behaviors and maturity level to handle a virtual working environment. Chapter 2 gives you plenty of tips and information about everything you need to know about putting your virtual team together.

Managing a Virtual Team

Not all managers excel at leading a team they don't see face-to-face every day; some people lead better in person. What you were able to do with your traditional team, you may find the need to do more of with your virtual team to build trust, open communication, and keep team members engaged in their work. Being successful as a virtual team leader requires tried-and-true best practices of building team trust and cohesiveness, being aware and emotionally intelligent, and focusing on creating clarity. Here are a few integral skills managers should practice to succeed in a virtual working arrangement:

» **Flexibility:** On virtual teams, work happens all times of the day and night. Accommodating team members who may be located around the country or the world requires a leader who is willing to be flexible to keep a pulse on what is happening with each team member. See Chapter 10 for more discussion about the importance of being flexible.

» **Trust:** Micromanaging when leading a virtual team is a major frustration for team members and a complete waste of time for you, the team leader. If you've done a great job hiring the right person for the role, setting clear goals, expectations, and objectives, and have a consistent communication plan and schedules follow up, it's time to let go. Chapter 12 examines in greater depth how you build trust with your team.

» **Communication:** The idea that technology hinders communication is outdated. My research shows that teams consider leaders of virtual teams successful who communicate most effectively and most often and who use technology appropriately. However, remote workers actually need more communication, feedback, and guidance than on-site workers, so as a leader you need to step up your game in this area. Chapter 13 discusses tips and strategies for communicating with your virtual team.

>> **Technical savviness:** A major obstacle a virtual leader can make is to not utilize, support, and champion technology tools. Whether it's for file sharing, videoconferencing, chatting, brainstorming, or managing projects, leaders must demonstrate proficiency using technology and encourage others to use it effectively on a regular basis. Chapter 16 explains in plain English why technology is so important and what tools you need to consider.

TEN STATISTICS TO CONVINCE VIRTUAL TEAM NAYSAYERS

Several years ago, as part of my work with teams and leaders on communication, trust, and leadership, I began taking note that more and more of these team leaders and team members had never met face-to-face and relied solely on technology to stay connected.

The use of virtual teams, fueled by advances in technology and the promise of reduced operational costs, was growing at a rapid rate. Businesses were launching headfirst into establishing virtual teams, with barely a backward glance at the issues of the virtual environment.

The more I investigated, the clearer it became: Virtual teams will continue to grow, but organizations needed to recognize the unique challenges of virtual teams and invest in ongoing training and support in order to realize the benefits. No research addressed this issue, so I conducted my own.

Over six months in 2016, hundreds of participants completed an online survey about their experiences leading or participating on a virtual team. Participants included virtual team members, virtual team leaders, executives that support virtual teams, and people who would soon be on a virtual team. Survey participants represented various industries and sizes of organizations.

Despite the growing data-driven evidence of the benefits of virtual teams, some cynics are still out there. Here are a few key data points from my findings and other sources that can help any virtual team advocate seeking upper-level support:

- Virtual teams have increased 800 percent over the last five years.

- Fifty percent of team members agree that productivity has increased being part of a virtual team.

- Virtual teams can save companies up to 25 percent of revenue.

- Teams with clear agreements are 18 times more likely to accomplish their goals.

- Teams with clear agreements are 28 times more likely to be highly productive.

- Teams with clear agreements are 39 times more likely to come up with innovative solutions.

- Newly formed virtual teams that communicate effectively were 55 times more likely to be responsive to customers.

- Newly formed virtual teams that communicate effectively were 12 times more likely to reach their goals.

- Teams that are effective at using collaborative technology are 98 times more likely to come up with innovative solutions.

- Teams that are effective at using collaborative technology are 74 times more likely to deliver on time and within budget.

» **Building the business case for virtual teams**

» **Drawing up your game plan**

» **Supporting your virtual team**

» **Attending to infrastructure and logistics**

» **Building community and culture**

Chapter **2**

Envisioning Virtual Teams in Your Business

Hiring virtual team members is a great business strategy for an assortment of reasons, including major cost savings on overhead expenses, expanded access to global talent, and jobs that are more appropriately suited for virtual work. Imagine each of these scenarios:

» **Scenario 1:** You live in Leavenworth, Washington, a town with a population of about 2,000 people. You have a proven business model and enough funds to start your business with five employees. You need to hire an experienced developer, project manager, engineer, and marketer, and your local search has turned up nothing.

» **Scenario 2:** Your software company that has an office located in downtown Atlanta has experienced record growth this year. Real estate costs are at an all-time high and investing in another large office and all the maintenance that goes along with it will cut into your financial projections significantly. Sixty percent of your open requisitions for the next few years will most likely be for software engineers and programmers.

Relying on remote workers to grow your business is also wise for other reasons, such as improving retention, having a positive social impact, and getting work done in less time.

This chapter builds the business case for virtual teams and helps you mull over the benefits and risks if you're contemplating this staffing strategy. You can put together a plan to start using remote workers and teams, perform a gap analysis to determine what roles you need to fill, and identify where you need to invest time and money to set up for success. This chapter helps you create a solid strategy for using virtual teams in your business whether you're in change of company of ten or ten thousand.

Contemplating Using Virtual Teams

Having remote workers can be a positive business strategy for many companies. The key is making sure that your virtual teams are designed thoughtfully and with solid collaboration strategies in place. The difference between virtual team success and failure is ensuring that virtual teams must support your business strategy. This strategic alignment is essential. For example, if establishing virtual teams helps grow your business by enabling you to access global skills and knowledge you need or reduces your expenses by 25 to 30 percent or helps to attract and retain key talent, then all the remaining logistical and technical decisions can flow from there.

REMEMBER

Virtual work isn't appropriate for every role or project 100 percent of the time. Certainly some examples require people to be face-to-face with team members or customers some or even most of the time. Think police officer, firefighter, surgeon, veterinarian, physical therapist, hair stylist, maintenance worker, attorney, or a highly complex development project to name a few. Even though virtual collaboration can be effective for a majority of situations, the more complex and uncertain the job role or project, the more it may require face-to-face interactions. Refer to the nearby sidebar that explains why virtual teams may not be appropriate for some professions.

TIP

If your business is ripe for using virtual or remote teams and you're ready to start, first focus your time and attention on creating crystal-clear goals and a strategy for accomplishing them. After they're defined, you can begin to ask yourself several questions:

>> What skills are needed to accomplish our goals and how quickly do I want to achieve them?

>> What tasks are required to move from point A to point B?

>> Are there many complex decisions involved in order to complete the tasks?

>> Do these tasks need to be completed in a collaborative way with input from others consistently?

>> Does collaboration have to happen face-to-face? Why?

Considering these questions and other key factors is part of the mindful process that can set you and virtual your teams up for success. Be sure to embrace this business strategy with your eyes open and have a clear picture of the benefits, challenges, and risks so that you're making educated, sound business decisions that support your success.

To help you begin to plan your strategy, the following sections examine key factors to consider if you're going virtual and highlight common challenges and mistakes that virtual teams make.

Thinking about these key factors

Perhaps you just have a particular area of your business where a virtual team makes sense, or perhaps you're a startup and considering going 100 percent virtual. Regardless of your situation, I want to bring these five key consideration factors to your attention.

AGILE MANIFESTO

A team of global leaders developed the *Manifesto for Agile Software Development* in 2001 and acknowledged that virtual work may not be the best business strategy 100 percent of the time. The leaders agreed on one key value: Individuals and interactions come first over processes and tools. People come first, always. And the good news: Technology has evolved and transformed the way people can now build relationships in a virtual environment.

In fact, many of these job examples where people expect face-to-face interaction as a customer, coworker, or community member, are progressing to include virtual options. Hospitals and health providers are offering "telehealth" and remote monitoring services where virtual nurses use phone apps to monitor and diagnose patients and can also call in prescriptions. Virtual pet visits using videoconferencing software, such as Skype, allow your vet to see your pet and provide care without you having to go to the hospital. Both of these examples are valuable, just-in-time options if you live in a remote area of the world or a mountain community where it can take several hours to reach a care facility. They can also save you valuable time from sitting in a waiting room when you already have a tightly scheduled day.

Find out if your in-office employees are ready to work virtually

Making the switch to a part-time or full-time virtual team after working in an office most of a career requires employees have a willingness to explore new opportunities and embrace change. Not all employees are change resilient and will do well in this scenario. Be that as it may, you can support your employees by laying out a clear transition plan that includes frequent and open communication, well-thought-out expectations and goals, recognition, and empathy for what will be lost, ongoing training and support, and a vision of success that is supported by leadership and team goals.

Get your leaders trained on managing in a virtual environment

Virtual team leaders make or break the success of your team. Their comfort level managing from a distance, building trust, holding people accountable, and establishing strong communication practices needs to be addressed. On a virtual team, the days of looking over someone's shoulder or checking in at her cubicle to gauge progress are long gone. This relinquishment of control can impact how a manager believes she contributes value, so part of your transition plan needs to address these mindset shifts through coaching and training in order to help managers establish a new way of leading.

Make sure you invest in technology

An absolute must for a successful transition to virtual work is to perform a technical audit on the systems you currently use. Can they easily transition over to a virtual team environment? If not, be prepared to invest in new software, systems, and training and be willing to have patience for the ramp up time your team will need to feel confident using them. See Chapter 16 for more in-depth discussion about what essential tech tools you need.

Focus your time and attention on building a culture of engagement

How much are you willing to focus on building relationship, community, and culture? Virtual teams are separated by time and distance, so an environment that encourages engagement is essential to team success and productivity. You must be willing to create a culture of engagement, complete with regular communication, clear expectations, employee training and development, trust, appreciation, and collaboration.

From all of the research I've done or I've seen, if you aren't willing to do the hard work that is required to make sure that your virtual team is connected, collaborative, and cohesive, then you're basically setting it up for failure.

Analyze your contracts, insurance, and benefits

Make sure you consult with your lawyer on what contracts and insurance is necessary for remote workers and what reasonable accommodations you may need to make to assist people in setting up a safe and productive at-home working environment. Chapter 6 delves deeper into these issues.

Embracing the challenges: The five flaws of virtual teams

Before you jump feetfirst into the world of virtual teams, you want to be knowledgeable about the common challenges that virtual teams face that can potentially render them as failures. Most of the research available on virtual team obstacles cites similar challenges, which I have deemed the five flaws of virtual teams. These flaws generally represent a lack of focus, commitment, and leadership by the organization.

You can easily address them by using the how-to strategies in this book. Pay close attention to Chapter 4 where I cover how to define your team purpose and set team goals and Part 4, which is focused on how to build engagement, trust, strong communication practices, and more.

Flawed leadership

Leaders of virtual teams who lack clarity on goals, purpose, and priorities will end up managing teams that are off track, second-guessing simple decisions and working on the wrong things at the wrong time. Team members make their best guess at what needs to be done and can create duplicate work, rework, or waste time and resources on something unimportant.

Without an investment of time and focus appreciating the diversity of gender, race, culture, age, thought, and style of your team, cliques can occur, and you may find yourself dealing with isolationism and disrespectful behavior.

If the team leader isn't a role model in establishing a strong relationship of trust and openness, team members may be afraid to speak up when they don't know the answer or feel as if they're drowning but are afraid to ask for a life vest. Team members also won't trust each other, which can have a significant impact on feeding the additional flaws.

Flawed communication

Virtual teams who don't begin with clear, consistent communication strategies that everyone agrees to are in for a world of trouble. These strategies can include the following:

>> How often the team connects and for what purpose

>> What communication tools are appropriate for different situations

>> How people like to get work done and receive information

In Chapter 13, I share best practices of communication and provide a variety of communication strategies to be a better communicator.

Think of it this way: You'll have different generations on your team who are comfortable using different communication methods and desire different amounts of connection and engagement throughout the workday. Not having any standards in place for what good communication looks like can feel like having a dreadful dancing partner where you're constantly out of sync, stepping on each other's toes, and eventually falling to the floor in a tangle of confusion. (Refer to Chapter 9 where I discuss ways to improve communication across generations.)

Flawed transparency

If team members aren't keeping each other updated on dependencies and deliverables, then your virtual team isn't really operating as a team. Rather, team members are operating in a silo with a lack of understanding that they are part of something greater and they have an impact on the success of others. In order to create transparency along with clear expectations and consistent feedback from you as the leader, rely on how technology can make your life easier. Refer to the "Flawed technology" section in this chapter for additional information.

Flawed commitment

Why does this work matter? Why do you matter?

These questions beg to be answered on a regular basis with virtual team members. Without daily connection with the manager or home office, team members can easily lose sight of their value and contribution to the bigger picture.

TIP

Make sure that you clearly define the virtual team's rules, responsibilities, and tasks for commitment to flourish. Evaluate each team member's skill sets and then carefully match them with the tasks that need completed.

In order to gain high levels of commitment from people who aren't working side by side on a daily basis, figure out the answers to questions, such as "Who does that task?", "When does Joel hand off work to Kyla?", and "How do we know that work has been completed successfully before that virtual hand off takes place?"

Flawed technology

Agile technology tools always need to be a topic of discussion for a virtual team to succeed. If your teams aren't assessing and analyzing what's working and what's holding them back, they will soon be using outdated technology to connect, communicate, and collaborate. Regular tech audits and feedback from your teams is an imperative process to make a habit in your business along with a willingness to invest in the right technology, at the right time for your team.

REMEMBER

Another key consideration — and often overlooked factor — is the requirement of fast, reliable Internet connection. All of the virtual team tech platforms are run on the web so all team members must live and work in an area where they can rely on full-time, uninterrupted web access.

Virtual work and cloud technologies also introduce security and compliance challenges. Many virtual teams work on highly proprietary projects in development that require security. Traditional management tools can leave your virtual team vulnerable.

When assessing using virtual teams as a business strategy, if you're not willing to put time and attention into considering these factors and challenges, perhaps moving toward a virtual team model isn't something your organization is currently ready for. Chapter 16 touches on the different technology features and how you can implement the right technology that your team needs.

Deciding Whether Virtual Teams Make Good Business Sense

In order to implement a virtual team in your organization, you want to ensure that you've contemplated some important considerations. Virtual teams can be a small part of your business or they can be integral to all of your business functions. You can begin with a pilot virtual team or decide to leverage your technical investment and go all in on virtual teams. You may be a startup who wants to build an exclusively virtual workforce or you may be from an established organization trying to modernize its recruitment and hiring. Whatever you decide, virtual teams must fit your business, culture, and management philosophies, and of course, they must be cost effective.

Keep in mind that not all benefits of using virtual teams are financial. Many additional benefits create a strong business case including recruiting experienced employees, retaining your star employees, and helping you meet your sustainability goals. People who work on a virtual team have also reported that it has reduced stress and conflict among team members, increased productivity and engagement levels, and improved overall job satisfaction. Furthermore, team members get the opportunity to build collaborative relationships with others located in different demographic areas or even different countries.

At the end of the day, incorporating a virtual team model in your company can build your reputation and street cred as a Best Places to Work on online feedback sites like Glassdoor. Site like these are one of the first places potential new hires will go to find out what it's like to work for you and your leaders.

REMEMBER

A virtual team is an iterative model, which means that it's meant to be adapted and improved over time. Don't expect seamless collaboration right off the bat. If having a virtual team is new to your organization, just know that it will take time, persistence, and patience, but the benefits are significant and the results are proven.

These sections take a look at where you may incorporate virtual teams in your business and evaluate not only the cost savings virtual teams offer, but also the additional benefits to your business.

Finding a place for virtual teams

Based on strong research that show virtual teams are a good business decision, you may be considering offering remote work options to your full-time employees. Here are additional ways you can incorporate virtual employees for special projects:

>> **Just-in-time project need:** You may have a project with a definite end date and you're in need of specialized skills to supplement your full-time team. Places like Flexjobs.com and Upwork.com can help you find someone quickly on a contract basis.

>> **New product launch:** Say that you're launching a new product line and your goal is to be the first to market. Bringing together a team of virtual freelancers or contract workers can help you get to market quickly without having to hire full-time staff.

>> **Seasonal staffing:** If your staffing needs change throughout the year, you may consider hiring virtual workers to support your busy season. Doing so enables you to scale your business at certain times of the year with remote workers and decrease staffing numbers as needed.

Each of these examples can save you time, money, and stress associated with recruiting, hiring, and onboarding full-time employees. However, the decision should be based on your business need. Ask yourself these questions:

>> What is the opportunity or challenge in the marketplace that I'm trying to address?

>> What are my clients asking for or complaining about?

>> Are these opportunities or challenges well suited for virtual or remote work (for example, customer service outsourcing)?

>> Do I have the resources internally to handle these issues?

>> Does my current staff have the knowledge, skills, and abilities to handle these issues or opportunities?

These questions can get you started thinking about what options to use for remote workers. After you're clear about your needs and direction, you can start creating your business model and game plan.

Counting the real ROI savings

Global Workplace Analytics has spent years developing research-based models and calculators to estimate the impact and return on investment of different workplace strategies, including telecommuting. Public companies, governmental agencies, and private sector employers have utilized its savings calculator to support the business case for virtual and remote work.

Based on 2017 Global Workplace Analytics data, it estimates that more than 3.9 million employees telecommuted part time or full time and collectively saved employers $44 billion a year, or an average of $11,000 per half-time telecommuter. That's an impressive number. But what's even more staggering is that if everyone who wanted to work remotely could do so even half of the time (85 percent of all employees), the savings to employers could total approximately $689 billion per year. That's a whole heck of a lot of money. Here are where some of the cost savings come from:

>> **Productivity savings:** The largest cost savings is from an increase in productivity. Productivity goes up significantly because people aren't distracted, they get more done in less time, and they can work a flexible schedule that suits them. This equates to $27.5 million per year in terms of savings.

>> **Real estate savings:** The second largest cost savings is from real estate, which has saved an estimated $7.6 billion a year for employers.

>> **Sick time/absenteeism savings:** When people aren't in the office spreading germs around, less people get sick. Even if your employee has a mild cold, she can still complete her work from home. Less sick time equates to $5.1 billion in savings for the employer. Furthermore, you don't have to shut down for snow days, floods, or other natural disasters, extending cost savings.

>> **Reduction in turnover costs:** With the flexibility that a remote work option provides, employees stay with their employer longer, which equates to $1.5 billion of savings in turnover cost.

>> **Commuter savings:** People who work full time on a virtual team can save more than $4,000 a year in commuting costs including auto maintenance, food, clothing, and dry cleaning. Don't forget the time people save by not having to commute to work every day. The average employee gains back the equivalent of 11 days per year, which is more than two weeks of work that she spends otherwise sitting in her car. How can you put a price tag on that?

>> **Meeting efficiency:** Working remotely certainly reduces your travel time to get to meetings. How many times have you been in a meeting and you're waiting for someone to come from another office because she's stuck in traffic, her car breaks down, or she was in an accident? The amount of time saved starting and ending meetings on time certainly equates to dollars saved when you consider the salary you pay every person in the meeting to be there.

>> **Reduction in parking expenses:** Parking in many U.S. cities is expensive. This continues to be a complaint in every crowded city I work in — there is nowhere to park. Working remotely eliminates this issue and the expense associated with it.

Thousands of companies around the globe have made 100 percent virtual and 50/50 virtual work for them. Most companies that believe in virtual teams and a distributed workforce are mystified by the need for an ROI measurement, stating simply that productivity in virtual teams is measured by results. That said, many organizations are looking to making a business case for going virtual.

Winning the recruitment and retention war

Going remote expands your access to a global talent pool and can help you fill capability gaps that you can't find in your local market. It allows you to recruit anyone from anywhere in the world and fill open position more quickly. Most Millennials seek out flexible work options and offering remote work opportunities provides a level of flexibility that makes employees more satisfied. And guess what? Happier employees stay longer at your company.

Remote workers are able to spend more time with their family and friends and improve relationships with the people they love. They can care for a sick child or aging parent while still checking in with their team and completing work, volunteer at their child's school, or participate in their community. Their quality of life overall improves because they're able to balance a multitude of responsibilities with more ease including family, friends, aging parents, pets, groceries, health and wellness, house projects, cleaning, and so on.

Impacting the environment

Virtual work allows you to expand your business without expanding your footprint. Companies use less electricity in their buildings and purchase less food, snacks, and supplies. Embracing remote work also saves on gas and reduces pollution by getting more cars off the road.

BASECAMP, A 100 PERCENT VIRTUAL COMPANY

Most virtual teams are created to achieve a specific goal – connect global teams, hire the best people, cut operational costs, or reduce its environmental impact. But some companies are built as a 100 percent virtual model because they believe being virtual is simply the ideal organizational work model.

One perfect example is Basecamp (formerly 37signals), a project management and communication software company. Based in Chicago where few of the company's employees live and work, Basecamp has more than 50 employees spread out across 32 different cities around the world.

Basecamp founder and president Jason Fired is evangelical about the benefits of remote work. Fried and his Basecamp co-founder David Hansson, blog about it and have presented a TedTalks on it, and they literally wrote the book about it. Two, in fact — *Remote: Office Not Required (2013)* and *Rework (2010)*.

Basecamp advocates a philosophy that if you hire talented adults, give them ownership, and provide them with the necessary environment for them to succeed, you can build something great. In fairness, Basecamp's product is perfectly suited for remote work — for both Basecamp employees *and* their clients.

Despite their distance, Basecamp makes their far-flung employees feel like family (and compensates them generously, paying all their people according to Silicon Valley scales), and they take care of their customers. Other core values include have fun, do exceptional work, build the best product, experiment, tell the truth, have a positive impact on the world, give back, and keep learning.

It's hard to argue with their results. Basecamp has 15 consecutive years of profitability.

In its State of Telecommuting 2017 report, Global Workplace Analytics found that telecommuters have saved more than 7.8 billion vehicle miles and avoided 530 million vehicle trips, which means less wear and tear on roads. The lack of vehicles on the road has helped avoid three million tons of greenhouse gasses, reduce oil consumption and dependence on foreign oil, and circumvent traffic accidents with a total environmental impact and savings of $1.5 billion.

Another important positive social impact is that virtual work enables disabled people, seniors, or people with special needs to work out of an accommodating home office. It also provides people who are living in remote or depressed areas of the country to find work as long as they have access to a reliable Internet connection.

Deciding on Your Plan

If you agree that virtual teams are a good fit for your company, the next step is to develop your plan. High functioning virtual teams don't happen by accident. They happen because the organization and leader put in the time and effort to build a solid foundation for virtual team success. This includes things like team purpose and goals, role clarity for team members, a transition plan for those co-located employees moving to a virtual team as well as overall communication recommendation to the rest of the company. Here I guide you through creating a strong foundation for your virtual team that includes all of these key strategies.

Defining purpose and goals

Like any well-planned business initiative, establishing and communicating clarity of purpose and goals for your virtual team is imperative for success. Be prepared to answer the following questions:

>> What do you want this team to accomplish?

>> What is the scope of work this team will be responsible for?

>> How will you measure team success and evaluate individual performance?

>> What other teams are impacted by the work?

>> Who are strategic stakeholders in the company that need to work closely with this team?

>> How does this team add value to the business?

>> How does this team positively impact the organization's strategic goals?

>> How is this team moving the company in the direction of its vision?

>> How will the team be structured? (100 percent virtual? 50/50?)

>> Why is the team structured this way?

>> Why is using remote workers the best business decision for this project or team?

>> Is this team a short-term or long-term strategy for the business?

Clearly defining the high-level purpose and goals for your virtual team can help you figure out the roles on the team you need to fill and how you'll communicate the game plan for the team to others in your company.

Figuring out the roles to fill

Getting crystal clear about the skills you need on your virtual team and what roles are interdependent and why is the first step to creating clarity around goals, workflow, hiring strategies, and more. With time and distance separating virtual team members, having the right roles established is even more important to reduce ambiguity among team members regarding who does what. It's difficult to manage interdependent tasks when team members are in different time zones and countries so the more clarity around roles, goals, and expectations for each role the better.

Building a mind map

A great way to determine the roles you need to fill on a virtual team is to use a mind map to decide what skills you need to accomplish your goals. A *mind map* represents a visual thinking tool that helps you map out your thoughts using words, phrases, or ideas, which can help you to make associations in the brain that spark further development of a goal or idea.

Figure 2-1 shows a simple mind map that considers what's needed to support a company goal of being known for customer service excellence. Here are the steps to build your own:

1. **Create a central idea or goal.**

   This is the starting point of your mind map and represents the topic or goals that you're going to explore. Put this in the center of your page.

2. **Add arteries or branches to your mind map.**

   These branches represent your main themes that support your central idea or goal. You can expand these main themes by adding more branches off each main theme.

3. Include keywords.

Keywords along your branches can help you to chunk information into core topics or themes and assist you in remembering a larger quantity of information.

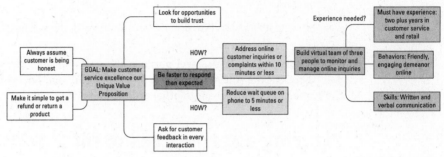

FIGURE 2-1:
A mind map.

I use this mind map to help my client home in on key focus areas to accomplish their goal of being known for customer service excellence. As a result, it shows you that a small virtual team of three people with key behaviors and skills will work well to handle all online customer service inquiries.

Performing a skill gap analysis

After you're clear on the skills needed for your virtual team, you need to perform a simple skill gap analysis to see if you have those skills internally or need to hire by following these four steps:

1. Identify what skills are needed.

Using your mind map, list all the skills needed on the virtual team. You can break this list down by key responsibilities, tasks, or functions. I recommend prioritizing how important each skill is to the team and what level of expertise in using the skill is required (high, medium, low).

2. Evaluate current team members.

Measure the level of skill you currently have available in your talent pool of employees. You can do this through interviews, surveys, assessments, or prior performance reviews. Figure 2-2 shows an example of a nine-box matrix to help measure current employee potential to fill roles on your virtual team. I recommend that you take into account other important behaviors such as coachability, attitude, and growth potential.

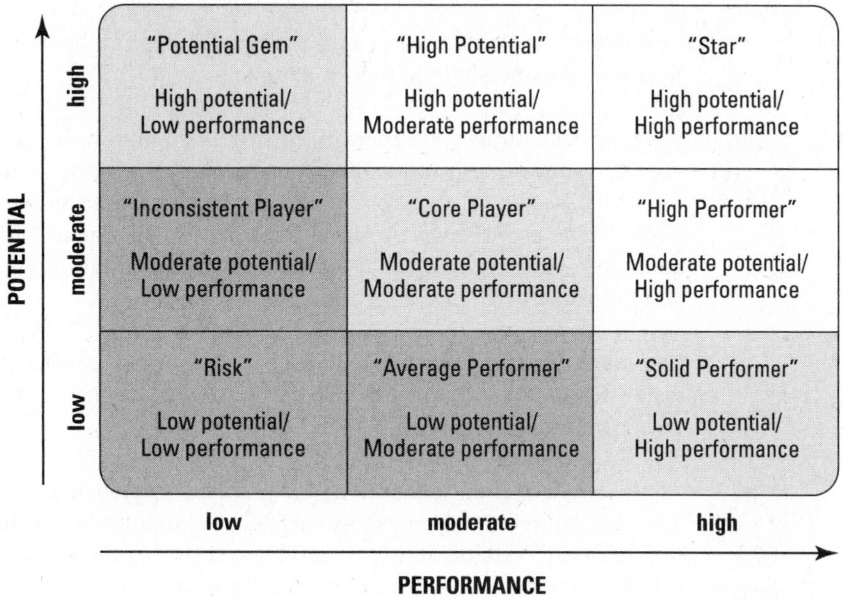

		low	moderate	high
POTENTIAL	**high**	"Potential Gem" High potential/ Low performance	"High Potential" High potential/ Moderate performance	"Star" High potential/ High performance
	moderate	"Inconsistent Player" Moderate potential/ Low performance	"Core Player" Moderate potential/ Moderate performance	"High Performer" Moderate potential/ High performance
	low	"Risk" Low potential/ Low performance	"Average Performer" Low potential/ Moderate performance	"Solid Performer" Low potential/ High performance

PERFORMANCE

FIGURE 2-2: A nine-box matrix.

© *John Wiley & Sons, Inc.*

3. Determine gaps.

Compare the skills needed on your virtual team and the skills you have available with your current workforce. You can do so with a skill assessment test or simple survey tool that assesses the strengths of your workforce. You can collect data from management and current employees. By using these tools, you can easily and quickly identify obvious gaps.

4. Develop or hire skills needed.

Create your plan of action — either develop the skills needed with the employees you already have or hire in new skills for your virtual team.

For each role on your virtual team, additional skills and experience may be necessary for the job including technology proficiency. Get more granular in terms of your employees' day-to-day responsibilities and tasks to ensure you don't have job roles on a team overlapping one another.

Communicating about virtual team adoption

In addition, getting people and leaders in your organization to champion virtual teams is imperative. Incorporating virtual workers can be a shift in mindset for people. Feelings of jealously and inequity can arise from those employees who can't work from home. Make sure that you're clear on how to communicate this new virtual team adoption in your company.

TIP

Some obvious terms you can include in your communication plan to support why virtual teams are a good idea for your business are *agile, faster to deliver, quicker resolution, speed to market, access to expertise,* and *expansion into new markets* to name a few. Think about how a virtual workforce is in alignment with your values and goals and articulate how you'll focus on hiring for cultural fit just as much as you will for skill.

Communicate in a way that will set people's minds at ease — talk about your vision for the team and what's possible. Remember that a powerful vision gets powerful results.

WARNING

Don't shy away from mentioning the fact that introducing virtual teams to your business will require change. The way people communicate, collaborate, and have influence will certainly require a paradigm shift. Highlight how you'll support the transformation through training, coaching, and technology. Address people's fears and allow them to speak up and be heard. The more weigh-in you encourage from employees, the more buy-in you'll have long term.

Using virtual teams will make you a more dynamic, diverse organization that is poised to serve your customers better than ever before. When communicating this significant shift to your employees, you really need to sell it. Not only are you evolving your business but you're also evolving mindsets.

Setting Up Your Virtual Team for Success

The early stages of your virtual team development are the most important. They require focus and support from leaders and executives at every level. And if you did your homework and to create a clear purpose, vision, goals, and roles for your team, then you're already off to a great start.

The next stage is equally important because it establishes the support structure to ensure that your virtual team has access to the right resources and is set up correctly to function, and you have established clear communication expectations.

Having the right resources in place

In order for your virtual team to be effective, make sure that your virtual team members have a few things in common: good communication skills, high levels of emotional intelligence, ability to work independently, and resiliency to recover from the snafus that inevitably arise when working remotely.

Being open to diverse cultures, ideas, and points of view is important to think about when choosing the right leader to manage your virtual team. Everyone has cultural and generational biases they may not even be aware of so identifying team members and leaders that come to the virtual table with an open mind, willingness to learn, ability to give and receive feedback, and a sense of curiosity is what you're aiming for. Refer to Part 3 for more information about assembling your team.

Arranging your remote office

A remote office is conducive to getting work done. For full-time team members working virtually, I recommend an at-home assessment to determine if their office set-up is appropriate. Can they participate in webinars, videoconferencing, and client or sales calls in a way that is acceptable to your business? Is it safe? Does it accommodate their needs? If not, what can you do to help them get there? Refer to Chapter 3 for more information about remote office setup.

REMEMBER

From a legal standpoint and based on your company policies, make sure you have proper legal documentation in place that states clear expectations about work hours, availability, time keeping, use of email and videoconferencing, data security, intellectual property, safety and compliance issues, hiring and firing process for virtual team members, and income and tax laws when working in different locations. Be sure to confer with a human resources lawyer and tax accountant about these topics and ensure you have the proper coverage and documentation in place.

Establishing communication expectations

Support for your virtual team includes setting up strong communication channels that everyone agrees to use to keep people engaged, involved, and feeling like they're part of your company.

Think about how often and by what medium you'll provide training on technology, leadership, or team development. What is your schedule for all-hands meetings, expectations for team meetings, or personal connection opportunities? Designing communication expectations that are accepted and effective in keeping your teams connected is important. Here are some expectations to consider from an organizational perspective:

>> How quickly does the team need to respond to each other?

>> How quickly does the team need to get back with customers?

» What expectations does the team have regarding communication in the evenings or during the weekend?

» What level of interaction or input does the team expect during all-hands meetings? Team meetings?

» What expectations does the team have for team connection other than work communication?

» What feedback channels or software does the team have in place to measure progress, impact, and engagement? How does the team expect this to be used and shared?

Spending time to establish clear communication expectations at the organizational level is one of the most important ways you can support virtual team success. Individual teams will set up their own communication expectations (refer to Chapter 13).

Paying Attention to What You Need

All virtual teams aren't created equal. Virtual teams are created for many reasons, and one size and structure doesn't fit all. The following sections talk about the organizational structure, size, and technology choices of the most effective virtual teams.

As a rule, virtual teams, both project based and functional teams, are structurally flat. Think about it — even traditional offices are phasing out the "too many chiefs" hierarchy, so you really won't see complex org charts for virtual teams, which by design are flexible, autonomous, and nimble.

REMEMBER

A manager, project manager, or team leader who oversees the progress of the project or functional team usually leads virtual teams. Some teams even make that leader position a rotating role.

Size matters: small versus large teams

Consider it the Goldilocks effect. Some virtual teams are too small and team members feel overworked, whereas other teams are too big and have no accountability, making it seem like nothing gets done. So what's the magic, just-right number?

From large corporations to tiny start-ups, the most effective virtual teams are small, with fewer than 10 to 12 people. With the growth of virtual teams, the size of teams has been getting larger and larger, sometimes exceeding 100 people for complex projects that aren't conducive to collaboration. Teams this large allow people to hide behind technology and not engage during team meetings because it's impossible for that many people to participate — a term called *social loafing.* On large teams, team members don't have to be involved, speak up, or give a lot of thought to articulating their opinion especially if other team members usually step up to the plate.

When projects begin to grow and more people from various departments are added, I recommend creating subteams that range from five to eight people. The smaller the team, the easier it is to communicate, collaborate, and make sure that everybody is participating in solving problems and coming up with innovative solutions.

Choosing the right technology

There is a myth that technology drives the success of any virtual team. The reality is that technology exists to enable team communication and collaboration, but it can't replace the impact of leadership, trust, creativity, time management, and plain good work.

That said, even the most tech-savvy virtual teams with the most talented workers and the best leadership can fail due to poor technology. In general, I recommend making functional-based technology decisions. Choose tools that support exactly what your team needs. Chapter 16 helps you navigate the technology field in greater detail so you know what tools are available to meet your team's needs.

Creating Connection and Community

Virtual teams can be a real boon for your business, but only if you're serious about building and maintaining community and culture. As the following sections explain, you can accomplish this goal in a variety of ways using technology, setting expectations, and tracking engagement, satisfaction, and happiness levels of the people that work for you.

Personally check in with your virtual team leaders and members a few times per year to find out what's going on with them, how they're feeling, whether they're happy with the work they're doing, and how they believe their team adds value. You want to keep a pulse on how connected people feel to the overall organization.

Connecting your virtual team to the larger organization

Here are a variety of ideas you can use to keep your virtual teams feeling connected to the larger organization:

>> **Hold all-hands meetings.** Use videoconferencing software, not audio, when having all-hands meetings where everyone participates. People need to see you and see others, especially if the team is global. Create opportunities for each location to provide feedback and ask questions if you have teams located in different offices. Provide time for each location to engage in some brainstorming while you're having your all-hands meeting, and then have each location choose a spokesperson to share insights and ideas. Ask all virtual team members to report what they're most excited about, have questions about, or if there is any recognition they want to mention for other team members.

>> **Plan a company retreat.** Even though costly, bringing everyone from your company together once a year for an in-person team building retreat can do more to build trust and open communication than you can imagine. I've facilitated many of these company retreats and can speak from experience that the relationships built during this time absolutely improve productivity and collaboration back at work. Face-to-face connection is valuable and makes a difference in building team camaraderie.

>> **Set up a buddy system.** Buddy people up located in different cities or countries. This idea worked fabulously when I built a mentoring program for a global scientific organization last year. We assigned everyone a mentor located in another part of the world after thoughtfully and specifically breaking down cultural barriers and helping team members understand the challenges and opportunities that people were facing in different areas of the company. It also helped people embrace the reality that even though the organization may be global, everyone was still one team, one company.

>> **Encourage employee resource groups.** Pinterest ran with this idea after looking at online employee boards where people were discussing and sharing common interests and hobbies. They used this information to create employee interest groups that have become a great way to develop culture and help people establish strong relationships through shared interests and things they care about.

Connecting virtual team members to each other

Creating a connection culture on every team is an organizational and team goal important to virtual team success. You can support this at the team level by letting each team figure out what its connection activities look like. The team members need to own it if you want them to adopt it as a common practice.

TIP

Encourage leaders to focus on nurturing relationships and build opportunities for connection to naturally occur. Support recognition by providing a budget for team members to support, recognize, and reward one another. I suggest teams use virtual collaboration tools as often as possible to build personal relationships and set aside funds for teams to get together face to face at least once a year.

Another idea for keeping teams connected is to support team personalization. Examples include coming up with a fun team name, team motto, or a phrase that represents the team. Although a tad kitschy, these ideas instill a sense of belonging to something that's personal to their team. They can help the team stand out in the company and create a true sense of camaraderie. (For more ideas about connection, don't miss reading my 50 surefire ways to create connection in Chapter 12.)

Fighting isolationism on your virtual team

You want to fight isolation on your teams like the plague. The only way to do that successfully is to make engagement fun and interesting. Because virtual work can be lonely, your virtual workers need to know consistently that they're valued, that you care about them, and that they're an important part of the company.

Fighting isolationism certainly starts with the relationships that team members have with each other, the relationship they have with their manager, and the relationship they have with your organization.

TIP

Use these tips to keep isolationism at bay and be sure to train each of your virtual team leaders to do the same with their respective teams:

>> **Establish frequent check-ins both personal and professional.** Get to know them, who they are, and what they care about.

>> **Use recognition and encouragement frequently when virtual team members are hitting the mark.** This could be a simple as sharing a story of a team member's contribution during your weekly team meeting video call or creating an appreciation blog space or award where team members can recognize each other on an ongoing basis.

>> **Offer engagement incentives and make it fun.** For example, the more they participate, engage, and reach out to their team to provide feedback, the more they get their names entered into a drawing for a weekend getaway.

>> **Set up virtual interactive huddles.** Like a sports team huddling on the sidelines during a game, your team members can do the same in the virtual world. During these interactive meetings, they can talk about weekly wins or lessons learned and everyone participates. You'll need a video meeting and some collaborative tools to engage all team members.

>> **Conduct home or remote office visits.** If budget allows, team leaders can go out to lunch with their team members and spend some time getting to know each other on an individual basis.

Keep in mind that research studies have shown human beings need social interaction to maintain the highest levels of productivity. In a virtual environment, you have to work harder to create social interaction and make it a priority. If it isn't a focus, team members will start to experience feelings of frustration and detachment, and engagement levels will quickly deteriorate, which means that results will soon suffer.

Don't leave connection to chance and hope that teams will figure it out. Provide support, communication, training, clear expectations, and many opportunities for connection to occur. If you're going to utilize virtual teams as a business model to grow your business, be sure to do it right.

Chapter **3**

Preparing for Your Career as a Virtual Team Member

Working virtually from a home office where you never have to get out of your sweatpants and your puppy gets to snuggle at your feet every day sounds dreamy. In fact, millions of people are attracted to virtual work options and thousands of people are living this reality around the world.

Just a decade ago, many businesses and organizations never would have considered allowing their employees working remotely. Today, remote work is on the rise and is the future of how the global workforce gets work done. According to the 2017 State of Telecommuting in the U.S. Employee Workforce report, 43 percent of U.S. workers now work remotely part of the time, up from 9 percent just 10 years ago.

Many reasons justify this shift, and this chapter focuses on you, the worker, who is interested in transitioning to working remotely in your current position or landing your next gig as a global team member with an organization that seeks virtual workers. Furthermore, this chapter helps you evaluate what mindset, positioning, and office set-up you need to make a virtual working arrangement possible, where to look for your next remote opportunity, and how to sell the concept of working virtually to your company, even if it's telecommuting just one or two days a week.

Note: I recognize that the terms *telework, telecommuting, working from home, remote work,* and *freelancing* are synonymous with virtual work. In this chapter, I refer to *virtual work* as the one consistent term to reflect them all.

Deciding If Working Virtually Is Right for You

Virtual work as a career choice is a decision that requires thought and planning. Although at first it may seem daunting to make the switch to working remotely, it can create a fulfilling and rewarding work experience for both the employer and the employee if done with care, clarity, and intention.

These sections discuss why virtual work is popular, how virtual work can affect on your life, and some questions you can ask yourself to discover whether virtual work is best for you.

Eyeing why virtual work is so attractive

For many people, the benefits of working virtually are obvious — no commute, flexible schedule, focused productive time to work, and of course, working in your PJs. But if you're considering switching to a virtual work model, take a closer look at the benefits you may not have considered. Here are six benefits for why you may want to work virtually:

Time management

Working virtually provides you with more personal time throughout the day. Because you're cutting down on the daily commute, you have more time to exercise, walk your dog, meditate, sleep, cook healthy meals, get your kids to school, enjoy hobbies, connect with family and friends, and do whatever else you like to do.

Virtual work also gives you more control over your schedule. To some degree, you can set and customize your work hours. For example, if you start work at 4 a.m. to connect with colleagues from Hong Kong and London, you may take a break from 9 a.m.–2 p.m. and then begin working again at 3 p.m. Virtual work arrangements enable you to meet other demands for your time during the day. If you find you do your best work at night or early morning, you can find a virtual opportunity that fits your schedule.

Self-direction

You can thrive in a virtual working environment if you're most engaged and plugged in when you're able to direct your workflow, plan your daily tasks and priorities, and hold yourself accountable for accomplishing your goals and your team's. The ability to control your schedule is a powerful opportunity to grow professionally and personally.

Money

When you work virtually, you can make a decent living working from home, no matter where you're located. Based on a special analysis of U.S. Census data conducted for FlexJobs by Global Workplace Analytics, the average annual income for most telecommuters is $4,000 higher than that of workers who don't telecommute.

Even if you live in a rural area of the country, with the right set of skills and technical savviness, you can work virtually in a role that compensates you well. You can also cut down on your personal expenses such as gas, auto maintenance, clothing allowance, and meals when you don't have to be in an office environment every day.

Happiness

Virtual workers report a higher level of job satisfaction and overall happiness and lower levels of stress when working from home. Due to a flexible work schedule and less time commuting, you have an ability to incorporate more things into your day that are joyful and fulfilling.

Virtual work eliminates much of the politics of working in an office so you can focus on doing the work without all the distractions. In addition, virtual work provides the opportunity to work in a more diverse team culture. You can work with teammates spread across the United States or the world. You can discover more about different cultures, work ethics, beliefs, and values. Diverse teammates share novel life experiences that can expand your awareness and appreciation of others.

Phase into retirement

Every company I work with is concerned with the real issue of *brain drain* in the workplace, which happens when you've been with a company for a long time and carry around years of institutional knowledge that hasn't been documented, written down, or captured anywhere and now you're ready to retire. If you're in this position, a phased approach to retirement, such as working in the office two days a week and at home three days a week, then going part-time virtual two to three days a week is a smart way to help you glide into retirement. More importantly, it helps your company transfer the cultural knowledge that you're carrying around in your head through opportunities to train, mentor, and coach others and gives you the chance to solidify your legacy.

World travel

If you're planning on being a virtual work freelancer, you have a lot of interesting options available, including choosing where you want to work. Depending on your role, traveling around the world while you work on various projects and teams is completely possible and thousands of people do it successfully every day.

Jobs that align nicely with virtual work and world travel include web designer, developer, online marketer, copy writer, blogger, digital director, data manager, engineer, SEO analyst, technical writer, account manager, sales, web hosting, marketing manager, customer success manager, grant and proposal writer, editor, and many more. These jobs represent an opportunity to see the world while working remotely, and to you this may sound like a dream come true. Certainly, this type of work situation is rich in benefits including:

>> Being able to relocate anywhere

>> Controlling your work schedule and the hours you work

>> Needing only a laptop to make a decent living

>> Never having to step foot in a corporate office setting

>> Meeting people from all over the world

>> Being able to immerse yourself in a different country with different customs and ways of living

>> Having more balance in life

Recognizing the personal impacts of working virtually

Despite the benefits of working remotely, being a virtual team member isn't short of struggles. Your mom will call and text you at all times of the day because she doesn't think you actually work. Friends not working will ask you to take the day off to go shopping or out to breakfast. Neighbors will politely ask if you can let their dogs out while they're away or drive them to a doctor appointment when their car breaks down because you're obviously not that busy. These requests will happen, and your success depends on how you handle them.

As a 17-year veteran of remote work, my daily struggle of working virtually is real. While writing this chapter, my daughters are screaming in the background while competitively playing video games. My new puppy is trying to scratch his way into my office, whining and barking for my attention. Kids from the neighborhood just rang the doorbell, and because I hesitated for a moment to finish a thought, they peered into my office windows, forcing me to stop what I was doing to answer the door and address them.

Losing focus can easily lead to multitasking and pull your attention away to deal with low priority items, which makes time management a challenge. The daily life of a virtual worker can be difficult and frustrating at times, but the benefits still far outweigh the challenges. Here are some ways being a virtual team member can impact you:

TIP

>> **Transition:** When you work in an office, your workday typically ends when you leave for the day. The transitional drive from work to home allows you to shift your energy and mindset so that you're ready to focus on your partner, kids, parents, roommates, or pets when you arrive home. That transition is more difficult when you work virtually, often feeling like work never shuts down, which can impact cultivating deep relationships with your family, friends, or pets because you're constantly distracted by work texts, emails, pings, dings, and rings.

Consider how you're going to make an effective transition when you're finished with work. If you have a designated workspace, close your laptop, turn off the lights, and shut the door to signal that you're finished with work for the day. Take a brief 30-minute walk around your neighborhood. Doing so can work wonders for a shift in mindset.

>> **Family:** Oftentimes family members don't understand that you're actually doing real work when you're home all day. Every day when my kids get home from school, they want to talk to me, share their day with me, or show me something they created. Occasionally after a rough day, they want to talk out their emotions with me. Unfortunately sometimes I can't stop what I'm doing right at that moment. When your children or pets can see you, but you're not able to give them your immediate time and attention because you're in the middle of working on an important project or leading a webinar when a family need pops up, it can be difficult for them to grasp. It's very conflicting. Juggling between the two can sometimes seem like you're drowning and no one is around to throw you a life vest.

>> **Boundary management:** *Boundary management* refers to the separation of work and home. When you're working virtually, managing boundaries can get extremely blurry. Choosing to shut off work and focus on personal interests

is one aspect of setting boundaries. Another more difficult task is to set boundaries with others. Virtual team members frequently complain about unspoken expectations imposed by themselves or others that they're always available in order to prove they're actually working. This mentality is aligned with issues of control and a lack of trust. Setting clear expectations with team members and your manager about your availability is an important aspect of working successfully in a virtual environment.

>> **Advocacy:** A recent *New York Times* article highlighted how people in the office exclude virtual workers, which can easily happen when the whole team isn't virtual. Virtual team inclusion requires a willingness to make an extra effort and consistently speak up and provide input, reminding your team, boss, and people in the office that you have something to contribute and can add valuable insight. Be your best advocate and work diligently to keep lines of communication open. When you're not included in a meeting invitation or a meeting gets rescheduled and you aren't notified, speak up even when doing so is uncomfortable. Make sure that your voice is heard even if you're not in the office.

>> **Distraction management:** Consider how you'll limit distractions in your virtual office. You may work from home, work in a remote office in another city, or work from a coffee shop. Make sure you create a workspace that allows you to get work done and be present for virtual calls and video conferencing. Ignoring this important aspect of working remotely will tarnish your performance, reputation, and long-term success in your role.

Predicting whether you'll excel as a virtual team member

Regardless of where you live, how old you are, or what your gender, race, or physical abilities are, virtual work is an option for you. Keep in mind though that not all jobs can be accomplished virtually, and current research reports that management, office, sales, and administrative jobs make up 43 percent of virtual jobs with the fastest growing remote opportunities in therapy, virtual administration, client services, tutoring, and state and local government.

It's difficult to know for sure whether virtual work will be a great fit for you or whether you'll be a productive, engaged virtual team member until you give it a try. If you desire and intend to succeed in this type of work environment, make sure you're aware of the challenges you may face and the proven characteristics of successful virtual team members. Use Table 3-1 to assess whether virtual work is a smart choice.

TABLE 3-1   ## Considering Working Virtually

Questions to Ask Yourself	Yes	No
Will I commit to presenting myself professionally over the phone and on video conferencing (such as making sure my office environment is presentable, limiting distractions, dressing professionally, and so on)?		
Will I manage conflict effectively with team members by asking questions, assessing emotions and feelings about decisions, and working to gain verbal agreement?		
Will I commit to communicating daily using various technology tools and agree to address important issues by picking up the phone or participating in videoconference meetings?		
Am I okay with limited in-person interaction on a daily basis?		
Can I be effective at brainstorming ideas and solutions with my team members over the phone?		
Am I willing to set time aside to get to know my virtual team members personally so that we can develop a strong, collaborative relationship?		
Can I organize my time effectively so that I have a productive workday that meets the needs of my team members?		
Can I commit to reasonable work hours and turning off work at the end of the day if I'm working from home?		
Do I have a practical workspace where I can get work done virtually without interruptions?		
Does my family support my desire to work virtually and do they understand what I need from them to be successful?		
If working on a global team, am I willing to shift when I work and sleep to connect with team members in different time zones?		
Am I self-directed and can I accomplish daily tasks and priorities without any check-ins or prompts from others?		
Am I willing to hold myself accountable for accomplishing my goals without my manager's daily support?		
Do I have self-confidence and trust with team members to self-advocate when needed?		
Am I willing to set clear boundaries of when I'm working and when I'm available with my family and friends?		
Can I commit to a transition routine that will help me shift from work to home and be present with those around me?		

Assessing your skills for virtual freelance work

Working with a variety of clients as a virtual freelancer may sound like the best gig around, and I'd have to agree. Yet, this type of remote work isn't always a possibility due to your life circumstances, and it requires keen social skills and a few strong character traits. Being a successful freelancer requires a high level of resolve, great communication skills, sales and networking ability, relationship building, time management, and organizational skills. You have to be willing to put yourself out there, market your services, ask for referrals, and deliver great customer service in order to keep a steady flow of repeat customers.

Most importantly, you need to be good with your money. Sometimes work opportunities will be plentiful and other times work will dry up. Be prepared to save your money when you're financially stable in order to coast through times when you want to take a break or can't land a lucrative project. Freelancing is a lifestyle choice. It's easy to feel alone, and it's up to you to make an effort to supplement your work with a rich, dynamic lifestyle.

Proposing Virtual Work to Your Boss and Teammates

If you're in a traditional 8–5 job and you've decided to pursue virtual work, you can start with your current employer and put together a proposal for your boss and teammates that highlights the benefits of working virtually and addresses all of their probable concerns. Be prepared to answer tough questions and work through issues to convince your boss and your colleagues that you working virtually will be a good move for the company and your team.

These sections identify how you prepare a proposal to working virtually including what benefits to include and what concerns to address.

Preparing your proposal

If you want to make any change to your work schedule, create a formal proposal that addresses the key issues — benefits and challenges — of the change. Figure 3-1 shows an example of a proposal for your boss and company.

Flexible Work Schedule Proposal Form

Employee Name	
Job Title	
Department	
Email	
Phone number	

Type of flexible work option being requested:
Fill in telework from home, hoteling, space sharing, part-time or full-time, contract or freelance, and so on. Be sure to include HR policies and practices, if any.

Reasons for seeking a flexible work schedule:
Here you will explain why you want this. Is it because you work better early in the morning? Or do you have an extremely long commute? Is it because you need quiet focused time to do your best work? Is it because you're seeking less stress/better balance in your life? Or maybe you have family issues that need attention every afternoon? Whatever it is, be honest about your needs and how a flexible work schedule will accomplish it.

Success factors:
Sell your plan by listing all the factors that will make this arrangement a success.

This list of factors will make this work arrangement a success both for me and for the team and overall organization.

- Weekly one-on-one call/video call with supervisor
- Weekly and/or daily written priorities; send to supervisor
- Highly detailed project management with daily reporting on where time was spent
- Private, quiet, distraction-free home office space complete with PC with mic and camera, headphones, ergonomic chair, printer, speaker phone
- A stronger focus on measuring success and progress based on measurable results like meeting deadlines and comparing the quality of work versus the perceived time at work
- Reliable, high-speed broadband Internet access
- Both clear, reliable mobile phone and a landline
- High degree of comfort with technology and troubleshooting technology hiccups
- Strong work ethic (proven history of meeting deadlines, working independently, creating high quality work, demonstrating strong collaboration skills)

Contingency planning:
Here you acknowledge how you'll respond if there are issues with working from home.

If anything should impact my accessibility or productivity while telecommuting, I have the following contingency plans:

- If home Wi-Fi is down, there is a power outage, or there is some other issue that prevents work from taking place at home, I'll switch my mobile office to a local coffee shop or I'll come into the office.
- I'll have in place service level agreements (SLAs) in place for when internal and external customers can't reach me. For example, I will respond to your voicemail/text/email within two hours.

FIGURE 3-1:
A sample virtual work option proposal.

Impacts to key job parts:
Here you identify your key job roles and explain how your flexible schedule can impact them.

The majority of my daily work involves working on my computer or participating in conference calls, video calls, or in-person meetings. In large part, working from home won't impact my ability to any of the key parts of my job. See these details:

- Weekly staff meeting: It's already handled as a conference call, so I'll dial in on days when I'm working from home.
- Complete _____ report: No change
- Collaborate with IT on _____ project: No change
- Write and edit quarterly business reports for all accounts: No change
- (Include any other job duties.)

Communication/collaboration technology:
Here you list all the ways you can be reached throughout your workday. Communicate that you'll block times on your calendar for focused work and meetings, but that other times you're available via these communication vehicles.

- Phone (landline and mobile)
- Phone (can office phone be routed to mobile?)
- VPN to access shared files on company server
- Text (on phone or online)
- Email (both personal and company accounts)
- IM/Hipchat (or other instant message/chat program)
- Calendar (shared calendar to see available times)
- Skype (or other videoconference program)

Advantage to the company/department:
There are many advantages to having flexible work schedules. Among them are

- More efficient work schedule
- Higher productivity
- Higher morale/less stress
- Reduced environmental impact
- Better able to handle calls from earlier or later time zones
- Still able to work on snow days
- Reduced contamination on sick days
- Work-life balance
- Better recruitment and retention

Flexible work schedules at _____ (fill in company's name):
Here you cite examples of successful flexible work arrangements within your organization as well as linking flexible work and its advantages to the organization's values and stated goals

FIGURE 3-1: *(better work-life balance, better recruiting and retention, lower carbon footprint, culture of*
continued. *trust, and so on)*

Proposed start date:

Proposed review date:
I propose a 90- day trial period after which we can review the schedule and make adjustments as necessary.

Proposed work schedule changes:

	Current work schedule:	**Proposed new work schedule:**
Sunday		
Monday		
Tuesday		
Wednesday		
Thursday		
Friday		
Saturday		

Employee signature: _____

Date: _____

Supervisor approval: _____

Date: _____

Supervisor's name:

Job title:

FIGURE 3-1:
continued.
Department:

REMEMBER

When putting your proposal together, consider the following:

>> Talk to HR to find out if your company is currently offering virtual work in any other positions that can help garner support for your proposal.

>> Interview managers and employees with established virtual work situations and find out what's working and what's a challenge. Inquire what measures are in place to determine success. Include these company insights in your proposal.

>> Research if competitor organizations are using virtual teams, to what extent, and what the results are.

>> How can you align your request to work remotely with company values and vision? For example, if your company values innovation, flexibility, and agility, then they align well with your request to work remotely.

>> Assemble your past performance reviews that highlight strengths that can help you be successful in a virtual work situation. For example, self-starter, goal oriented, focused, flexible, great communication skills, takes initiative, works without supervision.

>> If virtual work is new to your team or company, start with a request of working from home one to two days a week.

>> If you're going for a full-time virtual arrangement, present a detailed communication and engagement plan for your manager and team.

>> Propose a pilot of the new working arrangement for six months with suggested success measures to determine whether it's working. Measures can include

- Productivity levels

- Financial targets

- Deliverable dates

- Communication effectiveness with team members, customers, and vendors

- Participation and engagement levels

- Improved health, sleep, and overall job satisfaction

>> Consider what software, equipment, or other expenditures the company will need to make to set up your remote office.

Focusing on the benefits

After clearly stating your request, focus on how virtual work will benefit the company. Reinforce your commitment to the company and your value to the team, and then state your beliefs regarding how working remotely can help you be more productive and produce high quality work. Use the following key points to outline your proposal:

1. **Lay out reasons why working virtually is important to you.**

   They may be financial, health, family, and so on.

2. **Include any research that shows virtual workers are more productive and happier and stay with their employer longer.**

3. **If appropriate, discuss how working virtually will improve your ability to connect with your global customers or team members.**

4. **Track and analyze weekly how much time and money you waste by attending unnecessary office meetings.**

   Highlight how much it costs you and the company.

5. **For one week, keep a journal of the number of distractions that keep you from doing actual work.**

   Estimate the amount of focused work time that you'll have in a virtual work situation.

6. **Share with your employer that cost savings attributed to remote work is an average of $11,000 per half-time telecommuter according to Global Workplace Analytics.**

7. **Pick and choose from the vast amount of research data available that proves the positive impact and additional cost savings of virtual work for companies, employees, and teams.**

Possible key points to include are the following:

» **Positive business impacts:**

   - Better utilization of office space
   - Faster response times to team members and customers
   - Reduced carbon footprint
   - Reduced expenses (parking, office snacks, coffee, meals)
   - Improved company reputation in the industry
   - Reduced turnover costs

» **Positive team impacts:**

   - Increased engagement and productivity levels
   - Increased talent pool
   - Key employees retained
   - Happy employees

>> **Positive employee impacts:**

- Lower stress levels

- Improved work-life balance and relationships

- Enhanced creativity and innovation

- Eleven days gained per year by not commuting

- Reduced expenses (gas, maintenance, clothing, food) estimated at $2,700 annually if working virtually part time

Addressing key concerns

Don't shy away from addressing common key concerns in your proposal. Create an opportunity to have an honest conversation about them to continue to build the case for virtual work. Both managers and team members who aren't currently working virtually have some common concerns you'll want to address. Here are some common concerns and how to respond to them:

>> **You'll be sitting around eating bonbons all day instead of working.** Outline expectations to discuss and agree on with your manager and team on what needs approval such as availability, response time, and flexibility during the workday.

>> **You'll miss deadlines because you can't be self-directed.** For each project, priority, or important task, deadlines will be agreed upon, written down, and measured.

>> **You won't hold yourself accountable when your manager isn't looking over your shoulder.** Outline a plan for how you can keep track of deliverables, manage your time, and accomplish goals.

>> **We won't get your full participation and engagement when you aren't in the office.** Provide ideas for collaborating virtually and how you'll stay connected to the team. Clarify when you'll meet with each team member in the office during the week. If you're virtual full time, propose a plan for staying connected. Here are some ideas:

- Plan virtual one-on-one meetings with each team member monthly and with your boss weekly to check in on a personal level.

- Recommend that you'll visit the office in person for several days each quarter.

- Address concerns about cohesiveness and engagement and how you're going to make the extra effort to stay engaged and connected to your team members.

- Outline ideas for what's possible if a work emergency occurs and your team needs you in the office.

>> **It won't be fair to other team members.** After you prove virtual work is a successful way to work, you're creating opportunities for others to follow in your footsteps. It becomes a cultural shift for the company and will offer several positive benefits and significant cost savings. Plan to communicate and address jealousy, envy, or anger from your teammates and figure out how to support them in presenting their own proposal for remote work if appropriate.

>> **Communication will suffer.** Develop and share a plan for collecting frequent feedback from your manager and team. Having a feedback process is the most effective and proactive way to continually improve your working relationships when you're remote. Ask these feedback questions to your team members and manager:

- Is your virtual work arrangement working?

- What are your challenges and frustrations when I'm not in the office? How can I do a better job addressing them?

- Am I communicating with you enough? Where can I provide you with more information?

- Do you feel like our relationship is strong? Is there anything else I could do to build trust with you?

In your proposal, be sure to address these concerns and reiterate that you're willing to discuss and add other concerns after talking with your manager and team. Without their support, setting up a successful virtual working arrangement will be difficult at best, and you may soon be looking for another job.

THE STATE OF REMOTE WORK

If you've ever searched for a job with a flexible work schedule, you know that there are a lot of too-good-to-be true listings and just plain scams. Sorting through all the junk postings makes it hard for anyone to find the truly great flex jobs that are available.

Ten years ago, FlexJobs was created to solve this problem. By vetting the job opportunities, FlexJobs is now connecting thousands of people seeking flexible schedule jobs with companies seeking flexible employees. Everyone wins. Along the way, FlexJobs has become a leader in the flexible job movement. I met with Brie Weiler Reynolds, Senior Career Specialist at FlexJobs, for her take on the state of flexible jobs.

(continued)

(continued)

- **What are the trends for flexible work?** "More growth! All indications say that we will continue to see more — more people demanding flexible work schedules and more companies seeing the value to having flexible employees. Remote work has grown 115 percent in the last ten years, and it will continue to grow. For people currently working in the office, they'll have more opportunities to try out a flexible work schedule for one to two days a week. We'll probably also see baby boomers delaying retirement by seeking flexible work as a way to be active."

- **What's driving growth today?** "Ten years ago the biggest single driver of remote work was technology. Employees could dial in from anywhere and everyone had mobile phones. Now you have Millennials making a statement in the workforce — they have grown up with technology and connectivity their whole lives. They want to work when and where they want to work and, most importantly, they see it as a standard way of working — not a perk to be earned. This generational shift will drive the trend in the coming years."

- **What do remote workers need to know?** "There are a lot of things first-time remote workers need to know, from how to set up your office, the best products to have, and how to set boundaries and use technology so you can work efficiently. For great advice on taxes and insurance, we work with an advocacy group called 1 Million for Work Flexibility (www.workflexibility.org), and they have great advice and a community of experts to help. Or check out the blog (https://flexjob.com/blog/) where we have a lot of great information for freelancers and contract workers."

- **What do you say to the naysayers?** "Every time a major company speaks out against the benefits of telecommuting we revisit this issue. The reality is, it's pretty rare. Since 2013, we've seen six to seven major companies pull back — and in that same time, hundreds of companies have started or grown their remote programs. The success and growth of flexible work options far outweighs the impact of a few large companies who step away from it. In these cases, there is usually something else going on at the company, like a drop in overall performance, lack of product development, management turnover — it's not that telecommuting is the problem."

Determining Whether You Have a Workspace That Works

Your virtual work environment can look different depending on the project you're working on, your role, your remote working agreement, your company policies, and your living situation. You have several options when working virtually (at home, in a coffee shop, hoteling with your employer, and more).

Every environment offers pros and cons and can influence what you'll consider, what you'll propose to your boss, or what the next type of virtual opportunity you'll pursue.

Working from home

Many virtual workers chose to work from home. If this option is for you, you have several home office needs to consider. Think about where can you carve out a space that is private and quiet when needed and doesn't interfere with what your roommates or family is doing. Arranging your home office can be tricky, but with a little creative thinking, you can usually make it work.

Here are several essentials and a few nonessentials to make room for when scoping out a workspace in your home:

>> **Work desk:** Your can work on a kitchen table or a makeshift table as long as you can limit distractions and it's comfortable to sit at for six to eight hours per day. Seventeen years ago, my first desk was a piece of wood, propped up by two crates in the corner of my bedroom. I sat cross-legged on the floor to work. Of course, I don't recommend doing this, but I was determined to work from home and did whatever was necessary to make it work. (Waking up at 6 a.m. and checking emails did create issues with my husband.)

>> **Computer desk:** If you need a larger workspace for writing, drawing, or design work, you may need a separate computer desk or a standing desk.

>> **Computer or laptop:** Your employer usually supplies your computer or you need to purchase your own as a freelancer. Depending on the type of work you do, you may need an additional larger screen so you can always have more than one window open at a time.

>> **Phone:** You need a cell phone that gets good service. Furthermore, having a separate work phone and dedicated work number may be helpful. Depending on where you live, you may need to consider getting a backup mode of communication, such as a landline to ensure uninterrupted service, particularly for your conference calls, particularly if voiceover Internet protocol (VOIP) doesn't work.

>> **Internet service:** Reliable Internet is one of the most important things you need to work from home and can be a deal breaker if it's not effective. You may need to upgrade your Internet service to ensure you have the fastest and most reliable speeds available. Frequent videoconferencing may require that you connect to your modem using an Ethernet cord so you don't lose video connection. Be sure to check what is offered in your area.

- **>> Printer/scanner:** Most likely you need a printer available when working from home as well as a scanner to scan important documents to your company, clients, manager, or teammates.

- **>> Filing cabinets:** If you're not storing everyone on the cloud, you most likely need filing cabinets that are fireproof or that you can lock up to keep important documents.

- **>> Office chairs:** If clients ever meet at your home office, you need somewhere for them to sit.

- **>> Bookshelves:** Keep in mind that you'll need to have somewhere to store your work or you'll eventually be living with piles all around you. Keep your workspace tidy and efficient by using files and bookshelves to organize materials.

- **>> Lighting:** Make sure that the lighting in your office makes the workspace feel inviting and allows you to see your entire workspace clearly. Workspace lighting should include natural light, overhead, and task lighting. Natural light during the day is best and helps with your mindset. However, most virtual workers I know also work in the evenings, so having lighting that illuminates your workspace properly is important to steer clear of eye strain and headaches that can keep you awake.

If you're lucky enough to have a dedicated office space in your home, keep in mind that it should make a good impression about the company and you. For example, a dreary basement office isn't conducive to creative thinking or warm and welcoming for clients. If your office is in a busy area of your home, consider investing in some noise-cancelling headphones to reduce any unwanted sounds.

Furthermore, when working from home, having good organizational skills is a must or you'll quickly discover your work is spread out all over your house. Keep your space organized, have a place for supplies that is easily accessible, and institute a good filing system to keep track of your top priorities and projects. A messy desk makes focusing difficult. Each week, take time to organize your desk and manage filing. On a quarterly basis, go through magazines, articles, and other must-read items you have. If you can find the same information online whenever you actually need it, toss it. Annually, plan to clean your files, bookshelves, and office supplies and get rid of anything that you don't use frequently enough.

Considering hoteling

Hoteling has been a rising trend to cut office expenses and improve collaboration among coworkers and teams. *Hoteling* provides temporary workspace in the office, such as a cubicle, conference room, or open collaboration areas that employees or teams reserve for a short period of time. Studies show that traditional office space is only 50 percent utilized on average due to sick time, vacation days, and travel; hoteling works effectively for companies that already have people working virtually one to three days a week.

Hoteling requires you to use an online reservation system to search and reserve a space in the office for the day, and you never have the same dedicated office space. This trend has helped to improve collaboration between virtual coworkers, save cost, and allow companies to spend money on other important investments like technology, software, or hiring. If you're considering virtual work and your company offers hoteling as an option, give it a try.

Upsides to hoteling

Hoteling can be a great fit if you want to work virtually part time and with others in the office part time. It offers several benefits to both companies and employees as long as you approach hoteling with clear goals, expectations, and an open mind. Some pros associated with hoteling include the following:

>> **Cost savings:** Companies benefit from significant cost savings due to space utilization, which, as a result, allows them to grow without renting or purchasing more office space. It also permits them to invest in more important things like people, technology, and research.

>> **Project collaboration:** Hoteling can be perfect for collaboration on specific projects because you get to choose where you sit and what team members you sit by. Project teams can reserve an area together, such as a conference room to bang out a project or to solve an issue on a development initiative.

>> **Team building:** Teams can hotel on the same day by reserving an open collaboration area and work side by side for the day. It allows team members to know each other personally when most of the team works remotely and engage with each other on a more personal level.

>> **Quiet time/privacy:** If you're in the office and need focused work time, you can move if you need to and find a more quiet or private space to work.

Downsides to hoteling

Here are some cons associated with hoteling:

>> **Difficulty locating people:** Depending on the size of your company, finding people can be difficult. Because each space is assigned a number, you could roam the halls searching for someone's hotel space and waste a lot of time in the process.

- >> **Lack of cleanliness:** People can be dirty. Leftover food, wrappers, and even dirty dishes in a hotel space are common complaints.

- >> **Loss of belonging and personal space:** When hoteling, you don't get a space to call your own that you decorate with pictures of your kids, hobbies, and favorite vacations. It can seem impersonal and lonely.

- >> **Issues with having a mobile office**: Be prepared to lug around your work because you don't have a desk or drawers. Packing and unpacking can be time consuming and it's easy to lose something. However, some offices provide employees with a locker so they don't continually have to bring work back and forth from home.

- >> **Security concerns:** There's a greater risk of security violations or information getting into the wrong hands when employees are regularly moving sensitive documents from one place to another.

Being a successful hoteler: What to do

If your company offers hoteling or you're considering working for someone that does, here are a few things to keep in mind to be a successful hoteler:

- >> **Be proactive.** Plan to hotel strategically and in a way that supports your goals. With what team member do you need to build a better relationship? What project do you need more involvement? What space supports you in doing your best work? What space provides you with natural light next to a window? Set reminders to book your space in advance, depending on your goals.

- >> **Promote team building.** If you're located in the same city, encourage your team members to book a common area or conference room on the same day each month and use those opportunities to do a little team building. Suggest that out-of-town team members fly in quarterly to hotel onsite with the team.

- >> **Build cross-functional relationships.** Thoughtfully reserve space next to someone in another department that you should know better. Offer to go to lunch together to discuss insights about a recent project or idea that the company is launching. Break down cultural barriers.

- >> **Hold yourself accountable.** Clean up after yourself and think of the person who will sit there after you. Encourage your company to provide cleaning supplies for each hotel space.

- >> **Zen out.** Occasionally, you'll end up in a hotel space that's double booked. Work together with your space mate to come up with a plan or look for other options. Treat people with respect and kindness. Mistakes happen.

Becoming a globe-trotter

You may have the opportunity to work all anywhere in the world as a virtual team member. Keep in mind that not all coffee shops, libraries, or other places where you can set up shop may be conducive to getting your work done efficiently and on time. You need to scope out a workspace wherever you plan to live that has strong and consistent Internet.

If you'll be on team calls and occasional meetings, assess the noise levels or if you have access to a private room or area where you can have a productive conversation. Research these considerations ahead of time so that you'll have a workspace where you can set you up for success as a virtual worker.

THE BLESSING AND CURSE OF TECHNOLOGY AS A VIRTUAL WORKER

Alex Eckhart grew up in a beautiful but isolated part of the California Wine Country. His thirst for culture and desire to explore the world motivated him to get his bachelor's degree overseas in Europe. During his college years he even studied abroad in New Zealand and Australia, and he spent a summer in Argentina, all of which exposed him to different languages and cultures. From then he was hooked! After graduation, Eckhart looked for work in tech as a freelancer so he could continue to travel.

His remote work journey began on the Hawaiian island of Kauai where Eckhart gave himself 50 days to learn to code apps for the iPhone. He quickly realized how massive an undertaking that was and shifted his focus to smaller web projects where he was in complete control of the end-to-end process. He soon came upon a mentor who taught him how to use Wordpress to build websites in exchange for guitar lessons. With this new skill set, he spent the next several years as a digital nomad, building websites, living and working from Bali, Italy, and the U.S.

In Italy he learned an important lesson as a freelancer: you're always at the mercy of technology. If you're not on top of your tech needs and clearly research any technical limitations wherever you decide to locate, you'll quickly end up dead in the water. For months, Eckhart was forced to work from inside a small closet in the corner of the house he was renting in the Italian countryside in order to access his neighbor's Wi-Fi (with permission) and complete his work deliverables on time.

Eckhart continues to embrace his freelance lifestyle and travels for months at a time while working on client projects. It's empowering to realize that even if Alex lost everything, he could visit his local library, hop on the computer, and continue to make a great living.

Creating Your Remote Worker Brand

Building your virtual brand, otherwise knows as You, Inc., is an area that you want to give time and attention to developing strategically. You have a digital footprint that follows you everywhere you go, no matter where you are located in the world. Ask yourself these important questions: Does it represent you in the best way possible? Will it help you land your next remote job role and get you paid what your worth?

Gone are the days where your resume proved that you were the best person for the job within 50 miles of your office. As a virtual worker, you have to be the best person for the job in your entire state, time zone, and possibly the world. Virtual job opportunities by their nature create a more competitive environment. Your location, the way you position yourself, and your virtual brand aren't relevant. What's key is that you actively develop, manage, and grow your virtual brand with the intention to land your dream job.

The following sections discuss the key parts of your brand — your resume, portfolio, and online presence — and what you can do to make them stand out.

Reworking your resume

Almost every job you apply for will request that you submit your resume electronically either by email, by Internet job boards, or on the company's website. You need to know that many companies search their database of resumes for keywords related to the skills and experience for which they're looking. As a result, modify your resume, remove formatting for ease of submission into any database, and include keywords that can help you jump to the front of the line for any search teams related to the position you want.

TIP

Here are tips when rebuilding your resume that can help you land your next virtual job:

>> **Load your resume with keywords related to the position(s) you are interested in.** Carefully read the job ad and description to identify important keywords; many times employers repeat them more than once. Research several virtual opportunities and make a list of the keywords they mention in their ads. You can then rewrite your resume and include those keywords if you have the skills and experience required for the job.

>> **Focus on your accomplishments beyond the day-to-day tasks you do in your job.** No one cares about your job responsibilities; they care about what you did that was extraordinary or how you took initiative. For example, if

you've reduced expenses, led a major project, landed a huge client, or improved a process, highlight the financial impacts, time saved, or increases in efficiency. Here are a few questions to help you capture your accomplishments:

- What were you most known for in your last job?

- Is there anything you could do better than anyone else? What was it? How much better did you do it?

- Are there examples of projects where you were given an impossible deadline, problem, or issue and experienced success?

Building your portfolio

In addition to a resume, if you're poised and ready to go after the next virtual job opportunity, you also need to have a portfolio. A *portfolio* provides evidence that you've actually successfully done what you've listed in your resume. It shows samples of your work that demonstrate quality, level of expertise, and attention to detail; furthermore, a portfolio showcases your personal approach. Portfolios can be assembled and printed for face-to-face meetings, but it's far more common today to use a digital online portfolio that can be part of your personal website, LinkedIn profile, or blogspace. Here are some steps to putting together your portfolio:

1. **Decide what to showcase.**

   People who design creative works usually don't have any problem, but if your accomplishments are nonvisual, consider showcasing brainstorming sessions, progress updates, or a blog post about the problem you faced and the solution. You can also build a simple infographic that points out a process in which you were involved.

2. **Only pick the best examples.**

   Showcase only your best of the best even if it's just five examples. I made the mistake of posting videos of my early training days online. They were poor quality and honestly, and I wasn't that good.

3. **Keep your portfolio simple.**

   Make your portfolio easy to navigate with clear headings about what you're highlighting. Consider putting projects into categories so employers who view your portfolio don't waste time trying to find something specific.

4. **Be clear about what kind of work you want and how to contact you.**

   Clearly state the specific kind of work you're seeking, and make sure you provide a clear way to reach you. For example, "I'm looking to join a cohesive team that needs an innovator who can analyze trends and quickly generate new revenue stream ideas. Please email me at Tara@virtualwork.com."

5. **Share what makes you special.**

   Include a brief video or picture collage. Make a statement about who you are and why potential employer would want you on its team.

REMEMBER

Your portfolio is only a part of your bigger brand. Your resume, work experience, testimonials, and web presence are just as important.

Establishing your online presence

In today's job market, particularly if you want to be a virtual go-to person, having an online presence is a must. Your *online presence*, which includes everything from your social media footprint (Facebook, Twitter, Instagram, LinkedIn), says a whole lot about you. Because people make assumptions about things like your reliability, ability to communicate, professionalism, trustworthiness, and even cultural fit by checking out your personal sites, profiles, social media, blog posts and more, making sure your online presence represents you truthfully and completely is so important.

Here are some ways you can create an online presence that stands out and represents you:

>> **Build a personal website to share with potential employers.** If you're in development, design, engineering, marketing, or any job where you need to showcase your work to be competitive, a personal website that includes your resume and portfolio is the way to go. Highlight your experience and spotlight your best qualities. Use a simple landing page and break down your resume into key areas such as your bio, work experience, portfolio of examples, education, testimonials, and more.

TIP

You don't need to hire a professional web designer. Many professional, easy-to-use sites, such as www.squarespace.com, www.godaddy.com, and www.wix.com, are available. Just search online.

>> **Be consistent with your virtual brand.** Make sure that what people see on your personal website or in your portfolio is the same brand they will see if they visit your Facebook, LinkedIn, Twitter, or Instagram. If your goal is to be seen as a thought leader in marketing, recruiting, computer programming, or AI technology, then focus on creating blog posts, making comments, and writing articles that showcase your knowledge. Do a collateral review of anything about you online and determine what needs a refresh or an overhaul.

WARNING

>> **Keep your personal social media private from your professional online presence.** A good general rule: Live by the motto that what happens in Vegas should stay in Vegas and not online for the world to see. Remove or refresh anything online that doesn't position you in that light. For example, carefully scrutinize personal photos from your best friends' wedding, guys' fishing trip, or girls' weekend that could tarnish your online credibility and reputation.

>> **Engage with any company or people who you want to find out more about or potentially work for.** For example, share a recent accomplishment or featured news story about a company that you're following and add your thoughts about what makes the company a great place to work. Tag the company profile so it shows up on its feed.

Potential employers who plan to hire you without ever meeting you in person are going to do their due diligence and see what you're up to online. They will look at your posts and check out what and whom you follow, comment on, and even like. That's why you want to take your online presence seriously and build your brand the right way because it will influence their decision to hire you.

Keeping current on the latest communication and collaboration tools

If you're making every effort to experience success in a virtual work situation, make sure you're in the know about the latest trends in virtual technology. Employers are keen on understanding your level of comfort with different technology, but more importantly, they're interested if you have an open mindset to learning new technology.

TIP

Here are some tips for staying one step ahead of the ever-changing technology you'll most likely use as a virtual team member:

>> **Read.** Make it a habit to read at least one to two articles, blog posts, or whitepapers each week on tech trends related to virtual collaboration, communication, or project management.

>> **Network.** Join online community groups or attend virtual conferences where you can connect with other virtual workers and hear about what technology and tools are shaping their work experiences.

>> **Invest.** Attend conferences and seek out online courses, tutorials, or webcasts where you can get find out about the latest technologies.

>> **Volunteer.** Sometimes the best way to discover something new is to jump in and start using it. Search for volunteer groups that use virtual technology to connect and collaborate. Doing so is great way to experiment with collaboration tools to prepare you for the next opportunity and give back to your community.

Shopping for virtual worker–friendly clientele

If you're searching for your next virtual opportunity, look no further than FlexJobs (www.flexjobs.com) for the top companies with virtual work. They represent the innovators that are leading the way for virtual work around the world. Not only do these companies support virtual work, they embrace and promote it as a culture.

Research this list of companies and the jobs that they have available. This is a great place to find the kinds of jobs top companies want to fill with virtual employees. Identify key skills they're looking for, the keywords to add to your resume, and the most important characteristics they want. Align yourself with companies that you believe in and cultures that value their virtual employees. Research their values and why what they do matters to their employees, their clients, and their

INCORPORATING, OR NOT

Most virtual workers don't have to worry about this topic, but if you're starting you own freelancing business and you'll be working on different project for various companies, you'll need to consider options for setting up your business. Here are the two most common business structures for a small business to consider:

- **Sole proprietorship:** This is the most basic way to set up your business. It's easy to form and you control everything in the business. You also can be held personally liable for all financial obligations of the business.

- **Limited liability company (LLC):** An LLC offers a range of benefits for freelancers and entrepreneurs. The greatest benefit is that a corporation protects your personal assets if a client ever sues you. Another consideration is that an LLC adds instant credibility to your business and offers additional tax benefits and business deductions.

When deciding which business structure is right for you, meet with a tax accountant or attorney to make sure you're making the right decision. Depending on the work you'll be doing, risks involved and expenses you'll incur, incorporating could be a great business decision and can be done quickly and inexpensively if you're ready to start.

community. Finding a company that interests you and you're passionate about makes it easier to start the conversation about your next virtual opportunity.

Focusing on healthy work-life balance

Work–life balance is an odd term because in my opinion there isn't ever truly a separation of work from your life. Rather, work is part of your life. For me finding balance relates to the dynamic relationship between the achievement of reaching your goals and the fulfillment you get and the positive or negative influences that either support you or distract you.

MAKE YOUR ONLINE PRESENCE STAND OUT

Michael Hunter, CEO of PersonalBrand.com helps people build their personal brand to increase their influence, income, and impact. During an interview, he shared the importance of strategically and consciously building your personal brand and shared his top five red flags he watches out for when reviewing your digital footprint.

- Is your picture up-to-date?

- Do you showcase your work experience?

- Do you have a portfolio or personal website online?

- What does your profile say about you? If you have a party animal profile, are you going to come in every Monday morning with a hangover?

- How do you communicate, debate, discuss, and share your opinions with others? Are you looking to expand your perspective or just be right?

He knows that when building your personal brand, having an updated, rock star Facebook page is a must. Michael also shared five easy ways to improve your Facebook page immediately:

- Get an updated, professional headshot.

- Feature a cover image or video that boosts your credibility or positions you as a thought leader.

- Refresh your bio to make a wow impression right off the bat.

- Link to your landing page or personal website where viewers can see your full resume and review your portfolio.

- Include a featured video that shares who you are and what you stand for.

Influences can be external like friends, family, finances, coworkers, your boss, your neighbors, your house, and so on. Internal influences are things like your mindset, habits, thoughts, perspectives, beliefs, and emotions. Finding a sense of balance doesn't magically happen. Achieving a healthy work-life means making a commitment to frequently assess what is having a positive influence for you as a virtual team member and reducing or eliminating the things that aren't.

2
Building a Strong Virtual Team

Gain an understanding of the key team development factors and decisions necessary to set up your virtual team for success.

Find out what it takes to identify and recruit the right people for your virtual team.

Get tips and techniques for conducting effective virtual team interviews.

Cover all your bases when contracting with a remote worker.

Discover how to organize your team and choose the right team structure.

Uncover strategies for onboarding virtual team members and practicing behaviors that build trust quickly.

» Selecting a team framework

» Focusing on team goals

» Examining team member roles

Chapter **4**

Planning Ahead for Your Team's Success

Not surprisingly leading a virtual team versus a *co-located team* (one whose team members are all located in the same office) has similarities and dif- ferences. Many best practices for building a strong co-located team cross over to virtual teams, such as having a clear purpose for why the team exists, a set of strong values that team members agree to operate by, and clearly stated and understood team goals and priorities. Another common best practice is to ensure that team members understand their roles and responsibilities and how they impact each other's success.

Although these foundational best practices are important on both co-located and virtual teams, the amount of focus, attention, and adherence to these practices is what's integral when working and leading virtually.

This chapter discusses and assesses foundational best practices that build strong teams and how they differ with virtual teams. I explain steps for defining an inspiring team purpose, clear priorities, and the way to choose a team framework that incorporates both systems and people. I walk you through how to measure and articulate what team success would look like in relation to your goals and how to make sure that your virtual team members know exactly why they're necessary and valued.

REMEMBER

If you've been a manager of a traditionally co-located team that is now going virtual or you're managing your first virtual team ever, you may think that a lot of what I talk about in this chapter seems like common sense, which it is. It's just not common practice. And after working with thousands of team members, I can tell you with great certainty that if you plan ahead for team success by putting these foundational practices in place and you commit to them regularly, you'll already be leaps and bounds ahead of most virtual teams.

Defining Your Team Purpose

Having a clear purpose for your virtual team and every team member role impacts how you interview, who you hire, how you work with other teams in the company, and what your goals, priorities, decisions, problem-solving methods, workflow, processes, and more are.

REMEMBER

The steps to defining purpose is much deeper than simply stating your team exists to "find new business", "make the company money", "hire great employees", "handle customer service", or "build widgets". A powerful team purpose trumps everything in business. It attracts the type of team members that go above and beyond to make sure the team hits its goals. A strong purpose statement answers the age-old question: Why are you here and why is this team important?

The following sections walk through several steps to help you define a powerful purpose aligned with your company vision for your virtual team, communicate why your team is important, define your team priorities, and put a stake in the ground for how your team will be remembered.

Aligning with company vision and values

Often referred as the secret sauce to success or the glue that makes it all work, *alignment* creates the guiding path to what gets done, how it gets done, and how teams work together. It's a consistent message that flows between strategy and culture. It starts at the top by defining what your company stands for and cascades throughout your organization to impact even minor day-to-day tasks.

TIP

Think of alignment as golden thread that runs through your organization, down to every team, to every job role, and to every person. It should be apparent from your vision, values, purpose, culture, operating guidelines, strategy, systems, processes, tenants, and more. The Alignment Funnel in Figure 4-1 illustrates the importance of alignment.

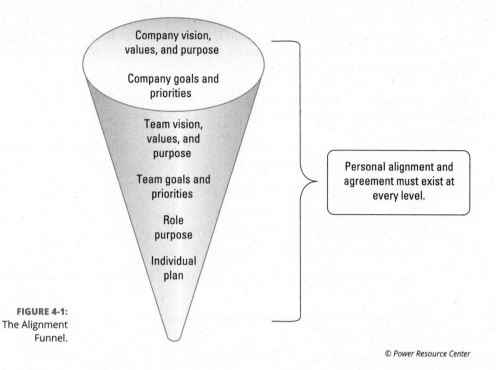

FIGURE 4-1:
The Alignment
Funnel.

Company vision, values, and purpose

Company goals and priorities

Team vision, values, and purpose

Team goals and priorities

Role purpose

Individual plan

Personal alignment and agreement must exist at every level.

© Power Resource Center

When strong levels of alignment exist across an organization, financial decisions, hiring and firing decisions, and even customer acquisitions are a heck of a lot faster, simpler, and dare I say, strategic. For example, if one of your top strategies as a business is product differentiation, then examples of alignment on your team could look like:

>> Hiring innovators and inventors

>> Setting up a team work culture that embraces a try-it mentality

>> Providing your employees time to research the latest technology and discover new ideas and then report back to the team about them

Establishing clear organizational and team alignment is critical for high performance on a virtual team because these two alignments drive the team purpose, goals, priorities, and day-to-day decisions and actions. Because you can't watch over team members, stop by their desk for a conversation, or meet with them regularly face-to-face, clear alignment provides virtual team members with clear guidelines when making decisions or solving problems on their own.

When I work with teams, I strongly advocate for establishing a habit of building, demonstrating, and discussing alignment. As a consultant, the first question I ask to understand the value of what they are asking me to do is "How does this team program, coaching initiative, or intervention align with your purpose, vision, or values?" If alignment doesn't exist, then they're probably doing something that isn't important or is a waste of time.

REMEMBER

Here are several questions you can discuss with your team and finalize the answers as you consider purpose and alignment for your virtual team:

>> What is the overarching directive or core purpose of our company other than making a profit? What are we here to do? Some examples include

- Walt Disney World: To make people happy

- Southwest Airlines: To connect people to what's important in their lives through friendly, reliable, and low-cost air travel

>> Why does our company purpose matter?

>> How does the work on our team support our company purpose? What is our team here to do?

>> How does each job role on this team support our team purpose? What is each job here to do?

>> Why are the company values meaningful?

>> How can our team live these values out loud every day, such as

- In team meetings?

- On team projects?

- When faced with conflict?

- When onboarding a new team member?

>> How do we agree to treat each other on our team?

>> How will we know that our team has been successful in living our purpose?

When building alignment for your virtual team, look for every opportunity to tie the work being done to what's important to the company. Doing so gives breadth and depth to projects, goals, and roles in your organization. Regularly check in with your virtual team members to discuss alignment and why what they're doing matters and how it ties into the bigger picture.

Communicating why your team exists

Even though your team may be 100 percent virtual or partially virtual, every team member needs to have a reason for getting out of bed in the morning and showing up. No matter the field your team is in — sales, software development, marketing, recruiting, or customer service — talking about what work you're doing, why it matters, and who it impacts is important.

REMEMBER

Being able to clearly articulate to all team members why your team is necessary and why every job on the team is necessary will attract team members who care about your message and show up every day because they believe they're making a difference. Everyone wants more than a paycheck; they want to know that the work they're doing matters.

Here are four questions to discuss with your team and help you communicate your team's purpose:

>> Who do we serve? Who is our customer? (Think both externally and internally.) You may serve more than one type of customer.

>> What product or service do we provide?

>> Why does this product or service matter? What problem does it solve? What benefit does it provide?

>> How are we different or unique? What are we known for?

Putting it all together, you end up with a statement or story that is meaningful and powerful. Here's an example:

> We provide the most up-to-date software development research before it hits the market to our developers and engineers, helping them to build best-in-class healthcare systems that save people's lives.

Communicating the team's purpose and the impact it has can change slightly from project to project or even shift mid-project. This clarity can provide focus, engagement, and momentum. It helps the team move forward in the same direction and in pursuit of the same goal. For example, in the movie *Apollo 13* rocket engineers quickly changed their purpose from sending astronauts to the moon and back home safely to getting the astronauts home alive.

TIP

Make sure your purpose is simple, concise, free of corporate jargon, easy to remember, and inspiring. Furthermore, it needs to highlight your team's uniqueness. Your purpose is what makes people on your team want to spend energy on moving in the direction of progress. A good team purpose makes people feel fulfilled and valued.

Having clarity around team priorities

Without fail, there will be more projects, goals, tasks, requests, and requirements than your team can possibly implement and focus on in any given week, month, or quarter. When considering how to help your virtual team achieve high levels of performance and success, focus on establishing, adjusting, and communicating priorities on a regular basis. And because your team is virtual, you must keep everyone on the same page with direction, focus, and shifting goals.

REMEMBER

Prioritization requires balancing the benefit of each task or goal your team is responsible for against the benefits, costs, and implications involved to decide what's more important. Having clear priorities for your virtual team will help the team:

» Focus on the most important requests and requirements

» Plan for workflow, handoffs, deliverables, timeframes, and so on

» Manage their projects more effectively

» Make decisions when presented with conflicting goals

» Allocate their time, energy, and resources

Most teams that I work with don't have a good method for prioritization, and it's not because prioritization is difficult. It's because prioritization takes a commitment of time and a structured practice to determine where to focus. Here is a seven-step method for prioritization that I recommend:

1. **Build a collective list of tasks.**

   List all team member tasks that significantly impact results. (After your team is established, you can do this together using a virtual whiteboard.) Remove any ongoing goals such as coming in under budget or hitting revenue goals.

2. **Identify tasks between urgent versus important.**

   Any tasks that have serious consequences to the team, business, or your customers if not completed in the next 90 days are considered urgent. Focus on the following to help you break down tasks into the two categories:

   - Put tasks in one of two columns: Urgent or Important.

   - Analyze the value for each urgent and important task to the team and business by assessing the level of impact each task has to people, process, or profit.

   - Rank them in order of urgency first, followed by value.

   - Analyze dependencies necessary to complete urgent tasks.

3. **Define tasks that always take priority.**

   These tasks can be major client requests, CEO requests, or system breakdowns that immediately move to the top of the urgent column.

4. **Determine time, resources, and effort required.**

   Making this determination is helpful when you have too many priorities. It helps you decide whether to check off the low effort priorities first or start on high effort priorities.

5. **Start cutting.**

   Only focus on priorities that your team can reasonably accomplish in the next three to six months with the time and people resources you have available. If accomplishing more priorities is necessary, ask for more resources.

6. **Assign tasks and review regularly.**

   Clarify what needs to be done to accomplish the priority, who is going to do what, and when the tasks need to be finished. Review progress on priorities consistently with your team.

7. **Be ready to adjust.**

   Change happens every day at a rapid pace. Prepare your team members for shifting priorities by keeping them updated on any recent developments or company decisions that may impact their priorities.

REMEMBER

Virtual team members can easily get off track if priorities aren't clear and progress isn't regularly assessed. Keep in mind that your team members should only have one top priority at a time or else they'll think everything is important, won't understand what matters most, and will have difficulty deciding on where to focus.

Always communicate to your team that although one person may be the expert assigned to complete a task or priority, the entire team is responsible for achieving it. This creates a shared team goal and support for team priorities, no matter where someone is located.

Considering what you want your team to be known for

If your virtual team doesn't have a good team brand or reputation from the get-go, changing poor first impressions can be an uphill battle. With a lack of face-to-face interactions, social outings (where team members can get to know each other), or personal contact with others, after your team has lost credibility, your virtual team leader and all team members will need to work hard to regain it.

That's why I recommend that in collaboration with your team members, you discuss and agree on what you want to be known for or what you want others — whether it's other teams, customers, vendors, or the CEO — to say about you.

Maybe your team wants to be known as the go-to experts or the fastest problem solvers in the west. Whatever it is, discuss and agree as a team on how you all can achieve this recognition in every interaction and with every opportunity.

Choosing a Team Framework

If you've ever tried to create a quality product without a defined, proven process in place, you most likely failed. That's because quality doesn't happen on accident. Quality happens when the outcome is intentional, habitual, consistently reliable, and repeatable.

Selecting a team framework is a quality process that is important for team success and helps build team culture, consistency, and trust. You may have different frameworks for different reasons. Regardless of the frameworks you use, the key to adoption is to collectively decide and agree on a framework that your team members are willing to apply in their everyday interactions with one another and when leading projects.

In this section, I share with you a simple framework I've used for team performance from my 20 years working with teams that you can discuss and customize together with your team. The suggestions I provide can help you lead this important conversation and make decisions that support high levels of virtual team performance.

Using a framework that builds trust and mutual respect

You may be thinking, "What's a team framework and why do I need one, especially if my team's values are clear?" Not surprisingly, high levels of team performance, trust, cohesiveness, and respect don't happen spontaneously or because of a divine intervention.

REMEMBER

High levels of team performance come from making choices about how your team works together and handles team dynamics, roles, responsibilities, and important processes, such as onboarding, decision-making, and so on. Team values align with and support your framework, but usually they don't focus on process, roles, and goals. Rather, values define how the team members agree to work together to achieve goals.

MY FAVORITE TEAM FRAMEWORKS

In addition to the custom team frameworks I've developed and the various agile project management frameworks available to use, here are some of my favorite team performance frameworks I use frequently with teams:

- The Five Behaviors of Cohesive Team from Patrick Lencioni: I use this framework with intact teams to discover what it takes to become truly cohesive and productive using a model of trust, conflict, commitment, accountability, and results.

- The Team Performance Model from Drexler/Sibbet: This framework illustrates the various stages involved in both creating and sustaining teams. It can create a common language for supporting a team-based culture.

- Stages of Team Development from Bruce Tuckman: This framework presents normal and natural stages of formation that every team goes through as well as the behaviors and challenges associated with each stage.

- Team Alignment Survey from Integro Leadership: I use this framework to measure team alignment and trust, including the degree to which team members are clear on their purpose, values, vision, and goals and the degree to which team members approve of where the team is going and how they're going to get there.

I frequently get asked to work with teams that are spinning their wheels trying to figure out why they aren't functioning at higher levels or why they continue to be dragged down by conflict, sabotage, and conflicting agendas. They usually spend a lot of time defining goals, deadlines, financial measures, expectations, and process. But what they're missing is a strong team framework as their foundation, which ties everything together and creates team culture.

Areas included in a team framework may include any of the following:

- The way the team is structured
- Workflow systems
- Communication systems
- Onboarding process
- Rewards and recognition systems
- Shared vision
- Integrated goals
- Defined roles and responsibilities
- Process for how resources get allocated

>> Process for how decisions get made

>> What measures define success

>> Agreement on how the team builds trust and demonstrates respect

Figure 4-2 shows an example of a team performance framework that I built for a team. Notice the key areas of focus that this team agreed on that would significantly impact its performance. The team used this framework to discuss and agree on behaviors, expectations, and success measures for each key area and decided how the team members would hold each other accountable for living this framework on a daily basis.

FIGURE 4-2:
A sample team
performance
framework.

© John Wiley & Sons, Inc.

TIP

Feel free to use this sample framework to start the conversation with your virtual team about the foundational stages, steps, or building blocks that ensure your team is set up for success. Take time to specifically define what your framework means for your team and how your team members live the strategies in the framework daily in every interaction.

Letting your team decide

The key to a strong framework isn't one predetermined by the team leader. Instead, the best way to develop a strong framework is to bring your virtual team together for a strategy session and decide on it together. The more team members weigh in on what to include in the framework, the more buy-in and acceptance they'll have for adopting it and living it in their day-to-day interaction with each other. They'll also feel more comfortable and confident calling out other team members when they notice they aren't operating in accordance with the agreed-upon framework.

Here are few questions to ask your team members to involve them in deciding on your team framework:

» What are the five most important questions you need to have answered to feel like a valued team member?

» What must exist for you to build trust and respect with another team member?

» How will we know that the team is performing at its optimal level? What would you notice?

» What poorly defined processes have contributed to dysfunction on other teams you've been a part of?

» How do you recommend we agree to resolve team conflict? Make decisions? Manage conflicting priorities?

Involve your team in building your framework for a strong foundation on which you can always fall back. Your team can use your framework time and time again to reset expectations about working together, handling problems, and building trust.

REMEMBER

Your framework is something to share with interview candidates and provide them with information about your team culture. It helps them consider what it will be like to work on your virtual team and what will be expected.

Establishing Team Goals: What Does Success Look Like?

Goal setting is a powerful process to use with your virtual team. Studies consistently show that individuals and teams who set goals achieve success at much higher rates than those who don't because by selecting to set goals, you're choosing a direction and determining a course of action.

REMEMBER

Setting goals and success measures with your virtual team should be based on your company strategy. Communicating what's expected of your team members and developing specific, measurable goals answers the question, "What do you need to do to achieve the expectations and how do you do it most effectively?" This level of clarity enables people to execute and complete tasks. When people know what to do and how to do it, they take ownership, stay focused, and remain engaged.

The secret for effective goal setting includes having an alignment discussion to clearly tie together how your team goals support the company goals. In addition, make sure that your goals are exciting, interesting, and motivating for your team or else you'll have a tough time keeping momentum in a virtual environment. You'll also want to be sure that you have the resources and skills in place to accomplish the goals.

Aligning virtual team goals with company goals

Establishing expectations and setting clear goals based on your organizational vision and direction as well as your teams purpose is an important step in setting up your team for success. When defining goals for your team, ask your team members the following questions to determine if alignment exists:

>> How do our team goals support our current business strategies?

>> Why are these goals important to the business? Who and what do they impact (revenue, customers, community, and so on)?

>> Are these goals meaningful to the team? Why?

>> What would happen if these goals weren't accomplished?

>> What benefits will achieving these goals bring to the company? Our team? Individuals?

>> How will we know we have accomplished the goal? What measures do we have in place?

Take goal setting a step further and build personal alignment with each team member. Inquire with each team member how the team goals align with her own personal direction, aspirations, or strengths. Building these synergistic connections around goals is what keeps people happy and keeps them working for your team and company long term.

If you can't answer these questions or are unclear with the answers, then alignment may not exist, which means you have to work on building better connections between what your virtual team is tasked with achieving and how those goals impact the business overall. At the end of the day if can't tell this story to your virtual team, you'll quickly find yourself with a team that is confused, demotivated, and disengaged.

Setting goals that are motivating, inspiring, and purposeful

Your team members should be excited and motivated to work on their goals, and you can influence their inspiration in several key ways:

>> **Make goal setting a collaborative effort.** When team members are involved in setting goals that are important to them, they have a greater interest in making them happen.

>> **Discuss, don't just tell.** Don't just announce to your team what your goals are. Discuss and arrive at the goals together. Challenge the assumptions of what is possible together. Be a thinking partner.

>> **Assess and discuss how the goals relate to the organization and department's mission.** Tie your team goals to the larger organizational goals. This kind of meaningful connection to a larger goal will define why your goals matter and help to drive motivation.

>> **Set stretch goals that will develop and challenge your team members in their area of responsibility.** Because you want your employees to experience success, set goals that are achievable. At the same time, encourage employees to set some *stretch goals*, which are goals that can only be achieved with extraordinary effort and can function as a motivational tool.

>> **Discuss current gaps to achieving those goals.** Brainstorm to identify any current gaps or obstacles that may get in the way of achieving them. Come up with solutions for removing any obstacles.

>> **Determine how the goals create value.** Look at the individual team member, you as the leader, your department, and the company as a whole.

>> **Confirm that the goals are comprehensive**. Ensure team goals fully represent all your team's responsibilities.

REMEMBER

When setting goals collaboratively with your team, be sure your goals follow common key principles that you may have heard referred to as SMART goals, which mean the following:

>> **S**pecific, Synergistic, Significant, and Shifting: Include details as to what, when, where, and how the goal will be achieved.

>> **M**easurable, Meaningful, Memorable, and Motivating: Define what the end result will look like after the team achieves the goal.

>> **A**chievable, Agreed-upon, and Action-oriented: Ensure that the goal is achievable given the knowledge of the team, each member, and the resources available.

>> **R**elevant, Realistic, Reasonable, Rewarding, and Resonating: Ensure that the goal is related to the role and purpose of the team and makes sense given the skills and abilities of your team members.

>> **T**ime Sensitive, Tangible, and Thoughtful: Establish a timeline with reaching the goal and thoughtful steps to achieve it.

Understanding what resources are needed to achieve team goals

The wind will quickly be taken out of your team's sails if your team members don't have the resources they need to be successful. Resources can include time, money, people, support, or technology. Without providing your team members with the resources, holding them accountable for hitting their goals isn't fair.

TIP

Keep the following tips in mind when determining what resources your team members need to accomplish their goals:

>> **Determine scope and impact.** The bigger the goal, the more team members are usually involved and the more time it will take. Take into consideration both time and resources needed from your team members and people and resources needed from outside your team or company.

>> **Set up a plan.** Work with your team members to determine milestones for each goal and estimate the amount of dedicated time needed by each team member each week to achieve each goal by the deadline. Crosscheck these milestones against all of the virtual meetings that your team members are expected to attend and make sure there is enough time in the day.

>> **Onboard others.** Communicate goals to others in the company and their part in offering support. Let people know the impact of not answering requests or

providing information in a timely manner. Your virtual team members who require the support of others to accomplish a goal need their buy-in upfront.

>> **Use your tools.** Put your plan into a project management tool so that you can easily track deliverables, handoffs, and notifications when something has gotten off track and set up instant updates on the progress of goals.

>> **Don't overcommit your people.** Be careful not to overcommit your virtual team members just because you can't see them working diligently each day. Always determine the scope, develop the plan, and work out your estimates before assigning more tasks to team members. Virtual team members can get quickly overloaded and may be afraid to say anything if the workload becomes too much.

>> **Know your team members.** What skills and experience do they have today and in what areas can they acquire new skills and stretch themselves? After you identify this gap, plan for appropriate resources, support, training, and coaching to develop needed skills.

>> **Monitor and check in.** The resources that your team members need could change as they hit obstacles or other priorities come up. Having a routine to check in on a regular basis and get progress updates on goals is important to keeping things on track.

Determining Team Member Roles

Defining your team members' roles, the function they will perform, and the way they need to interact with other team members can help you hire the right people for the job and create a sense of clarity and calmness for your virtual team. With clearly defined roles for your team, you'll quickly be able to identify the type of people you need and use that information to attract and hire the most qualified candidates.

You also have a higher chance of collaboration and sharing of information when people know exactly what is expected of them and of their teammates. Without the daily oversight on a virtual team, roles and responsibilities can easily overlap and redundancies can occur without anyone being the wiser, which can create confusion and frustration on a virtual team.

In this section I help you define roles on your team by looking at what skills you have and what you need. I also discuss how to help team members understand how they interact together to accomplish team goals.

Ensuring team members understand their roles and why they're important

You never want to hear a team member say, "I didn't do it, because I thought it was Dan's job." That's why going through some type of role clarification exercise at least yearly is important for your virtual team. Here are some steps to help you with role clarification:

1. **List the two to three key deliverables or objectives each role produces for the team, the impact of those deliverables, and the resources required for their success.**

   For example, a team member may be responsible for creating and distributing monthly sales forecasts using data from your SalesForce Customer Relationship Management platform. This data impacts her sales team's focus and efforts, and it also impacts the overall sales goals for the company.

2. **Assess what's missing and what you need.**

   Questions to ask include the following:

   - Are there any functional areas in which you're lacking?

   - Are there important priorities that continually get put on the back burner or don't get done because of a lack of resources?

   - When comparing your goals for the upcoming year with the skills on your team to achieve them, what gaps exist?

   - Are there objectives that are no longer important and relevant that would free up more time for a particular role?

   - Are team position descriptions accurate and a strong guide for what each job is responsible for?

3. **Recalibrate current roles.**

   You may find some tasks should be reorganized based on a team member's skill set.

4. **Hire for new roles as needed.**

After you've clearly defined the roles and responsibilities of each team member, you'll have a clearer picture of team roles and responsibilities. This activity also helps you define the relationships between team members. Team members will know their key tasks and responsibilities as well as with whom they're expected to work or collaborate.

Incorporating systems thinking to support how your team works together

Systems thinking is an understanding that any small change in how your team operates could significantly impact the rest of the organization. Teams that use systems thinking make it a habit to consider all the links, connections, and interactions between people and components that make up the system. The *system* can be your team, your company, or the entire industry you serve.

The importance of systems thinking for your team is that it helps to move you away from using a bandage approach to solving problems and making knee jerk reactions and decisions. With systems thinking, your team develops a theory as to why something is happening or what may happen and then engages in innovative thinking to discover different ways of changing the system to improve performance.

This systems thinking approach can help virtual team members adopt a much more integrated and holistic view of their work. They spend thoughtful time analyzing, considering, and discussing the interconnectedness of tasks, processes, roles, practices, and decisions that need to work together for the whole system to function optimally. It keeps teams from making a decision in a vacuum without considering the full impact to the rest of the system (human or nonhuman).

So, your virtual team may be at risk for a system failure. You're probably asking yourself, "What the heck does that mean?" A system failure occurs when a team or team member fails to see the connections between people or processes needing to work together for success. Sometimes those failures can be traced back to confusing goals, lack of commitment, a flawed process, lack of feedback, or lack of collaboration on a team.

The key is to practice good team habits where systems thinking begins to just happen naturally. Here are some suggestions for doing so:

>> **Implement rewards.** Award the team or the group rather than individuals so that members focus on what everyone needs for success, not just what they need.

>> **Set goals and priorities together.** Agree on top priorities together and allow the chance for input and debate. Doing so provides an opportunity for team members to explain how others impact their priority or why their priority needs to happen first to support other goals.

>> **Encourage virtual lunches.** During these virtual lunches, team members showcase their work and how others' roles and responsibilities make their work possible.

>> **Commit to discussions after problems, issues, or mistakes.** Support all team members in discussing their contribution and what they could do differently in the future.

>> **Address team conflict early.** Don't let conflicts break down the system. Support team members in having virtual meetings where they discuss what they need from each other for success. Consider hiring a third-party coach to help them navigate the conflict effectively.

>> **Ask great questions.** This is the best way to help your team think more holistically and understand how any decisions made can impact others or where the root of the problem exists. Here are a few questions you can ask your team members the next time a problem arises:

- What has been happening or what has happened?

- Have we seen this happen before or something like it?

- What are all the contributing factors as to why this is happening (for instance, people, processes, policies)? Why do you think that?

- Are there any patterns that keep reoccurring?

- What is the impact?

- What about our thinking allows this situation to persist?

- What assumptions are we making? Why?

The primary goal of using these questions is to expand the thinking of your team members so that they may notice where a small change or shift could have a significant impact. This shift could be around a communication approach, a policy, or a process.

» Filling roles on your virtual team

» Knowing what qualities to look for in a virtual team member

» Conducting interviews in person and remotely

» Performing your due diligence

» Discussing your expectations and theirs up front

» Making an offer

Chapter 5

Finding and Hiring the Right People

Hire smart. Train hard. Manage easy. These three statements aren't truer than when you're hiring for your virtual team. Making sure that you start off with a rock-solid selection process that includes smart recruiting strategies and a strategic interviewing process is essential.

Finding and hiring the right people, for the right role, at the right time isn't only critical to traditional team success, but it's also crucial to virtual team success. Every virtual team wants to strive to have high performing individuals. And if you've made great hires, you'll have a motivated team of people doing their best work without a lot of oversight. That equals success for a virtual team.

WARNING

right people to work on your virtual team, and most teams don't put the appropriate time and effort into their selection process. Bad hires end up costing thousands of dollars of wasted time, training, and resources. In fact, the U.S. Department of Labor puts the price of a bad hire at 30 percent of the employee's first-year earnings. For small companies, an investment in the wrong person for your virtual team can be a threat to your business. Putting a warm body in a virtual team seat may work for a short-term project, but it's definitely not a strategy for long-term team success.

In this chapter, I walk you through a solid selection process, including recruiting tools and interviewing techniques to help you attract and hire the right people for your virtual team. How much you adopt this process as a matter of doing business is completely up to you. But what I know for sure is that the steps in this chapter work. They're based on proven methods, data, and research. Oh yeah, and don't forget that you'll end up with a team of rock stars that accomplish more in a virtual environment than most traditional teams ever will.

Attracting Your Virtual Team Talent

By embracing a virtual workforce, you open the door to attracting talent that can live and work anywhere in the world. Virtual working arrangements are transforming the modern-day workplace as you and I know it. Being knowledgeable about what motivates someone to seek out a virtual work situation is important.

REMEMBER

Certain motivating drivers can be deal breakers for potential virtual employees, so you want to make sure that they're part of your recruiting strategy in order to attract the best and brightest to your virtual team. In a recent survey, remote workers identified several important reasons they prefer to work virtually. They include:

>> Having more time for self-care and exercise

>> Being able to find a happy work-life balance

>> Getting rid of stressful commutes

>> Spending less money on gas, clothing, and food

>> Experiencing more happiness and less stress.

These sections discuss things you should consider to attract the right virtual workers to your company and create an environment where they will thrive.

Making your business attractive to teleworkers

The reasons people prefer working remotely has benefits and positive impacts for both the employee and employer. I suggest that you discuss those benefits throughout your recruiting process to shine a spotlight on alignment with your potential new hire.

TIP

Here are several tips for discussing benefits that your candidates will find valuable:

>> **Clearly articulate why your company loves having virtual workers.** What benefits have you experienced or expect to experience using virtual team members (Chapter 2 discusses the specific benefits)? Being transparent about why you value virtual workers confirms that they'll get the support they need to be successful in their new role.

>> **Share your onboarding process and how you plan to help them get connected with their team members and others in the company.** For example, if you have an office, do they visit in person during their first 30 days? What training will they receive on company services and products? How will you introduce them to the values or guiding principles of your company? Chapter 7 delves deeper into what to cover during the onboarding process.

>> **Discuss with them how you're leveraging technology to support virtual team effectiveness.** Are you using *unified communications (UC)* — interconnected systems that enhance communication, collaboration, and productivity between people and teams? Do you continue to research and stay on top of technology trends and innovative tools for keeping a virtual workforce connected? Chapter 16 discusses the important technology concerns for your virtual team.

>> **Share what's unique, innovative, or appealing about your work culture.** Remember talented employees have choices. What are the perks about working for your company that they may care about such as bonuses, recognition opportunities, career paths, tuition reimbursement, and so on? What are other virtual workers at your company saying about their experience? See Chapter 8 to find out more about culture considerations.

Composing virtual worker–friendly job ads

Choose a killer job title with key statements that make it attractive to a remote employee. Communicate the why, tell your story, and motivate people to notice your job ad.

REMEMBER

Keep in mind that the job ad is selling the job so you're not focused on a job description at this point. Your goal is to get people to take notice of your ad and keep reading.

Here are some guidelines to follow when creating an attention-grabbing virtual team job posting:

1. **Start with a strong job title and one to three words or statements that *grab the attention* of your desired talent.**

   The goal is to be short, creative, enticing and a little provocative. For example, Senior Story Teller, Talent Curator, Detail Enforcer, Chief Problem Solver.

2. **Follow up with key details that *hook* the potential candidate into reading the full job ad.**

   Provide more details about the job role without losing the creativity. For a job title of Brand Evangelist, you may add "spreading the gospel of the brand through consistency of message and design."

3. **Talk about your *why* and tell your company story.**

   This is where you tie the job role to the overall company story. For example, the Creator of Opportunities for an innovative home furnishings company is responsible for seeking out new people and places and helping them create a better life. Clearly expressing the *why* in your job ad will separate your virtual opportunity from an ocean of possibilities and attract someone that personally aligns with your story.

4. **Focus on the *perks or benefits* using the tips that I discuss in the previous section.**

   These perks and benefits are specific to the virtual job role, such as zero commute time, opportunity for personal development, and working in a creative, supportive, and collaborative environment.

Consider your current or next virtual job opportunity. How can you write a job ad that immediately demands attention? Hooks the reader? Tells your story and why it matters? Sells all the perks and benefits of working for your company in a remote setting?

Recruiting Online

Numerous online job sites focus on remote work opportunities specifically, and you can bet that's where your potential new hire is hanging out. Make sure that you're advertising on one or more of these job sites and know the resources available in order to find your next virtual hire:

- » **Flexjobs.com:** More than 50 job categories ranging from freelance to full-time executive.

- » **Weworkremotely.com:** This site focuses on remote opportunities at high tech companies.

- » **Workingnomads.co:** Choose daily or weekly emails focused on your job search criteria.

- » **Remotive.io:** This site offers a weekly newsletter and additional resources for remote workers. Features jobs in engineering, marketing, product support, sales, and human resources.

- » **Staff.com:** Visit this site for longer term remove work in a range of industries from personal assistants to programming.

- » **Skipthedrive.com:** This site has multiple resources for remote workers.

- » **Virtualvocations.com:** Advertises jobs that are 100 percent virtual and hosts a popular blog on remote jobs.

By using the recruiting strategies from the previous section, you can find a perfect match for your virtual job opening. And don't forget to drop me a line to let me know how these recruiting ideas worked for you.

Hiring Based on Skill, Behavior, and Fit

After the resumes start flowing in for your virtual opening, the important work begins. The interviewing and hiring process is the most important task you'll do when hiring a virtual worker. Your goal when hiring for your virtual team is to find a rock star who has the highest chance of achieving his goals, has proven experience working virtually, and is comfortable solving problems on his own and in collaboration with other virtual team members.

REMEMBER

All great hiring managers spend time up front clearly defining the purpose and expectations for the role. Then the hiring manager uses the interviewing process to determine if the person has the skills, ability, and motivation to do what is required for that job, and if he is a great fit for your culture. Key areas to define before you begin the interviewing process include the following:

- » **Job purpose:** Why does this job exist? How does it impact business goals? What is the job's core purpose?

- » **Success measures:** What needs to be successfully accomplished, created, built, improved, developed, and changed over the next 6 to 12 months? Two to three years? How will success be measured? Can you explain what success looks like?

» **Job challenges:** What are the biggest challenges in the job? Who will the position be working with and what types of projects will he be working on?

» **Critical competencies and behaviors:** What skills and behavioral attributes are key to successful performance in the job role?

» **Shared values:** What values do you need to look for that will help to ensure culture fit with your company and team?

Focusing on these key areas to develop a well-thought-out job description before starting the interviewing process can help you find the best person for the job, ask the right questions during the interviewing process, and give you confidence in your hiring decision for your next virtual team member.

In the following sections, I walk you through how to hire for skill, behavioral competencies, and cultural fit.

Hiring for skill

Consider the skills that you expect your virtual workers to have to fulfill the day-to-day requirements of the job role. Skills include their abilities, experience, or knowledge to be the right fit for the job.

A great way to identify key skills needed for the role is to assess current rock-star performers that you already have on your team. What are the skills that have made them successful in the role such as technical skills, math skills, presentation skills, verbal skills, project management experience, proficiency in certain areas, industry knowledge, or know-how?

Take time to identify must-have skills versus nice-to-have skills. When you're reviewing resumes for your virtual job opening, if the candidate doesn't have the must-have skills, then he isn't a good fit for the role.

TIP

Be sure to send all candidates that applied for the job but aren't a good fit, a thanks-but-no-thanks communication. It's important to maintain a good reputation and follow-through by thanking them for taking the time to apply for the job.

Hiring for behavioral competencies and interests

Understanding what behavioral competencies are needed for the job can be more important than having the right skills for the job. You may have heard people say that it's easier to teach someone a new skill then to teach them a new behavior. In my experience working with thousands of leaders and teams that is absolutely true.

Personal background, habits, and life experiences all shape who you are and how you show up in the world. They create patterns of behavior that can help or hinder you in any given job role, and it takes a lot more time and energy to change ingrained behavioral habits and patterns after you've hired someone for the job.

Similar to identifying the right skills, paying attention to the behaviors and interests that your high performers demonstrate in their roles will help you determine what behaviors are most important. Then you can develop situational interview questions that can uncover if the candidate already operates using these competencies.

Here are some examples of behavioral competencies and interests:

>> Ability to manage and develop others
>> Adaptability
>> Approachability
>> Business acumen
>> Creativity
>> Communication skills
>> Cultural sensitivity
>> Conflict resolution
>> Customer focus
>> Decision-making ability
>> Delegation ability
>> Ethical
>> Flexibility
>> High standards
>> Innovative
>> Integrity and trust
>> Leadership
>> Negotiation skills
>> Organizing and prioritizing

- ≫ Perseverance
- ≫ Proactive
- ≫ Problem solving
- ≫ Relationship management
- ≫ Results driven
- ≫ Self-composure
- ≫ Sense of humor
- ≫ Stress management
- ≫ Team player

Hiring for cultural fit

Because you're hiring for a virtual environment, you can easily overlook the importance of cultural fit, which can be a costly and time-consuming mistake. Cultural fit is what can make or break team trust, respect, and overall team cohesiveness. It also impacts job satisfaction, performance, retention, and turnover.

WARNING

The Society for Human Resource Management (SHRM) has stated that the result of poor culture fit due to turnover can cost an organization between 50 to 60 percent of the person's annual salary.

UTILIZING SELECTION TOOLS DURING HIRING

Using a selection tool during the hiring process can provide the hiring manager with insight into a candidate's cognitive abilities, behavioral traits, and interests, including tips about the candidate's potential job fit and relevant job-specific interview questions. We provide our clients with a selection tool called PXT Select that can help you to hire for positions and job types at all levels and in a myriad of industries. It measures thinking style, behavioral traits, and interests, which represent what has been described as the total person — the three areas that impact an individual's approach to situations in the workplace. It compares the candidates results to a defined performance model for the role. Armed with this information, you can determine if the candidate falls within the performance model range for the job role and may be able to meet important skill and behavioral requirements for the job.

Cultural fit is sometimes hard to define, but you always know when it's missing. It's been described as the glue that holds an organization together. A simple way to think about *cultural fit* is that it represents the spoken or unspoken norms, beliefs, or agreements that people have decided to live by in a company or on a team.

When assessing cultural fit during an interview, you're determining the likelihood that someone will reflect and/or be able to adapt to the core beliefs, values, attitudes, and behaviors that make up your organization. Keep in mind that he is assessing your culture and whether it's going to be a great fit for him too.

Here are some questions that can help assess culture fit in an interview:

>> In what type of culture do you do your best work?

>> What does your ideal team look like and how do they treat each other?

>> What attracted you to our company?

>> How would you describe our culture based on your experience so far?

>> Tell me about a time when you worked for a company where you didn't fit in. Why was it a bad fit?

Seeking Out the Right Qualities in Virtual Team Members

Your goal when hiring for your virtual team is to find a strong candidate who has the highest chance of achieving his goals, has proven experience working virtually, and is comfortable solving problems on his own and in collaboration with other virtual team members. They also need to excel at written and verbal communication because that's how they'll communicate with others a majority of the time.

With a virtual team you don't have the option of a quick hallway conversation or happy hour drinks to work through a problem or assess an opportunity. People who excel in a virtual work environment need to be self-directed, deadline driven, comfortable working alone, and trustworthy. They also need to have no hesitation picking up the phone or using collaborative technology to engage and communicate, get things done, and build team relationships.

Here I provide several areas to focus on when interviewing your candidates that can help to determine if they have the important qualities that would make them successful in a virtual role.

Determine whether they're self-directed

One of the most important behavioral characteristics of virtual workers is their ability to self-direct, organize, plan their work, and meet deadlines. Working virtually in the comfort of your home office in your sweats is a great perk, but it comes with a lot of distractions.

Pets, kids, laundry, cleaning, groceries, delivery people, neighbors, parents, and personal phone calls can be constant distractions for a virtual worker. Your virtual worker needs to have a plan to focus, shut out all distractions, and get down to business. Here is a list of interviewing questions you can ask to assess if the candidate is self-directed, can keep track of his work, and stay focused:

>> How have you managed your daily workflow in the past?

>> What do you do to manage or limit distractions in your environment?

>> Can you provide specific examples of projects that you have worked on independently and how you stayed on track to meet your goals?

>> What do you do to stay motivated when working alone?

>> Tell me about a time when you were under a tight deadline. How did you hold yourself accountable and keep your team updated on your progress?

Be on the lookout for strong communication skills

Effectively communicating in a virtual environment is paramount for building trust, engagement and cohesiveness. Candidates with strong communication skills will always do better in a virtual environment and usually establish strong relationships with their manager and coworkers.

Knowing when to text, IM, email, pick up the phone, or have a virtual face-to-face meeting takes a high level of awareness and emotional intelligence. I've worked with virtual teams that hide behind the wrong technology rather than picking up the phone or having a virtual face-to-face meeting to resolve a conflict, ask for help, or deal with a relationship snafu. Poor communication skills on your virtual team will have long-term consequences and can slowly erode trust, impact team productivity, and success.

TIP

When interviewing for a virtual role, pay close attention to the candidate's overall communication skills. Evaluating communication skills in written form, over the phone, and in a videoconference interview can help assess if the candidate communicates clearly and articulately. Additionally, here are some valuable communication questions you can ask:

>> How do you stay in touch with your team members and build relationships?

>> What form of communication do you prefer? Why?

>> Provide me with three examples when you would pick up the phone or have a virtual face-to-face meeting with your peers or manager?

>> Share a time when your communication was misunderstood or created a conflict. Was there a different method of communication that would have worked better? Why?

>> How do you proactively communicate to keep your manager and team members updated and ensure they know what you're doing?

Specify the importance of engagement

In a remote work environment, engagement takes on a whole new meaning. *Engagement* is the emotional commitment the employee has to the organization, the team, and its goals. Emotionally committed virtual employees stay in their jobs longer, get sick less often, and surpass their goals. Check out Chapter 11 for best practices on building virtual team engagement.

Use these questions to assess how important engagement is to your potential new hire:

>> How do you stay engaged with your team and other key stakeholders without face-to-face interaction every day?

>> Tell me about a time when you were disengaged in your work. What could your team have done differently to support you?

>> We expect high levels of engagement from our virtual team members. What does that look like to you?

>> If you were feeling disengaged from the team or your manager, what would you do about it?

HIRE FOR BEHAVIORAL STRENGTHS AND MAKE ENGAGEMENT THE MAGIC WORD

Jim Padilla is the CEO of Gain the Edge, an outsourced sales force and leadership training company. With close to 100 employees located around the United States, Padilla's team is 100 percent virtual and continuing to experience record growth. He is a big believer in hiring for values first, strengths second, and then skills. This strategy has led to a pattern of rock-star virtual hires that stick with the company and create a culture with astonishing levels of engagement and success.

Throughout Padilla's multistep selection process, he approaches each candidate as if he is naturally curious, extremely optimistic, and possesses a resiliency mindset — all must-have qualities of sales professionals in his organization. Candidates go through a series of steps before they ever get to the actual interview in order to assess cultural fit and behavioral characteristics:

1. Submit a video regarding the job ad and what inspired them to apply. They explain why the outcomes for the role are important to them and why they matter.

2. Watch a video about the meaning behind the company's five value propositions (ownership, results, partnership, optimism, flexibility), who they serve, why they do what they do, and expectations of team members. If a candidate is still interested, they book a ten-minute preview call.

3. Participate in a "preview" call that is focused on creating challenge and assessing resiliency. The goal is to evaluate how well the candidate handles objections (which they'll face on an hourly basis in their role) and what steps they take to qualify any questions or objections. More than 70 percent of all candidates are eliminated during this step.

4. Participate in a role-play call with a group of employees. This call is designed to see if the candidates can handle a high paced, volatile sales environment.

After hired, Padilla's onboarding process puts his virtual new hires on the path to success immediately. A series of automated videos, online courses, and emails outline the vision, values, and culture of Gain the Edge. Live training calls using Zoom are set up with operations, technical, and team leads within the first 30 days where subject matter experts provide virtual tours of project management software, sales methods/process, and how-tos that are integral for their success. The new hires are assigned a buddy who is financially incentivized to help the new hires experience success on their first campaign as well as a mindset coach who is available to offer support as needed.

Most importantly is getting and keeping the new hire connected and engaged. In fact, engagement is the magic word at Gain the Edge because according to Padilla, before results slip, engagement slips 100 percent of the time. On a daily basis, employees post their wins, losses, questions, and concerns in a private Facebook community and receive valuable feedback from teammates. They attend weekly virtual training calls to hear about what's happening globally and what's working with other clients. And they have regular virtual office hours where they get individual help and training if needed.

His process is thoughtfully designed to attract and retain top talent in a virtual environment. It's not surprising that his company continues to be successful in a highly competitive market.

Holding the Candidate Interview

You may conduct interviews in person or remotely to find your next virtual team member. Regardless of your process, make sure the hiring team members prepare for the interview together; review the qualities, skills, and cultural fit to assess for; and align around what a high performing candidate looks like.

During the interview, setting expectations puts the candidate at ease and lets him know what to expect. These sections explain in greater detail what you can do to get ready for the interview, what you can ask during the interview, and how you can evaluate the candidate.

Preparing for the interview

Before the interview, have the hiring team conduct a briefing meeting to ensure accuracy when evaluating the candidate against job needs. Doing so helps everyone involved in the interview process better understand the real job needs and apply a standard benchmark based on measurable and objective selection criteria. Refer to the earlier section, "Seeking Out the Right Qualities in Virtual Team Members" for information about the important aspects of the job role such as job purpose, success measures, challenges, critical competencies, and shared values.

The briefing meeting also provides the opportunity to review any key findings from earlier HR interviews or communications with the candidate. This can help to point out any areas that the hiring team specifically needs to investigate during the interviews.

Knowing what and what not to ask

Use the STAR interviewing method as a quality check to ensure you're digging as deep as you can into a candidate's past experience in relation to the skills, behaviors, and values that you defined important for success in the virtual role.

STAR stands for:

>> **S**ituation: Ask the candidate to explain a situation where he used the skills or behaviors that you're inquiring about.

>> **T**ask: Ask the candidate to provide details about the specific tasks for which he was responsible.

>> **A**ction: Ask the candidate what actions he took or steps them implemented to solve the problem or move forward.

>> **R**esult: Ask the candidate about his results.

This method of interviewing helps you to:

>> Make sure that the candidate's experience proves he can handle the virtual job

>> Understand how the candidate thinks and solves problems

>> Easily compare job candidate responses

Table 5-1 breaks down STAR a bit more:

TABLE 5-1   **Interviewing with STAR**

Interview method	Questions to ask
Situation	What was the project you were working on?
	Tell me about the problem you were solving?
	What was the situation and who was involved?
Task	What specific tasks were you responsible for in this situation?
	What sequence of steps were you specifically involved in?
	What was your part in the decision-making process?
Action	What were the steps you took to solve this challenge?
	How did you think through any problems?
	How did you overcome roadblocks and follow the situation through to get results?
	Was there anything unique about your actions or your methods worth mentioning?
Results	What was the outcome?
	What would you have done differently?
	How were things better because of what you did?
	What did you learn from that experience?

When you use STAR, pay special attention to your candidates using these responses:

>> Specific or measurable tasks they performed

>> A conclusion and final accomplishments

>> Reflection on the situation

>> Use of "we" and "I" to compare team orientation versus individual accomplishment

>> Ability to articulate a point, tone, inflection and delivery

>> What they learned from the experience

In addition, be aware of these responses:

>> A focus on what others were doing or should have done

>> Changes in communication or how they describe the facts

>> Lack of specifics or accomplishments

Be sure to steer clear of any of the following topics during your interview and focus on keeping all interviewing questions job related:

>> Disability

>> Gender and gender identity

>> Health

>> Marital status, age, dependents

>> Nationality

>> Politics

>> Religion

>> Sexual orientation

Discussing your expectations and theirs up front

When you start an interview, take a few minutes to build rapport with the candidate and make him feel welcome, comfortable, and at ease. You can then set expectations. Candidates are likely to feel a bit anxious, so ease their nerves and let them know what to expect. I recommend explaining your method of interviewing using the following example:

"Before we begin the interview I want to walk you through some of the questions I will ask about previous roles you've held. These questions may include:

>> What were your key roles and responsibilities in this job?

>> What were your greatest challenges in this job?

>> What were your greatest accomplishments?

>> How would you describe your relationship with your manager?

>> Why did you leave?

"When providing examples, I would like you to provide a **STAR** answer: This is an acronym we use to understand the *situation* that needed to be addressed, the *task* that needed to be done, the *action* you took, and the *result* of your actions. Usually, these come out in your overall answer, but I will remind you to answer the question if you were unclear on one of the **STAR** components.

"At the end of the interview we'll discuss your career goals and aspirations, and you'll have a chance to ask questions. Although this sounds like a lengthy interview, it will go remarkably fast. I want to make sure you have the opportunity to share your full story, so it's my job to guide the pace of the discussion. Sometimes I'll go into more depth, and other times I'll ask that we move on to the next topic. I'll try to make sure we leave plenty of time to cover your most recent and most relevant jobs. Do you have any questions about this process?"

Evaluating responses

Hiring teams need a simple method for evaluating candidate responses that they agree on and are clear on what different rating level looks like in terms of performance. Be sure to go through examples of your rating scale with the hiring team to ensure alignment for what each rating means. I recommend a rating of 1 through 3 as such:

>> **1 – Doesn't meet requirements:** Past performance and examples of work and accomplishments are less than expected. Will struggle to meet job expectations.

>> **2 – Meets minimum expectations:** Past performance and examples of work and accomplishments meet most job expectations most of the time. Overall performance will be acceptable.

>> **3 – Consistently exceeds expectations:** Past performance and examples of work and accomplishments consistently exceed expectations. Overall performance will be consistently high, sustained, and recognized by others as a high performer.

Checking Out the Past

Companies are spending more time and effort making sure they get the right virtual talent into their workforce, and background and reference checks have taken on a much larger role before extending an offer to a candidate. In fact, one out of five job candidates (around 21 percent) get knocked out of consideration after speaking to their professional contacts. When you have narrowed it down to a few potential candidates, the reference check and reviewing work samples often becomes the deciding factor. In the next sections, I provide important best practices that help you to make a final determination if have found your next hire.

Reviewing work samples

Depending on the job requirements, more than likely you want to ask the candidate to share recent samples of his work to assess quality, attention to detail, and technical savviness. Examples may include a presentation deck, project management plan, marketing copy, corporate communication message, or software code written to solve a technical issue.

TIP

Some candidates may exaggerate about their participation on a project. Be sure to ask them if anyone else was involved in creating the sample they shared and specifically what their role was in completing it.

Contacting references

Checking references is an important opportunity to gather fact-finding information about the candidate. Verify that he can work well in a virtual environment and validate information from his resume and interviews. The hiring manager needs to conduct in-depth reference checks and answer the following questions. When you call the references, be sure to introduce yourself, your role, and the job the candidate is interviewing for.

>> In what context did you work with (candidate)?

>> What were (candidate's) biggest strengths?

>> What were (candidate's) biggest areas for improvement?

>> In this virtual position we need someone who is very strong with (include skills here). How would you rate (candidate's) skills in this area? (Repeat this question as needed to validate additional skills.)

>> How would you rate (candidate's) overall performance on a scale of one to ten? Can you give me an example as to why you gave him this rating?

>> (Candidate) mentioned (include weakness here) as a weakness. Can you tell me more about this?

>> On a scale of one to ten, how would you rate (candidate's) level of (include the most important behavioral traits)?

Making an Offer

If you're ready to hire the candidate, it's time to make the offer.

TIP

Use these tips when doing so:

>> Congratulate the candidate and let him know why he rose to the top. Reinforce your confidence in his ability to excel in the job.

>> Highlight why this virtual job opportunity is a great match and revisit any concerns or objections the candidate may have had during the interview process and the solutions to overcome them.

>> High performers are looking for at least a 30 percent improvement from their current position. This may include an increase in pay, better perks or benefits, improvement in work-life balance, a shift in job responsibilities, quality of team dynamics, quality of manager relationship, growth opportunities, and company reputation. How can you communicate the full value of the role?

>> Sell your company and your team. What are the recent accomplishments, accolades, and opportunities that you can share with the candidate? How can you give him confidence that this is a great decision?

>> Focus on growth and career development opportunities that he'll have available. Explain the support he'll receive during the onboarding process and how you'll set him up for success.

>> Communicate your confidence in him as a new member of the team and make the offer.

After you make the offer, you can expect most candidates to engage in some negotiation. Today's candidates are savvy about what they want, and salary is only part of the package. The entirety of a job offer may include salary, health benefits, a possible sign-on bonus, profit sharing, paid vacation time, investment in professional development, and the framework of their remote work schedule. Be prepared for the candidate to ask to take 24 to 48 hours to respond (or counter) the offer.

TIP

Hopefully, you're starting with a competitive employment package; I don't recommend beginning negotiations with a low-ball offer. Rather put together a fair and equitable package given the candidate's experience level and skill set. Keep in mind that employment negotiations should always stay positive and professional on both sides of the table. The bottom line is to find a balance between what the candidate is worth and what you can offer.

» **Working with independent contractors (ICs)**

» **Using nondisclosure agreements (NDA) or not**

» **Understanding the noncompete agreements**

Chapter **6**

Contracting with Contract Workers

I ndependent contractors. Freelancers. On-demand workers. Consultants. Self-employed. Solopreneurs. Flex-jobbers. Side-giggers. Call them what you want. In this gig economy and with the rise of virtual teams, independent contractors (ICs) represent a valuable pool of flexible, on-demand talent who specialize in performing specific tasks for a company without actually being an employee. By nature of their agility, independence, and expertise in their field, they're ideally suited to be members of virtual teams.

More and more, people are opting out of traditional employment and choosing instead to contract their services to multiple clients. And companies reap the benefits. These highly skilled professionals can come onto a team and immediately get to the task at hand with little to no training or investment of time to get them up to speed.

This trend is here to stay. In fact, many economists believe that nearly all the job growth in recent years is from the rise in contractor and temp jobs. But how does that increase affect your company recruitment and hiring practices, management training, legal compliance, insurance, and so on?

This chapter walks you through all the considerations that employers need to consider regarding hiring an IC on a virtual team. Here you can find advice to help you make the decision whether contract workers on your virtual team is right for you and for your organization. Before you take any action, make sure your own legal counsel reviews any policies, practices, insurance, and contracts. *Note:* There are different rules and regulations when contracting with people and companies outside the United States. This information is specific to the United States.

Deciding Whether You Need a Contract

Contracts are put in place to protect both parties. An *employment contract* is an agreement between an employer and employee and is the basis of the employment relationship. In general, employees don't need a written contract. ICs definitely require contracts to clearly define the roles and responsibilities of the professional relationship.

These sections explain what independent contractors and employees are and how they're classified. With this information, you can determine whether you and the worker need to sign a contract.

Differentiating between an employee and independent contractor

Employees and ICs are two different classifications for workers, no matter whether they're on a virtual team or in a traditional work environment. Knowing the differences between the two and their definitions is extremely important because you risk expensive class action lawsuits for wage, hour, and other labor code violations including fines and penalties from the IRS and/or the Department of Labor (DOL).

Here is an overview of the two so you can see how they're different:

>> **Employee:** An employee is someone provided with guidance and oversight about how and when she works. An employee has a strong employee-manager relationship with regular and frequent check-ins. The company trains the employee on how to do her job, and her work is evaluated and measured on a regular basis. The employee is furnished with the equipment necessary to perform her work and is generally guaranteed a regular hourly or monthly wage or a yearly salary. The employee's work relationship is expected to continue indefinitely, and she receives benefits such as sick leave, vacation time, and insurance.

>> **Independent contractor:** An IC is someone who isn't an employee and her work isn't supervised on a day-to-day basis. How the IC performs her work isn't detailed or measured by a performance evaluation system. ICs can have specialized skills, usually set their own schedule, and are free to seek out

additional clients. They don't receive benefits or insurance from the company and don't need training to perform the basic tasks of their job. They purchase and have their own equipment, tools, and materials to perform the work.

REMEMBER

A company and an IC always have a contract that outlines the IC's pay for the project or monthly fee. An IC usually works repeatedly with a company whereas freelancers may be contracted to work on short-term or long-term projects or on a temporary basis. Contracts always specify an end date at which time the contract can be renewed if both parties agree.

From a financial perspective, employees and ICs differ in two key ways:

>> For the employee, a company withholds federal and state income tax, Social Security, and Medicare from wages and usually pays for insurance and benefits.

>> For the IC, the company doesn't withhold taxes so the IC must pay her own income taxes, and companies usually don't provide benefits.

Other differences between an employee and IC are evident by your organization's work-at-home policy or remote working agreement with employees. More than likely you have more standard policies in which employees have to agree that many times ICs don't have to, such as:

>> **Attendance:** Hourly or salaried employees often have attendance requirements.

>> **Use of social media:** As a representative of the company, there may be standards for how long employees are on social media during work hours and how they present themselves relating to pictures, alcohol and drug use, and political opinions.

>> **Code of conduct:** Similar to social media, employees are oftentimes considered a brand ambassador for the company. As such, they may be held to standards of behavior consistent with the company's values.

>> **Data protection and confidentiality:** Employees often have access to company proprietary information, so security measures are in place for employees in the handling of confidential information.

>> **Vacation-time requests:** Employees accrue paid vacation and sick time so requests for time off are usually required.

>> **Noncompete agreements:** Employees may be asked to sign noncompete agreements where they agree to not work for or share trade secrets with competitors for a certain amount of time after they leave the company.

>> **Office and computer equipment:** The company provides the use of office and computer equipment to employees and shows how to do so responsibly.

Figuring out a worker's status if you still aren't sure

If you're still not certain whether the workers on your virtual team are employees or ICs, ask yourself these questions:

>> Does the company control or have the right to control what the worker does and how the worker does the job?

>> Is the company setting the worker's work hours?

>> How difficult will this person be to replace?

>> Will the role have access to highly confidential company information?

>> Should the company control the business aspects of the worker's job? These include how the worker is paid, whether expenses are reimbursed, and who provides equipment, software, and supplies.

>> Are there employee benefits such as a pension plan, insurance, or vacation pay the worker expects or will receive?

>> Will the relationship be ongoing or is it short-term?

>> Is the company providing the equipment, tools, and resources to perform the job?

>> Does the person need training to perform the job?

TIP

If you have any question of whether a worker is an employee or IC, consult the IRS website (www.irs.gov/businesses/small-businesses-self-employed/independent-contractor-self-employed-or-employee). You can review many factors and each situation individually to determine status. However, the most important and consistent factor the IRS and DOL use is whether or not the employer exercises control over how the work gets done, when it gets done, and by what means the work gets done.

Choosing to Work with an IC: What You Need to Do

If you determine that you're working with an IC, having a contract in place is an important part of doing business and establishes expectations for pay, deliverables, performance, termination of contract, and more. The process and paperwork required is much simpler than for employees, with only a few important documents needed. You don't have to set up payroll taxes or benefit forms, and in most cases you don't have to perform skill tests or drug tests, or handle other legal documentation necessary when hiring an employee. However, you want to be sure that the IC you're considering for hire is qualified for the role, will be able to perform as expected, can maintain confidentiality, and has a good reputation.

These sections delve into what is essential when you decide to use an IC, including what credentials to verify, what records you need to keep, and what to include in your contract.

Checking credentials

Just like you would check references when hiring an employee, you want to be just as diligent when hiring an IC. Many virtual teams use long-term ICs to supplement the skill set on their team, and the ICs are considered key team members. They have the same impact on culture, communication, and engagement that any team member would, so make sure you perform your due diligence before you sign on the dotted line.

REMEMBER

Do your homework and check the following before hiring your next IC:

>> **Background check:** Make sure that the IC doesn't have any felony convictions. If her work involves financials, sensitive data, or specific clientele, she could pose a major risk.

>> **Social media:** Check out the IC's social medial sites to get a feel for cultural fit and if she's actually someone you feel comfortable having on your team.

>> **Online presence:** Many ICs build an online presence to showcase their work, provide testimonials, and more. Check out if the IC has a personal website or LinkedIn profile.

>> **Work samples:** Ask for work samples or even hire the IC for a short project (say, five to ten hours) to assess her work.

>> **Reference check:** Follow up with references and ask questions about work ethic, meeting deadlines, quality of work, and team engagement.

>> **Better Business Bureau:** If the IC is set up as a business, you can check with the BBB to see if any complaints have been filed against her.

>> **Business insurance:** If the IC is doing high-level work where risk is involved, she should be able to provide you with a copy of her business insurance. This insurance is meant to protect the IC from being personally sued. It also demonstrates a credible IC that takes her work and relationship with clients seriously and shows she's done her due diligence as well.

Keeping records

When you hire an IC, you're required to collect and keep on file a few essential documents. If the IRS ever audits you, you must verify the status of your IC with these documents. I recommend creating a file for each IC that you hire. Here are the documents that you need:

>> **Application and resume:** Keep a copy of the IC's application, resume, or professional qualifications on file. The application should clearly state that the job is contractor status, not an employee, which is for your protection.

>> **W-9 Form:** All ICs must sign this form when they start working for you. On this form they're required to provide a tax ID number, Social Security number, or employer tax ID number if they're a business. (Reputable ICs should have an employer tax ID number.) You must have this form on file so you don't have to withhold income taxes from the IC.

>> **1099-MISC form:** For tax purposes, you use the W-9 information as well as what you paid the IC over the course of a year to create a 1099-MISC form. These forms are sent to the IC for her income taxes and must be given to the IC no later than the last day of January the following year.

>> **Form 1096:** Your business must document all payments made to ICs for the year, and a Form 1096 must be sent to the Social Security Administration by the end of February the following year. Copies of all 1099 forms should be included.

>> **Contract:** Keep a copy of the signed contract by both the IC and the company.

Knowing what to include in a contract

For every IC that works for your company, your contract should outline key terms and agreements that both parties sign (and then kept on file; see the preceding section). You may be thinking to yourself, "Do I really need an agreement with every IC I work with?" The answer is *yes!* It protects both you and the IC in the event of a conflict, dispute, or termination.

Terms to address in the contract agreement include the following:

>> The scope of work that the IC will be performing and what she is responsible for

>> Who owns any intellectual property that is developed: IC or employer

>> Who the IC will be working with to complete the requirements

>> Deadlines for when the job needs to be done

>> Payment terms, amounts, and what happens if payments aren't made within the terms of the contract

>> Clear statement that the person is an IC and not an employee and won't receive benefits, vacation pay, and so on

>> Confidentiality and what information the IC is responsible for keeping private

The following lists IC inclusions for a contract and a foundation for what you should include in your contract. You may want to add your own company policies. Make sure to have a lawyer read over it to verify you've covered all your bases because I'm not a lawyer and I don't play one on TV.

» Date contract is entered into

» Who the contract is between (company and an individual or company and a business)

» Terms, including the date when the contract starts and ends

» Services to be rendered by the IC

» How services will be performance (unsupervised, at own expense, remotely)

» Compensation and when it will be paid; check out the next section for more information

» Equipment and supplies the IC will need for the work

» Insurance requirements from IC, such as workers' compensation and business insurance (amount needed can be specified); refer to the later "Understanding insurance requirements for ICs" section for more info

» Obligations of the company to the IC

» Ownership of intellectual property

» IC status; see the later "Clarifying contractor status" section

» Measures of success, performance, or required deliverables

» How and when the contract can be terminated

Specifying compensation

Deciding on compensation for an IC is fairly easy. You negotiate and agree on an hourly, weekly, monthly, or by-project rate. This rate is outlined in the contract and signed by both parties. Because you're usually not withholding any taxes (check with your state laws to be sure), the IC receives payment for what was agreed upon at the timing interval stated. You can also include in the contract any *success measures* or milestones that the IC must accomplish before payment is made. Be sure to outline in the contract what happens if work isn't done on time or isn't acceptable. All of these terms should be agreed on before the IC is hired.

REMEMBER

Determining what is fair and equitable pay for an IC takes into account a lot of things, including experience, expertise, knowledge, past performance, specialized skill set, and more. ICs have many more nonreimbursable expenses than an employee does; and this amount is usually incorporated into their rates.

Compensation will usually require some level of negotiation for the company and the IC to come to agreement. Doing your research ahead of time to understand what the market is willing to pay an IC for a similar job role with similar experience is an important part of preparing for negotiation.

Understanding insurance requirements for ICs

For employees, health insurance is usually part of an overall benefits package offered during the hiring process. Virtual workers who are employees need to make sure that their home office complies with the company's health and safety policies and may need to provide an up-to-date homeowner's policy to their employer. It's also possible that the company will conduct an inspection of the home office to check that furnishings and equipment are ergonomically designed for safe work and that lighting and ventilation are sufficient.

However, this process differs for ICs, who need to consider options for purchasing health insurance on their own. An independent insurance agent is a good option for creating a personalized solution. Group health insurance coverage is available through groups like `FreelancersUnion.org` or the `National Association for the Self Employed` (`www.nase.org/`). ICs can also compare health insurance coverage rates online with major carriers and comprehensive sites such as `eHealth Insurance` or `HealthCare.gov` (which is managed by the U.S. Department of Health & Human Services) can help too.

Liability insurance is another major consideration for virtual workers. ICs need to be aware that their homeowner's insurance won't cover issues related to their home-based business. Just like setting up a separate work space and creating separate bank accounts, ICs need separate business and personal insurance. Typically, ICs should carry general liability insurance, but depending on the work they do, they may also need a commercial property policy (for business equipment), errors and omissions (recommended for writers and consultants), and workers' compensation insurance (if they have employees who work for their home-based business).

Clarifying contractor status

Be sure that your contract clearly states that this virtual job role is as a remote IC and that as the employer you don't provide any benefits, paid vacation, or sick time. In addition, ensure that the contract clearly states the following:

» The company doesn't control, direct, or otherwise supervise the IC in performing her services.

» The IC will use her own tools and equipment.

>> The contract isn't exclusive, which means the IC can perform services for other clients.

>> Any necessary insurance requirements the IC must have including workers' compensation insurance or business insurance.

Requiring a Nondisclosure Agreement (NDA) or Not

A *nondisclosure agreement (NDA)* is required when the company plans to share important confidential information with the IC or vice versa. The NDA legally prevents the IC from sharing or using sensitive information discovered or obtained during the course of her contract work and can require her to maintain secrecy even after her contract has ended.

NDAs can protect proprietary information such as trade secrets or as nebulous as a business concept. They can even involve a pending law enforcement investigation. The NDA, which is legally binding in a court of law, should outline what specifically shouldn't be shared with others. An NDA should set a time frame and spell out consequences if the agreement is breached.

Here are some situations where you may want to use a NDA with your IC:

>> When sharing or presenting a new idea, product, or invention with an IC to get her opinion on what's possible or how to market it

>> When sharing confidential company information such as financial, customer data, marketing, or strategy decisions with an IC

>> When the IC has worked with your competitors in the past or may work with them in the future

>> When the IC will have access to sensitive information as part of her work

When writing your NDA, remember that it doesn't have to be long and complicated. In fact, the good ones usually don't run more than a few pages long. Here are the key elements to include in your NDA:

>> Who's involved in the agreement (for example, your company and the IC)

>> Definition of what is deemed to be confidential or not generally known by the public

>> The IC's confidentiality obligation (who she can and can't talk to and share information with)

>> What's excluded from the NDA and okay to discuss

>> Length of time of the nondisclosure obligation

Numerous sources for free NDA templates are available online, which you can customize to meet your needs. A few options include the following:

>> www.rocketlawyer.com

>> www.legaltemplates.net

>> www.formswift.com

Navigating the Legalities of Noncompete Agreements

One way that employers can get into trouble with ICs is by using noncompete agreements. A *noncompete agreement* is an agreement between two parties where one party agrees not to compete in the same profession, industry, or with the same clientele as the other party. The agreement also has reasonable limits regarding how long it's in place and its scope.

Although many employers have ICs sign noncompete agreements (I've signed many), they have to be able to enforce the agreements in a court of law. What can get quite confusing is that different states have different laws regarding the enforceability of these types of agreements. The key is that the agreement needs to make sense for the party that is requiring it. Examples where a noncompete seems to make good business sense include:

>> When you're sharing trade secrets, special formulas, or client lists with an IC

>> When your IC will be introduced to your clients that she could potentially solicit as customers down the road

However, the validity of noncompete agreements can get tricky when considering how the IRS and DOL determine the employer-employee relationship. Generally, a noncompete agreement is an indicator that the employer is exercising control over the IC that looks like more of an employee relationship. Remember ICs are in business for themselves, and you can't ask them to forfeit their ability to grow their business because you decide to work with them.

A good employment lawyer can help you formulate a noncompete agreement if using an agreement makes sense for your business and the ICs you're working with.

Chapter **7**

Structuring and Assembling Your Team

A ssembling your virtual team requires thought about what quality processes and structure you want to have in place. Your decision depends on the type of team you're leading, the work you're performing, the level of skill and experience on the team, and the culture and values of your organization.

Your team exists to solve a problem or address a need, and defining a structure for your team directly relates to solving that need. Every team needs a foundational structure and frameworks that dictate how the team is organized, how communication and work flows through the team, and who has authority to make decisions. If structure isn't defined or frameworks aren't in place, lack of clarity will lead to inefficiencies, missed deadlines, and poor team performance.

Beginning with the onboarding process, develop a strategy for getting your new team members engaged and up to speed as quickly as possible. Agreeing on team values and trust-building behaviors helps the team connect, collaborate, and get results, and it's one of the most important exercises you can do with your team.

This chapter takes a closer look at the importance of deciding on a team structure, the approach to build a strong onboarding process, and the way to lead the discussion of team values and what they mean for your team. This chapter also examines the importance of setting clear team expectations and how feedback can help you create a culture of accountability on your virtual team.

Organizing Your Team the Smart Way

Choosing a structure for your team is vital. It outlines the way people relate to one another, how your team is organized, how roles are assigned, and how people communicate and make decisions.

Selecting a team structure involves a variety of frameworks that are flexible to shift and change in order to support changing team goals and priorities. Basically, your team structure is the glue that holds everything together and helps your team grow. The following sections help guide you in creating the optimal team structure for your virtual team.

How teams are structured

Teams can be structured in several ways, and the way a team is structured usually depends on company culture, goals of the team, roles and responsibilities, and the way team members interact and communicate. Some structures are more rigid than others, and with a virtual team, it's important that your structure is flexible to allow for much more self-directed work. Here are the most common team structures:

>> **Hierarchical:** This is the old-school team structure where a clear chain of command exists from the leader down to the front-line employee. Decisions are made at the top and passed down to the bottom of the structure. Team members at the bottom of the structure don't have authority to make decisions on their own, and this type of structure is slow to make changes and adapt to quickly shifting market conditions. The military and some traditional companies still use this structure.

>> **Matrix:** Most large companies today like Starbucks, Apple, and even Wal-Mart have moved to a matrix structure to be more adaptable to market needs. In a matrix structure, people report to different managers or teams for different reasons. It may have some level of a hierarchical structure for reporting purposes and performance management, but it allows for more flexibility on a daily basis to get the work done. For example, an accountant may report into the CFO for performance purposes but she also reports to the project team manager for specific projects that the accountant supports, which allows for faster communication and decision-making.

>> **Flat:** A flat structure removes any hierarchy and spreads out decision-making and responsibility. Teams are self-managed, and employees have freedom to decide how to get their work done and when. Communication is faster and direct.

>> **Holacracy:** This is the newest organizational structure made famous by Zappos. In a holacracy, responsibility is distributed among groups called circles. The circles make their own decisions about what gets done without reporting up any chain of command. Employees can have different roles in different circles based on their skill set and what a particular project needs.

REMEMBER

Your team structure should support your team goals and how you want communication to flow on your team. On a virtual team, I most often see a combination of a flat or matrix structure for getting work done and a hierarchy structure for reporting purposes. The key to success is that everyone on the team is clear of the structure being used and the leader is flexible, adaptable, and willing to shift gears if things aren't working.

The importance of frameworks

Team *frameworks* are used for things like product development, communication, high performance, decision-making, feedback, coaching, team building, and more. Team frameworks are extremely common, and a leader usually recommends them based on positive past experiences. Many frameworks presented in popular leadership books are researched and proven to work, all with the same goal: to assist your team in building trust and efficiency and accomplishing results.

In Chapter 4, I take a deep dive into what's included in team frameworks and provide an example of a team performance model that I've developed. I also discuss why it's important that your framework aligns with your goals, priorities, and roles.

Focusing on the Onboarding Process

Taking the time to develop and implement an organized, integrated, welcoming onboarding process for your remote employees is something I can't stress enough. Onboarding your virtual team member is a delicate point in time when new hires either feel a connection to the company and their team or they feel left to their own devices and put in a position of sink or swim, as if they don't really matter. Your onboarding process significantly impacts the initial impression that your new team members have of you, the team, the company culture, and their place in it. If that first impression is negative, changing it can be difficult.

The Society for Human Resources Management shared that according to research, 90 percent of all employees make a decision whether to stay or leave a company within the first six months on the job. Hence, companies with a good onboarding process experience higher rates of successful integration into the company culture, faster time to productivity, and higher levels of employee engagement.

TIP

Don't leave a good onboarding process to chance with the hopes that one or two team members will take your new hire under their wing. If this is your strategy, you may quickly lose employees within months of their start date, which is a costly mistake. In fact, turnover costs on average 1.5 to 2.5 times a person's salary, depending on the employee's job level, which is due to the enormous amount of time, costs, and resources it takes to recruit, hire, train, and onboard a new employee. A new hire quitting has a significant impact on everyone and your company's bottom line.

The good news: You can create great strategies to address turnover, and it starts with the onboarding process, which I discuss in the following sections.

Creating an onboarding process that works for your team

The onboarding process is a time when employees need to feel welcomed to the team and have everything clearly explained to them so that they can hit the ground running in their new role. Here are some important steps you can take to develop a strong onboarding process for your remote employees:

1. **Have tools and technology ready.**

   You may provide a laptop, phone, or other office equipment to your remote employees. Make sure you send them to your new team members' remote offices before the first day. Whether you like it or not, not having the tools and technology ready to go communicates some unsettling messages like "we weren't really ready for you," "we were too busy to focus on you," or "we have more important things to do than to get you set up."

2. **Send a welcome care package.**

   Ship your new hires a care package full of company swag and a message from the team to arrive on their first day to welcome them and showcase a bit of your culture. Your newly hired remote employees will love it because they immediately feel a part of team. Some of the best welcome kits that I've seen include these ideas:

   - Company mugs, water bottles, T-shirts, hats, pencils

   - Company journal with the values on the front and an explanation of the values on the inside cover

- Leadership books that the team members have read and reference frequently to improve team culture and relationships

- Team welcome cards signed by everyone (ideally, handwritten but electronic signatures can work too)

- A welcome message from the CEO or founder

- A calendar of important company events, including all-hands meetings, company retreats, and so on

- A checklist of tasks to complete in the first 15 days that includes connecting with different people in the company, doing research on the company website to answer trivia questions, taking pictures of their remote office, sharing where they live and a story about themselves, and completing important HR paperwork, nondisclosure agreements, or benefits.

TIP

Even if you don't have a bunch of company swag, look to several online companies that specialize in beautiful care packages for onboarding. The one I use frequently is www.baudville.com. Whatever you decide, just be sure to make your new hires' first day special.

3. **Plan and budget for one in-person meeting the first month.**

Many virtual companies I work with swear by the practice of investing in meeting their new employees in person the first week or month. The manager may visit the new team members at their home or town, or the new team members may journey to the home office (if one exists) to meet the company executives. Doing so provides a chance to hear stories about the company culture, vision, and values. Furthermore, it speaks volumes to the new team members about how important they are to the team. If time and expense is a deterrent, have a face-to-face meeting using videoconferencing technology.

4. **Create a training and coaching plan developed for their role.**

Develop a training plan for your new hires to introduce them to the company, culture, products, and their role priorities. This plan most likely includes self-study, online training, coaching by the manager or other team members, and more. The key is to get them up to speed on the most important aspects of their job role and the company culture and values. See Chapter 15 for more information on training your new virtual team member.

5. **Have them meet the team.**

You can get creative with this one as well. When introducing the new team members, you may do a virtual conference with the whole team and have each team member share a snapshot of what's out his or her window or an interesting hobby. You can also schedule each team member to have a one-on-one meeting with the new team members during their first week. You want to make them feel part of the team family quickly so build ample opportunities for the team members to engage with them early and often during their first 30 days.

6. **If you're the manager, be savvy with your touch points in week one.**

The first day is super-duper important when onboarding your new team members. If you're the manager, the best-case scenario is to meet your new team member face-to-face. If that's not possible, meet with them via a videoconference call first before anyone else, which is your opportunity to build the relationship, discuss expectations of working together, help them understand how the team and company are organized, explain what they need to know about the culture, and share some personal insights about each other. I also recommend you plan a meeting at the end of their first week to answer all their questions from week one, dive deeper into job level expectations, discuss more about the company and team culture, and chat about their priorities, goals, and measures for the first 90 days. (Refer to the section, "Focusing on the first 90 days" for more specific guidance.)

7. **Watch out for the new team members being overwhelmed.**

Starting any new job can feel like you're drinking from a fire hose. Schedule frequent and regular check-ins to touch base and keep a pulse on how your new hires are doing. Keep in mind that if they're struggling, they may keep quiet about it because they want to be seen as competent. Make sure you ask open-ended questions to check for understanding or confusion.

8. **Partner them up with a buddy.**

When you read this list for onboarding, you're probably a bit overwhelmed. You may also be thinking about where will you find the time to accomplish everything. I understand, which is why I strongly suggest having a buddy, also known as a mentor, for every virtual new hire for the first 30 to 60 days. Having a buddy is a powerful way to make sure that your new remote employees don't slip through the cracks the first few weeks and feel isolated and alone. I discuss the importance of having a buddy in the next section.

Using the buddy system

Assigning a buddy in your company who will be a confidant, friend, mentor, and supporter for your new hires immediately establishes a strong connection for the new team members and makes them feel part of the company and the team. These sections examine how a buddy system can help you, how to choose buddies, and how to establish expectations.

Eyeing the benefits of buddies

Your team can benefit by designating a buddy for your new team members in these ways:

>> A buddy provides the opportunity for the new team members to ask questions that they otherwise may be afraid to ask for fear of looking incompetent.

>> Your new team members are more likely to gain confidence and understand what's expected of them when they have a buddy watching out for them, encouraging them, and checking in on them regularly.

>> A buddy shares some of the responsibility with you to ensure the new team members are moving through the onboarding process successfully.

Having a buddy system is one of the most effective ways I know of creating a sense of belonging and trust for new team members, especially if they're remote. Using a buddy system is a nonnegotiable because of how effectively it fosters strong workplace relationships beginning on day one.

Choosing buddies

Select a buddy who understands the culture of the company and team, has a good understanding of processes and procedures, communicates well, enjoys their job, and most of all, wants to be a buddy. I recommend that you choose someone who has been with the company at least one year. Keep these other questions in mind when choosing a buddy for your new team members:

>> Does the prospective buddy have the time?

>> Does she communicate well?

>> Is she familiar with the new team member's new job and the team?

>> Is she a strong performer and can she handle the additional responsibility of being a buddy?

>> Does she demonstrate the company values?

>> Does she have a good attitude, enjoy her job, and speak well of the company?

>> Do the other team members respect her?

Establishing clear expectations

Setting expectations for buddies and what their role entails is important. To be clear, they're not supervising. Consequently, the new team members should discuss anything to do with pay, promotions, job responsibilities, performance measures, evaluations, and so on with their direct manager.

However, you can discuss and agree on certain expectations that will ensure an effective buddy system on your team and at your company. Here are some common expectations for buddies:

>> Schedule several key touch points during the new hires' first week, including in-person breakfast or lunch if possible.

» Orient them to the company history, organizational structure, such as who's who and how to get needed resources, company policies, culture, values, and so on.

» Plan social connections that include connecting outside of work to check in and see how things are going. You can have a virtual happy hour or meet virtually for breakfast or lunch.

» Introduce them to key stakeholders in other areas of the company to build cross-functional communication.

» Support them as needed to answer questions or concerns, or be a sounding board.

Focusing on the first 90 days

The first 90 days is a sweet spot for you to focus on with your newly hired remote employees. If you've put in the work to find great hires (see Chapter 5), most likely you have self-directed, self-motivated employees working for you. They're ready to start, and setting clear expectations, goals, and priorities for the first 90 days can help them to begin.

TIP

Use a crawl, walk, run strategy with more check-ins planned upfront to make sure the team members are doing okay. Then you can spread them out after you both feel comfortable, clear, and in sync with each other. At the end of 90 days, you can recognize whether you made a great hire, your new team members need more support and coaching from you, or maybe the team members weren't the best fit.

Focus on the following for the first 90 days when onboarding new virtual employees. Doing so during this initial time is can open communication and trust with your new team members and make them feel at home:

» **Have frequent check-ins, both formal and informal.** Schedule more formal check-ins the first week. You can then progress to every two weeks and then at 45 and 90 days. These check-ins focus on their progress, offering coaching and support as needed, and assessing how they're feeling about the new job. The informal check-ins should happen daily as soon as the new team members join your team, and then weekly to keep them feeling connected to the team and to you.

» **Set short-term goal.** Does it feel amazing that after your first 90 days on the job, you hit your goal or knock it out of the park? Of course, it does! That's why setting a short-term goal for your new team members to work toward and accomplish is so important. Doing so allows the new employees to assess their strengths, work pace, and skill set. If they get the goal done ahead of schedule and the task seemed simple, you can set a *stretch goal* (a much more ambitious goal that exceeds the established goals) the next time.

>> **Break it up.** If you're onboarding a virtual employee with many responsibilities, break up the tasks into different parts and introduce them in steps. Confusion and misunderstanding can interrupt workflow, but with organization and clear instructions, you can make sure that employees know exactly what you expect from them. When you gradually introduce responsibilities, your employees can master them more quickly, resulting in more efficiency and productivity. Consider what to focus on during the first week, and then during the first, second, and third months.

>> **Share knowledge resources.** Being new can be incredibly overwhelming, especially in a virtual space with far fewer watch-and-learn opportunities. Mitigate this challenge by sharing as many resources and how-to documents as possible with new hires. Having these resources at hand helps to address common questions and concerns.

>> **Discuss the importance of engagement.** *Engagement* in terms of a virtual team means communicating with team members daily, collaborating on team decisions, and actively participating in video chats, brainstorming sessions, and nonwork message boards. Talking frequently about your expectations concerning engagement is essential. Point out to your employees where they could engage more and where you loved how they contributed. You can also ask them what they need from you or the team to feel more comfortable engaging. Refer to Chapter 11 for more discussion on engagement.

>> **Do a personal assessment.** Find out how your new team members are thinking and feeling about their job, team, and you. Assess their confidence level and survey whether they feel happy with their decision to work for you. You can use a simple survey tool like surveymonkey.com or surveygizmo.com. Make sure you conduct at least two in the first 90 days.

>> **Ask about the culture.** Don't be afraid to talk about the team culture and company culture with your new team members. Do they feel accepted, welcomed, and valued? If not, ask them to describe a time when they felt that way and what happened for them. Discuss how you can bring those feelings into their work with you. What have they noticed that they love about your company culture? What don't they appreciate or is a struggle?

REMEMBER

Using these onboarding strategies work to get your new hire up to speed, connected, and quickly engaged with your team. If you've made a good hire, you'll end up with a rock star virtual team member who stays with your team long term.

Establishing Team Values As Your Bumper Rails

Imagine riding the bumper cars at an amusement park. The bumper rails protect you from getting hurt, but they also keep you in the game. Team values are your bumper rails. They're agreements between team members that create the foundation for how the team will work together as well as provide guidance for how to steer clear of any offensive or inappropriate behaviors. Furthermore, team values help a team stay on track and make decisions about solutions to problems, provide guidance on the kinds of people to hire, and specify how to treat customers, suppliers, and partners.

More than likely if team members on the team are acting disrespectful, disengaged, or not fulfilling commitments, their behaviors aren't in-line with your team values. That behavior, when it happens, creates an opportunity to have a constructive conversation about living the team values and getting the team member back on course.

Team values are different from your company's core values, which are deeply ingrained principles lived by your company. Core values create and impact culture, whereas team values are custom to your team. Your team agrees on them together, including what they mean and how they show up in your everyday interactions with each other. Team values are only effective and influential when developed together.

These sections examine how you can establish your team values by setting specific ones for your team and making sure you live them everyday.

Defining your team values

Your virtual team will no doubt be a blend of cultures, beliefs, and mindsets. And most certainly, you have an expectation that the team will work together to make progress, make a difference, and achieve its goals. How to bring together a diverse group of people and get them moving in the same direction in a way that is positive and inclusive is what's essential. Linking your team members' personal values and what's important to them to team values is the best way to build congruence, alignment, and overall job satisfaction.

Follow these steps in this exercise to define your team values by using collaborative technology such as a virtual whiteboard to take your team through the value discussion and identification process. *Note:* This exercise could take more than one meeting.

1. Clarify and share personal values.

Provide each team member with a sample list of personal values (see Table 7-1). Ask team members to choose their top five values and share what they mean with the team.

TABLE 7-1

Personal Values Clarification

Values	Values	Values
Security	Advancement	Contribution
Independence	Service	Wealth/Prosperity
Recognition	Environment	Variety
Health	Balance	Power
Leadership	Freedom	Creativity
Relationships	Adventure	Spirituality/Faith
Challenge	Risk-taking	Integrity/Honesty
Pleasure/Enjoyment	Fun	Open-mindedness
Humor	Communication	Happiness
Peace	Achievement/Success	Friendship
Teamwork	Connection	Decisiveness
Love/Affection	Family	Health
Wisdom	Truth	Trust
Strength	Simplicity	Respect
Quality	Productivity	Patience
Loyalty	Intelligence	Innovation
Hope	Beauty	Competence
Competition	Courage	Flexibility
Growth/Learning	Autonomy	Harmony
Dependability	Diversity	Effectiveness
Empathy	Equality	Curiosity
Discipline	Kindness	Charity
Expertness	Excellence	Honor
Humility	Loyalty	Safety

2. **Discuss everyone's personal value alignment.**

   After team members have shared their personal values and what they mean, make the link of alignment to the team. Here are some questions to ask:

   - Do you currently live these values daily in your work? In what situations are you not living your values?

   - What values do you need to integrate and live more often in your work? How?

   - How do your values contribute and support the team culture and goals?

3. **Identify team members' shared values.**

   Capture shared values on a virtual whiteboard. Ask team members to clarify what values are central to their work and what they believe the team should focus on exhibiting in its day-to-day interactions, decision-making, problem solving, and conflict. Here are a few examples of shared team values:

   Accountability

   - We show up on time to meetings and come prepared.

   - We keep team members updated on our progress.

   Trust

   - We provide honest and regular feedback to each other.

   - We respect that everyone has a role on the team and that their contribution matters.

   - We always offer support and recognition when we see an opportunity.

   Commitment

   - We contribute ideas and support to every project even if we aren't the lead.

   - We can be counted on to deliver even in difficult circumstances.

   - We make decisions in alignment with our vision and values.

4. **Vote and agree on the top three to five team values that all team members are willing to live by.**

   Discuss what living these values looks like and sounds like. Questions to discuss include

   - Do these values capture what we stand for and want to be known for?

   - Do these values tell a story about our team culture and what it's like to work on this team?

   - What would these values look like in action on a daily basis?

   - What behaviors express these values?

- How do we demonstrate these values when in conflict? With customers? When having to push back with other teams?

- How do we agree to recognize each other for living these values?

- How do we communicate and call out each other when we aren't upholding these values?

- When should we talk about or revisit these values to keep them top of mind?

- How do we explain these values to new hires?

5. **Create your team values map, chart, or other reminder.**

Make sure all team members receive one and can hang it in their office. I recommend talking about the team values at the start of any new project, when faced with problems, or when giving recognition when you notice people living them. Don't let your values become something that you never look at again.

Living your team values

Your values support and guide your team culture. Hence, keeping them top of mind, relevant, and inspirational is important. Here are a few reminders to ensure your team values are front and center:

» **Lead by example.** As a leader, you're always in the spotlight. Setting team values and then failing to abide by them is worse than not establishing them at all.

» **Remember that talk is cheap.** Plastering your values on coffee mugs, business cards, and motivational posters is fine, but it's far more powerful when team values are a cultural team norm and always in practice. That starts with you, the leader.

» **Integrate values everywhere.** Include your team values in literally everything you do and say. Recruiting, hiring, ongoing training, performance reviews, success stories, customer service, recognition, team blogs, team meetings, and so on.

» **Step into the spotlight.** Celebrate and reward values-driven behavior and nominate coworkers for successfully living the values with public recognition, bonuses on the spot or gift cards, peer-voting opportunities to, and written recognition in newsletters or on your company website.

» **Know when to let them go.** Recognize that team members who violate the values may not be a good fit for the team. When an employee engages in behavior that contradicts your values, the other team members notice, and it almost always has a negative impact on team dynamics. Don't be held hostage by a high performer that doesn't live by the team values. Leaders must put their ethical nonnegotiables ahead of everything, including performance and profits. Demonstrating how important your team values are is vital. When a team member isn't willing to abide by them, it's time to let her go.

MAKING YOUR DREAM TEAM: WHAT TRAITS ARE KEY

In 2017, Google released its findings from a two-year study on what makes a "dream team." Google conducted more than 200 interviews, looked at more than 250 team attributes, and narrowed the research down to five key characteristics that successful teams shared. Not surprisingly the results align with much of what I've espoused to teams during the past 20 years. Google's research uncovered these five traits that make the best teams work:

- **Dependability:** Team members are accountable and meet expectations.
- **Structure and clarity:** The team has established clear goals, defined roles, and rules of engagement.
- **Meaning:** The work has significance to each team member.
- **Impact:** The team's work makes a difference and have a positive impact
- **Psychological safety:** The team works in an environment where team members can safely be vulnerable; the environment is a place to be authentic.

The one success trait that really struck me was what Google called "psychological safety." You can call it trust or a safe space to take risks, but it basically boils down to the same thing: acceptance, with no fear of judgment, recrimination, or competition. Psychological safety can be established either formally or informally as the team's team culture, and quantifying it is tough, but you know when it's there. Google's researchers concluded that what distinguished these good teams from the dysfunctional teams was how teammates treated one another. And perhaps most importantly, psychological safety — more than any other factor — is critical to making a team work.

Google's intense data collection and analysis led to a conclusion that many good leaders have always known. On the best teams, members know each other, listen to one another, and show empathy to other's feelings and needs. Google's insights aren't necessarily original; they validate the fact that emotional intelligence, inclusion, and authenticity are critical to team success. These traits are important whether your team is virtual, located in the same office, or spread around the world, which is only possible if clear expectations, a role, and a strong sense of values and purpose exists. When these success traits are present on a team, it creates an environment where people aren't afraid to speak up, offer constructive feedback, and hold each other accountable.

Identifying Team Traits That Build Cohesiveness

Creating an atmosphere of trust and camaraderie between employees when they're all in the same building for eight hours a day is one thing. However, when your virtual teams rarely see their coworkers, if at all, then keeping your virtual teams connected to the larger organization — and to each other — is even more important. And with more and more people working remotely, team leaders need to find ways to instill team values and build cohesiveness on their virtual teams. The following sections help you recognize and build cohesiveness among your virtual team members when you're first assembling your team.

Building trust is an inside job. On a virtual team, building trust takes a higher level of commitment and persistence because the team isn't in the same location. Building trust starts with the leader setting the example, leading the way, and developing trustworthy habits into the team culture. See Chapter 12 for more detailed information and ideas on how to build trust and rapport on your team.

Having clear expectations for success

Too often, I notice that team leaders are surprised when team members aren't mind readers and don't know exactly what is expected when joining the team. Rather than set and communicate clear expectations that define the milestones against which team performance is measured and rewarded, team leaders assume people know exactly what to do and how to do it. The result is that healthy teamwork, initiative, engagement, and productivity take a back seat whereas hesitation, indecision, and lack of focus on the wrong priorities rules the day.

TIP

Don't rely on unspoken assumptions and expectations. Rather, remove the ambiguity by setting clear and consistent standards for the team and for each individual role. Here are a few examples of topics where setting expectations for your virtual team is valuable:

>> What you measure (examples include performance levels, revenue targets, customer satisfaction scores, hold times, time to resolution, and so on)

>> Expected time frame for responding to emails and voicemails

>> Updating project status and progress

>> Engagement and participation levels

>> Personal reach out and connection frequency

>> Subject matter experts and their role

>> Behaviors that align with team values

>> Adherence to process or policy

You may have several other expectations that are important for team success, but these topics can get you started thinking about what areas you want to discuss with your team. Refer to the Cheat Sheet at www.dummies.com and search for "virtual teams" for how to set clear team expectations and create a story about what those expectations mean for your team.

Getting real with feedback and accountability

Virtual team members who succeed at their job tend to be self-directed and take more individual responsibility to meet their goals and deadlines. High-performing remote employees are usually supported by a leader who sets clear goals and expectations, gives the team the freedom to make choices about how to design and take ownership for how the work gets done, and trusts them to make it happen. When accountability is present on a team, people are willing to call out performance or behaviors that hurt or inhibit the team. When this level of trust and transparency exists, a lot less time and energy is wasted on wondering what people think. Furthermore, team members are more willing to accept feedback and own their mistakes, and a strong sense of team exists.

However, if your team has traditionally worked in an office environment, this mindset shift to self-directed work and a strong sense of ownership can be tricky for both the leader and the team. Team members may be waiting for the leader to tell them what to do, may give them approval to do it, or may be afraid to take any risks on their own. Team leaders may have traditionally imposed accountability by directly supervising the work, creating elaborate incentive plans, or always making the final decision.

So, the question of the day is how do virtual teams create accountability practices that are healthy and transparent and supported by everyone on the team? Even though holding one another accountable can be uncomfortable and challenging, doing so is critical for virtual team success. Try these tips for creating healthy accountability on virtual teams:

>> **Recognize that accountability is everyone's job.** It's not just the leader's job.

>> **Create clarity on roles and responsibilities.** Teams that have a high level of clarity find it easier to hold each other accountable and point out behaviors or performance that are impacting the team in a negative way.

- » **Measure success on results, not on time worked.** Involve employees in setting realistic deadlines and schedule check-ins for progress updates.

- » **Establish a strong level of commitment to goals and expectations.** Help your virtual team members understand what everyone is doing and what is expected of each team member.

- » **Provide direct feedback.** Some people are uncomfortable providing feedback because they haven't practiced it enough. Check out a simple process of giving feedback in Figure 7-1 that focuses on solutions for the future, rather than past behaviors that didn't work. Practice this regularly with your team members to increase their confidence in giving feedback.

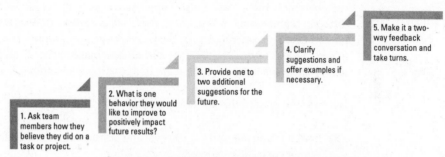

FIGURE 7-1:
How to give future focused feedback.

1. Ask team members how they believe they did on a task or project.

2. What is one behavior they would like to improve to positively impact future results?

3. Provide one to two additional suggestions for the future.

4. Clarify suggestions and offer examples if necessary.

5. Make it a two-way feedback conversation and take turns.

Remember to always focus on what you want to see in the future, not what happened in the past.

© John Wiley & Sons, Inc.

- » **Encourage the team to notice, support, and positively reinforce when team members engage in peer-to-peer accountability in team meetings.** Although pointing out when another team member makes a mistake may feel uncomfortable to hear, doing so establishes a habit of transparency and honesty that is ultimately necessary for virtual team success.

- » **Use technology appropriately.** Technology is an effective tool for visually mapping both team and individual progress and where things are getting stuck. Project management software can facilitate who sees who isn't pulling their weight, meeting deadlines, and moving the project along. Shared calendars can help team members understand what other team members are doing — whether they're out of office, traveling for work, and so on.

Using these tips to set up your virtual team to practice an accountability culture can help you build a virtual workforce that has high standards, exceeds goals, and has a strong bond. You can identify problems quickly, and poor performers will feel pressure to improve. In addition, team members will freely offer honest feedback to one another. The high level of respect team members have for each other will amaze you, and you can steer clear of politics, hidden agendas, and secretive conflicts that can easily take down a virtual team.

Rotating leadership

As the virtual team leader, you're a key player in determining initial structure and roles, communicating direction and goals, leading the discussion around team values, and providing ongoing coaching and feedback.

Because virtual team members are required to have a high level of self-management skills, leaders of virtual teams often act more as a coach — providing guidance, measurement, and feedback as needed. This relationship between virtual team members and their leader also supports the idea of *rotational leadership* where different team members who are subject matter experts (SMEs) act as the leader or go-to person on key projects or decisions. Depending on the task, the SME is the expert at hand. Giving the SME the authority to make decisions on goals, strategies, and problem resolution for the team in a rotating leadership role makes sense.

Here are the pros to this rotational approach:

>> It allows team members to discover and practice important leadership skills through real-life experience.

>> It identifies *bench strength* (employees who have the right skill and attitude to move up in the company) and who is your next in line leader.

>> It builds respect and trust with team members and garners support for future promotions.

>> It improves *systems thinking* (a holistic philosophy that analyzes how a task or decision is interrelated and linked to the larger system) because the rotating leader gains insight into all the moving parts and individual impacts on team goals.

>> It increases the comfort level of providing feedback and builds an account-ability culture.

Meanwhile, be aware of the cons:

>> When you rotate leaders, you may never know what you're going to get or how adept different team members will be at leading.

>> Some leadership styles work well for the team, and some don't. Unless you have a highly emotional intelligent and flexible leader, trust and communication can break down quickly and can take a long time to rebuild.

>> A loss of consistency can be detrimental to a virtual team.

» Some team members may not want to lead. They would rather succeed at the tasks they were hired to do then have the added pressure of leading a project.

Rotating leadership on a virtual team is a good practice that keeps all team members engaged and builds a keen understanding and awareness of various team roles. Discuss this strategy and expectation with people during the interview process. Then after hired, follow up with development, coaching, and mentoring to prepare each of your team members to lead.

3

Creating and Nurturing a Productive Team Culture

Crack the code on building and maintaining a healthy virtual team culture.

Leverage the benefits of having a cross-cultural team and improve ideas, innovation, and success.

Discover how to navigate the different genders, generations, and culture on your virtual team with ease.

Identify ways to build and practice cultural competence so you can expand your worldview.

Find out how your old-school management approach needs to shift to lead a virtual team.

Anticipate and prepare for the most common virtual team problems you'll encounter.

» **Recognizing your culture**

» **Deciding on the kind of culture you want**

» **Nurturing the desired culture**

» **Embracing a cross-cultural team**

Chapter **8**

Making Work Culture Considerations

The topic of culture is near and dear to my heart. It's what has allowed me to have a thriving consulting practice for close to 20 years, and healthy work cultures create healthy communities, families, and ultimately a healthier world. What I know for sure is that every leader at every level must be intentional about developing and nurturing the culture she desires.

When you work for a company that has a healthy culture as opposed to a dysfunctional culture, the results outside of the workplace are tremendous. They include more connected families, increased volunteerism and sense of community, continuous learning, less stress, more active adults, less disease, stronger relationships, less divorce, and a competitive advantage for your company, just to name a few examples. Unfortunately by some estimates, as many as 95 percent of today's workplaces exhibit some form of dysfunctional or toxic symptoms in their culture.

Much has been written about workplace culture, but nearly all has focused on C-level executives and their responsibility in creating a healthy organizational culture to drive results and reduce turnover. In the virtual world, teams have to discover how to work effectively and in alignment with the overall company culture, but they also need to create their own microculture that defines how their team thrives and operates.

Building a healthy workplace culture involves a commitment of focus, time, and energy that is ongoing and integrated into everything you do. Sustaining a healthy culture needs support from the top with leaders setting the example.

This chapter convinces you how important virtual team culture really is, helps you identify what type of culture you already have, and assists you in determining what behaviors, tools, and practices will build the culture you want. Furthermore, this chapter provides ideas that you can put into practice immediately to foster a positive, productive, engaged culture that is rampant with people who love their job and their team members.

Grasping Why Company Culture Is Key

Because everyone defines company culture just a little bit differently, when I talk about *company culture,* I'm referring to the spoken or unspoken beliefs about the environment in your company or on your team, the values that people live by, and the most prominent behaviors witnessed in company meetings, on projects, in conflicts, with clients, and between leaders and their teams.

Culture is holistic in nature and builds organically over time through workplace experiences, common character traits of the people you hire, and the way leadership communicates and interacts with each other and employees. Culture can be influenced through intentional effort and is one of the most important sustainability strategies for every company and every team. Don't take culture lightly; approach it thoughtfully and with purpose.

Culture is about how people operate and treat each other every day. It's about the stories you tell and what you focus on creating between people and teams like competition, trust or fun, or a maniacal focus on service, results, or innovation. Culture is most apparent when you notice how people behave under pressure or when they're faced with a difficult situation, irate customer, or failed project.

No doubt, culture can make or break your company and how the world views you. At a team level, a toxic culture can destroy your team and impact the health and happiness of everyone who is a part of it. On the other hand, a healthy culture can support you in attracting the best and the brightest, create a sense of value and contribution on your team, and build a reputation that positively impacts the bottom line.

Company and team culture can be a blessing or a curse. A positive culture can make your work life a delight, but a bad culture can be toxic. The following sections examine how to spot culture problems.

Recognizing toxic cultures and the mess they create

The negative effects of a toxic culture can be far-reaching and have a lasting effect on many areas of your business, including employee depression, mental health issues, on-the-job accidents, absenteeism, turnover, low productivity levels, and medical and legal fees. When employees are faced with trying to function in a toxic environment, they become reactive just to be able to get through the day. Additionally, a toxic leader can do more to poison a team culture than any other factor.

Take Wells Fargo for example, a company caught encouraging at least 5,000 frontline employees to commit fraud by opening more than a million fake bank and credit card accounts on behalf of unaware customers. Or Uber's unchecked culture that produced serious accusations about harassment and discrimination and was an example of what culture looks like when you incite people to do whatever it takes to reach the top. These examples of toxic cultures trickled down to every team and every employee. The toxic cultures gave people unspoken permission to behave unethically and created dysfunction at every level.

REMEMBER

By identifying the warning signs of a toxic team culture, you can immediately develop strategies for correcting potentially hazardous results. Here are some signs to watch out for on your virtual team:

>> **Some of your best virtual workers have quit in the past 18 months.** When a team loses a key player, you can't always easily replace that person's expertise, even in today's virtual workforce. Projects stall, motivation of team members drops, and the hiring and onboarding process is time consuming and costly. Even more devastating, those past employees tell their friends and colleagues that your team isn't the place to be.

>> **Your team has developed a CYA culture.** CYA (Cover Your A**) describes a culture where most employees are out for themselves. Team members and leaders in this type of culture often practice CYA tactics through holding unnecessary meetings or crafting memos or emails solely to generate a record to protect themselves to the point of creating a strongly risk averse team culture and fueling employee disgruntlement and paranoia.

>> **Employees don't share information with one another; instead, they work in silos.** Where virtual team members exchange little to no information, they have high potential for rework, misinformation, incorrect assumptions, and overall ineffectiveness. Distrust spreads, gossip ensues, and relationships crumble. Employees don't get access to information they need to do their jobs with no way for them to understand how their role fits into the bigger picture and impacts other teams. This type of behavior undermines strategic growth and goal attainment.

>> **Recognition, feedback, and expectations are impossible to come by.** You don't have to always shell out the cash or give big-ticket awards to get your team members to make them feel proud of their accomplishments. As one virtual team leader shared with me, "If somebody on my development team goes the extra mile, I write a personal thank you note and mail it." Your people will feel more like part of the team if they know your expectations and you find meaningful, sincere ways to let them know when they're doing a good job.

>> **Work-life balance on your team is just a rumor.** Most people tout virtual work as a way to support a healthy balance. But if the only way to get ahead on your team is be available day and night and never be offline, you'll quickly end up with burnt-out team members looking for a different job.

>> **Virtual team leaders think that having very few touch points is sufficient.** Back in the day, people in a company thought that if they hoarded information they had power. On a virtual team, all that has changed. As a virtual leader, use the technology and communication tools available to solicit and share information with team members — through scheduled, ad hoc, and one-on-one meetings, whatever it takes to build stronger, more connected teams.

>> **Employees don't respect most leaders in the company and the company in general.** A quick review of Glassdoor can reveal more about your company culture than you realize. Having a mountain of complaints about leaders in your company may deter good people from coming to work for you.

>> **If asked the question "Why is what you do important?" less than 50 percent of virtual employees could answer.** On a toxic team, members aren't sharing how others make a difference. In return, employees aren't proud of the work they're doing because it doesn't seem to have meaning or add value. Even on a virtual team, employees will leave if they don't know why they matter.

>> **Team meetings are viewed as a waste of time, and innovative ideas are dismissed, ridiculed, or even nonexistent.** Virtual team meetings are a time to connect, provide feedback, discuss progress, and build relationships. When your team stops giving input, coming to the virtual table with solutions, and offering suggestions for change, take a hard look at the level of trust with your staff.

>> **Abusive behavior and bullying is ignored and allowed to continue, regardless of the impact.** Don't think that just because your team is virtual, people don't bully. Sometimes the behavior is noticeable and sometimes it's hidden. If you notice a team member shuts down when a certain person speaks up on a call or becomes unproductive when having to work with a particular employee, her energy isn't going into brainstorming, innovation, or producing a result; it's going into dealing with the emotional fallout of that coworker's behavior.

Identifying a healthy culture and how to build one that thrives

Most people think establishing company culture is easier when everyone is in the office versus everyone is virtual. What's more true is that culture forms quickly and sometimes accidentally when people are located in an office and has the opportunity to be much more intentional when people are virtual.

Making a commitment to building a thriving culture on your virtual team will be rewarded in spades. The following lists what a healthy company culture looks like:

>> Team members are engaged.

>> Employees and managers share mutual respect and trust.

>> People feel they're being treated fairly.

>> Everyone has a clear sense of purpose.

>> Employees can balance their work and personal responsibilities.

>> Employees feel safe and respected.

>> You have a fantastic reputation in your industry, and people are knocking down the doors to work for you.

>> Employees stay in jobs longer, and the company enjoys a low attrition rate.

Building a healthy culture begins with a desire to create a great workplace from the top, which means the organization supports and expects open and honest communication and feedback on every team. Furthermore, employees are given control over their work, and performance is based on results and relationships rather than stepping on toes and leaving dead bodies to get to the top.

In order to sustain a healthy culture at the team level, you must consistently recognize the right behaviors and immediately address the wrong ones. Don't make the mistake of thinking that because you're virtual, issues between team members will magically fade away. You have to address them and support others in doing the same. If not, bad habits will seep into your culture that can be difficult to correct.

Consider what steps you can take to intentionally build a virtual work culture that thrives. Here are a few ideas:

>> **Keep your pulse on the climate of your team.** Survey your team by using a tool like Survey Monkey. Recommended questions are as follows:

- Do you feel valued by your leader and team?

- Are you excited and inspired by the work you do?

- Do you believe you're making an impact?

- Does trust exist between team members?

- Do you know team members on a personal level?

- How would you describe a healthy team culture?

- What three words would you use to describe the team culture?

- What is one idea for improving team culture?

>> **Use a combination of digital and social tools to stay connected and agree to how and when to use them together as a team.** Make it so easy to get in touch with each other that doing so is quicker than if your team members were in person. Set clear expectations about how often team members are using their communication tools to stay connected (refer to Chapter 16 for more info).

>> **Make staying engaged fun.** Create incentives for people to offer their feedback or support on a Facebook group. For example, have a raffle for team swag at the end of a training event where participants get tickets for participation throughout the training call.

>> **Knock it out of the park with your onboarding process.** This process is the first peek under the hood, where new hires discover your culture. As a result, clearly communicate to new hires how valued they are to the team and how people treat and care about each other. Spend time making this transformational. If you need ideas, check out Chapter 7.

>> **Host in-person meetings at least once per year and focus on several days of team building and trust building.** All work and no play makes for a missed opportunity. Team building doesn't need to be over the top to be successful. Allow time for some structured creative activities and informal, social time together.

Taking Note of Your Existing Organizational Culture

Just as each team member has his or her own unique style, your virtual team also needs to develop its own style and culture. Your team culture has a tremendous impact on how people feel about what it's like to work on your team. One team member may think that your team's culture is a perfect match and another person may feel uncomfortable. An inclusive culture appreciates, even celebrates, diversity and variety, and all team members operate from a set of shared values. Your team culture also impacts intangibles, such as the pace at which works gets done, the level of attention to detail or rules that people follow, the risk people are willing to take, and the way other teams, customers, or vendors are treated.

REMEMBER

After culture is in place, team members will feel pressure to conform to the established cultural norms. A number of different factors influence and shape your team culture, including:

>> Your leadership style

>> The pre-existing style of the group (such as creative and informal, progressive and risk taking, conservative and traditional, competitive and results-driven)

>> Team purpose and values

>> The type of work for which the team is responsible

>> Past experiences or history of the team

>> Level of trust, collaboration, or conflict on the team

Before you begin to shift or shape your culture, know what you're working with. Be sure to understand what type of culture you already have before you try to change anything. If this team is brand new, consider your company culture and whether it works for your virtual team. If not, assess the culture you want to create that is aligned with your team's purpose and then build an engaged, thriving environment for everyone.

The following sections examine the four common types of team culture that I discuss with my clients on a regular basis so they can have an educated conversation about the advantages and drawbacks of their culture and what shifts they want to make. The team leader's style influences them, and depending on the work your team is responsible for, all of these cultures can thrive.

Commanding culture

In a commanding culture, a focus on results and growth is number one. The leader sets ambitious goals for the team with control mechanisms, such as incentives, measures, processes, fear tactics, or a heavy dose of micromanagement in place to make sure goals are achieved.

There is an expectation that decisions will be made quickly, problems will be solved swiftly, and the competitive, driving spirit of the team usually ensures the team members get right down to business. People who thrive in this culture enjoy overcoming challenges to achieve success, love straight talk and a focus on results, and give trust and respect to others that do the same. However, interpersonal relationships and communication may suffer. This culture tends to operate under a high level of stress, which can result in burnout and turnover.

Energizing culture

What makes an energizing culture stand out is the team's vibe. The culture tends to be optimistic where people love brainstorming and enjoy socializing both during and outside of work. The team uses a collaborative approach to problem solving and decision-making and believes that by working together the team will accomplish the best result.

In this culture, team members view you as trustworthy when you use your social skills to create an atmosphere of openness where people feel comfortable expressing themselves. However, team members who aren't as social may find this culture difficult to handle and get frustrated with the amount of group collaboration or brainstorming that takes place. They may also feel that the team isn't concerned with process or planning and has trouble assessing risk and maintaining consistency.

Supportive culture

A stable and harmonious environment is most important to the supportive culture. With this type, people like to follow a systematic process and sincerely want to see the team succeed. Team members are friendly and loyal to the team and will avoid conflict or disagreement, choosing to brush things under the rug. This can cause a lack of innovation when people don't speak up in order to keep the peace, even though they disagree. This culture values consistency, so sudden or frequent changes can be overwhelming. This type of culture ensures that everyone is included and supported but may avoid difficult decisions that could hurt someone's feelings.

Analytical culture

If you aren't a perfectionist, then you won't do well in the analytical culture that values high standards, accuracy, and analysis above all else. Quality is what you can always expect from a team with this type of culture, but members can also get stuck in analysis paralysis. This culture may scoff at ideas that aren't backed up with data or facts and can miss out on potential innovation opportunities. Trust has to be earned through high quality deliverables and few mistakes. People who enjoy this type of team culture tend to be professional and serious, which can dampen the mood of others who are motivated by enthusiasm about the work.

Deciding What You Want Your Culture to Be

When your team is spread out across the country or the world, you want to be purposeful about creating and maintaining a healthy work culture. The first place to look for direction is your values. Your company values are the guiding principles behind culture. They set the expectation of how the company operates with customers and internally with each other. Your team values are your guideposts that define how team members agree to treat each other. All team members must share and agree on the values. Make sure to discuss your values in the interviewing process to determine if you're hiring someone that supports those values and can live by them. If not, you'll soon be struggling with someone on your team who isn't a cultural fit.

REMEMBER

In a virtual environment, developing a healthy work culture that is desirable for team members who come from multiple generations with different approaches and a diverse team demographic may be challenging. Everyone on your team may have different needs, and building something special will take nothing less than a devoted commitment to culture. (Refer to Chapter 9 for working with people from different generations.) When thinking about how to build a healthy culture at a high level, consider the following:

>> **Past experiences:** What worked for you in the past and think about companies that are revered for their culture like Zappos, Disney, and Southwest. What can you discover from the past that didn't work? What innovative ideas can you find out from those that are succeeding?

>> **Alignment:** Whatever you want your culture to feel like, look like, and be like, has to align with your values at every level. If operating in your culture isn't supporting the values everyone has agreed to, you're basically setting yourself up for turnover, poor performance, mistrust, and a bad reputation.

For example, the Honest Company has a value of Service Matters. Therefore, every employee on every team should focus on customer service as her top priority. As a customer for more than eight years, I can confirm that everyone lives this value. However, if one of their team leaders was more interested in the quickest path to launching the next best beauty product and service took a back seat, you'd immediately notice and feel a disconnect. People on the team would be making decisions based on a set of values and behaviors that weren't aligned with putting service first. Eventually, the amazing service-focused employees that the company carefully hired would leave in droves because the work wouldn't be enjoyable and not what they signed up for.

>> **Hiring practices:** Hiring for culture is more about hiring for values first. Does the potential new hire align with the values and can she share how she exemplifies the values that your company and teams cherish? If you hire a bad apple, her attitude and poor behaviors can spread like an infection and your team culture can quickly go downhill.

>> **Making it fun:** Your culture should be something in which people want to be a part. They should find it unique and extraordinary and discover that working for your team is a privilege. That's what attracts the right people and keeps them.

TIP

When you're ready to get more descriptive about the culture you want to create, start by thinking through these questions:

>> What are the benefits of your current team culture?

>> What are the drawbacks?

>> Do you believe that your current team culture supports or inhibits team success?

>> What type of culture would improve team success? Do you have examples or experiences to back it up?

>> How are your team members responding to the team culture? Are they engaged? Connected? Do they collaborate when necessary?

>> How do team members react when something goes wrong?

>> What cultural differences may impact your team members? How should they be addressed in a positive way?

>> How can your team leverage cultural differences to be even more awesome?

>> What does good communication look like?

>> What is fun, unique, or quirky about the team's culture that would attract the right people to the team?

>> Based on the work you do, what behaviors are most important for the team to demonstrate? For example:

- Risk taking

- Quick decision-making

- Constructive and consistent feedback

- Perfect deliverables every time

- Innovative ideas

- Healthy work-life balance

- Follow-through

- Organization and efficiency

- Proven processes

- Thorough analysis

- Structure and stability

- Collaboration

- Strong personal connections

- Comfort level with constant change

- Systematic pace or fast pace

These questions can help you start to outline the behaviors and beliefs that will affect your team culture. You can begin to define norms and the attitude required by team members to build the culture necessary for success.

Building and Maintaining the Culture You Want

After you figure out what type of team culture you desire, you need to build cultural expectations into everything you do, including how you hire; what your values are; how you communicate, collaborate, problem solve, handle conflict, celebrate, recognize each other; and so much more.

Knowing the culture you want is just the start. Now you need to create it and keep it going. In the following sections, I provide ideas to get you started.

Establishing principles to guide mindset and behavior

You have several tools and techniques at your disposal to help you establish guiding principles that shape your team members' cultural mindset and their behaviors they exhibit daily with each other and your customers. Consider the following:

>> Decide together as a team the three words that you want people — your customers, vendors, and other teams that work with you — to say that describe your culture.

>> Use your values as a guide to outline expectations of how people work together and treat each other. Be sure they align perfectly with the culture that you're trying to create.

>> Collaborate with your team to discuss what it looks like to live your values out loud. Be specific with defining behaviors that support your values.

>> Set clear guidelines for communication, such as:

- How often does the team connect daily or weekly and for what purpose? For example, projects, progress updates, or personal.

- How frequently should a team member connect or follow up with customers? What do team members want to be sure they communicate to customers every time they connect?

>> Agree on performance standards that aren't negotiable for the team. For example, a team member responds to questions from the team within 60 minutes during the workday, or if it's urgent, the team member should pick up the phone.

>> Agree on the use of technology tools for collaboration. Chapter 16 takes a deeper dive into technology.

>> Build team recognition into monthly meetings to acknowledge culture champions. Refer to "Pinpointing culture champions" later in this chapter.

>> Define what to look for in an interview. How can the team assess cultural fit? Make sure you're all looking for the same things.

>> Establish a habit of focusing on culture-building activities when the team gets to together face-to-face. I recommend face-to-ace events at least annually.

>> Offer training and development opportunities that support your desired culture. For example, if innovation is a cultural aspiration for your team, have a budget for sending team members to conferences or events that focus on progressive topics, technology, or trends. And certainly have a follow-up process that allows team members to share their insights with the rest of the team.

Ultimately, you want to look at every team practice, habit, and process to consider if they support the culture you want to create or if they present an obstacle. The key is to have clarity around what a healthy culture looks like and to make your conversations about culture authentic and inspirational for your team.

Putting the right HR policies in place

Culture is unquestionably defined by your people, but company policies can have a huge impact. Human resources play a key role in driving the culture of your company, and HR policies can impact your cultural aspirations. Areas in which HR are involved in setting policy or practices that impact culture include the following:

>> How performance reviews are handled

>> How poor performance and employee relation issues are addressed

>> How bad behavior or unethical behavior is managed (regardless of level)

>> The amount of coaching and support provided to leaders

>> Training and coaching budgets

>> Executive communication strategies

>> Level of corporate transparency

>> What feedback loops are in place and whether or not feedback is anonymous

>> What the company does with engagement or employee satisfaction survey data

>> Recruiting, hiring, and onboarding practices

>> Termination practices

>> Policies for responding to Glassdoor comments

>> Community involvement

>> Compensation practices

>> Company goals

The goal of HR is build an environment that is productive and inclusive and that enables people to do their best work. However, many times restrictive policies and practices get in the way of allowing a healthy work culture to flourish. Question any policies that don't align with the culture you're trying to create. Remember that change is good and can help your company and team evolve and grow.

Pinpointing culture champions

Of course, all team leaders should be champions of your culture. If you aren't, you probably have made some bad hiring decisions that you need to address quickly. In addition, you want to identify others on your team that exemplify your cultural aspirations and are trusted and respected team members. *Culture champions* usually stand out as your high performers because they're aligned with your values, and the environment supports how they work and cherishes who they are. It seems like a perfect match.

If they don't feel they're able to use their strengths, authentically lead, and contribute on a regular basis, they'll leave your company, which is why a strong team culture will be flexible enough to honor and respect the unique differences and talents of everyone on the team and will foster several culture champions.

Your culture champions will quickly make themselves known by their behaviors and actions. Here are a few characteristics to identify the champions on your team. They

>> **Live the values.** They consistently demonstrate your values in their actions and words. They probably discuss the values frequently.

>> **Are the first to support change.** They help to sell the benefits of change to others and empathize when there is fear or concern due to change.

>> **Mentor and coach new team members.** Without asking, they take new hires under their wing and spend time getting to know them and helping them integrate with the team.

>> **Are viewed as leaders.** Other team members deeply respect and pay attention to what the champions think and feel.

>> **Have influence.** Because they're well respected, their thoughts and opinions influence others.

>> **Speak up.** They care about the team, the company, and the work, and they believe in the impact that you're having in the world. They have no issues speaking up when they don't agree or feel strongly about something.

>> **Engage.** They're highly engaged when making decisions and solving problems, and they approach everything with the goal of accomplishing the best possible outcome for the team.

REMEMBER

Your cultural champions drive the acceptance and integration of your culture. No matter how many policies and guidelines you have in place, your champions make the greatest difference in building and maintaining a culture that is healthy and authentic and supports the diverse needs of all team members.

Noting the Benefits and Challenges of a Cross-Cultural Team

Even though world politics seemingly are trying to divide people, forward-thinking companies know that cultural diversity is necessary to compete on a global scale.

Technology has made the world global with no going back, regardless of the political climate. And companies that already embrace cross-cultural teams are changing everything about the way business happens.

When a company is culturally diverse with team members hailing from different countries, backgrounds, and races, people and teams experience both profound benefits and surprising challenges. However, you can properly address most challenges with strong corporate values and culture in place, along with an emotionally intelligent leader at the helm. And in my experience, the benefits always outweigh the challenges bar none. Here is a list of benefits and challenges to be mindful of if you're planning on building a global team.

Benefits of a cross-cultural team

The pros to having a cross-cultural team are as follows:

>> **Organizational efficiency:** Make decisions quicker and adapt to changes in the market more effectively when your global team has a pulse on what's happening.

>> **Competitive advantage:** Insight into local world markets, legalities, and competition provides your company with a competitive advantage.

>> **Closer to the consumer:** Spot consumer trends, issues, or opportunities faster when you have people on the ground in global locations.

>> **Innovation and creativity:** Diversity drives innovation. New ideas evolve from having different perspectives and ways of looking at the world.

>> **Profitability:** A range of expertise and problem-solving methods can lead to higher levels of productivity. Culturally diverse companies have shown higher levels of profitability.

>> **Attracting talent:** Cross-cultural teams can attract the global thought leaders you need.

>> **Emotional intelligence:** Practice cultural sensitivity in your marketing and hiring practices. Build high levels of emotional intelligence in your global leaders.

>> **Personal growth:** Get exposed to other cultures and perspectives. Elevate your awareness of global issues and build a portfolio of experience that can take your career around the world.

Challenges of a cross-cultural team

Some trials that cross-cultural teams may face are as follows:

>> **A knowledge of cultural norms:** What is acceptable and unacceptable in different cultures is usually discovered through trial and error and requires an inquisitive mindset and continual openness.

>> **Language barriers:** Difficult accents and misinterpretation of body language can quickly become frustrating. High levels of patience are required for effective communication.

>> **Conscious and unconscious bias:** Stereotypes and prejudice can play a role regarding the openness and effectiveness of multicultural teams. A commitment to education, story sharing, rapport, and trust building is the best approach.

>> **Differences in style and approach:** Traditional organizational structures may look different from country to country. Using a highly flexible approach to communication, problem solving, and decision-making is necessary and can be challenging for team leaders and members.

You can successfully address these challenges with sensitivity, respect, and appreciation for learning about other cultures. The key to making cross-cultural teams work is to leverage the exquisite differences that make the team unique. From personal experience, I've never felt as alive and present as I did when I worked with leaders from more than 10 countries. I looked at leadership through a different lens, saw things in a completely new way, and built innovation into my development process.

If designed intentionally and with emotionally intelligent leadership, global virtual teams will be an asset to any company and never a liability.

Chapter 9

Managing Differences in Gender, Generation, and Culture

There is richness in diversity.

No statement is truer, whether it's in schools, in communities, or on work teams. Savvy business leaders know that diversity on a team produces more innovative ideas, taps into a greater range of knowledge and experience, and ultimately develops better solutions. After you decide to go virtual, you have access to people from all walks of life who are potentially living anywhere in the world and coming to your team with differences that range from gender, ethnicity, culture, generation, experience, religion, language, education, geography, nationality, disability, gender identity, sexual orientation, style, and personality type.

That's a lot to consider, which is why having strategies for managing diversity and fostering inclusion on your team is important. The key to managing diversity is recognizing that it's a constant evolution of understanding, education, and compassion for each team member, and the work of creating an inclusive virtual team environment is never done. Although this chapter highlights things that make people unique, I include it in this book in the spirit of building awareness and emotional intelligence rather than providing labels for differences that continue to divide people and teams.

In this chapter, I focus on the most common variations you may find on virtual teams, including gender, generation, and cultures and how you can make all those differences work. I provide ideas for creating an environment that is healthy for all and where team members feel valued, respected, and appreciated.

Managing Gender Differences

Across the world, a gender gap continues in companies and on teams. In fact, only 3 percent of Fortune 500 CEOs are women, and women make up only 15 percent of executive leadership teams worldwide, even though gender-balanced teams tend to outperform teams made up of mostly female or male members. The good news is that your virtual team has the opportunity to transform these statistics and leverage the strengths of all genders, resulting in better ideas, solutions, and teams that are more satisfying for team members.

REMEMBER

Challenges can exist on teams when gender differences exist. In some cases these challenges can cause conflict, miscommunication, and misunderstandings. In order to prepare yourself to manage these challenges, you have to understand the playing field and the variety of ways that men and women may contribute differently to your team.

To discuss these differences, I reference common assumptions in the following sections based on research, regarding gender on teams. That's not to say that there aren't diverse teams out there with a phenomenal leader, emotionally intelligent team members, and a sure-fire hiring process who have effectively leveraged the value that both genders bring to their team. These teams have invested time and energy on creating an inclusive environment, and it has paid off.

Recognizing gender benefits

Rather than discuss the differences, this section focuses on the talents, abilities, strengths, and assets that different genders bring to a team. Table 9-1 looks at the most common benefits that men versus women bring to a team.

When reviewing this list of benefits that men and women bring to your team, think about the positive impacts of having both genders represented and where you have an opportunity to create an environment where both are free to bring their natural tendencies and approaches to work. Yes, men and women are wired differently, and that is a good thing. The more you can tap into diversity of thought, action, and style, the higher levels of productivity and results you'll experience.

TABLE 9-1 **Common Benefits Men Versus Women Bring to a Team**

Benefits of Women	Benefits of Men
Emphasize communication and relationships	Emphasize role and status
Build trust through relationship	Build trust through results
Will recognize team members for their accomplishments	Will recognize their own skill, commitment, and hard work for their accomplishments
Appreciate team rewards	Appreciate individual rewards
Want opportunity to be heard and sharing of information	Want clear expectations and objectives
Like working cooperatively to complete a task	Like working individually to complete a task
Enjoy face-to-face contact	Enjoy solving problems on their own
Desire to work through conflict together	Desire to detach from conflict
Are comfortable with a more democratic process	Are comfortable with a more direct or controlled process
Like to work within a flatter organization	Can work effectively when authority levels are clearly defined
Are process focused	Are goal focused
Accept more challenges	Have more confidence

Eradicating gender bias

If you're excited to successfully manage the gender differences on your team, the first place where you can make a difference is to thoughtfully review your company processes to see where gender bias may exist. Take time to discuss and analyze these processes and carefully consider if bias may be unconsciously built into the process and is impacting your team makeup, retention, or results. Pay attention to the questions you ask, expectations you have, and even what gets rewarded in the following areas:

>> **Recruiting:** Consider where you advertise, what pictures you include in your ads, and what words you use.

>> **Hiring:** Review questions or situational examples you cover during an interview, the people included in the interviewing and hiring process, and the personality styles and strengths most valued.

>> **Onboarding:** Think about who is assigned to mentor new candidates, how those mentors are introduced to the team, and what key ways build trust from day one.

>> **Training:** Look at your training process. Is it collaborative or goal focused? Are their opportunities to train employees based on their most effective learning style?

>> **Communication:** Consider what expectations you have of your team, how you communicate them, and what you are doing to build open communication on the team and allowing for two-way feedback.

>> **Goal setting:** Analyze whether your goals include a balance of results and relationship, whether progress toward goals is appreciated along the way, and whether goal setting is collaborative.

>> **Recognition:** Review when and how you give recognition to individuals and teams. Do you customize the message and delivery to the person or is it a one-size-fits-all reward? Do you recognize teams throughout the process or only at the end of a project?

>> **Performance measures:** Remember that what gets measured matters, so consider whether you're measuring the right things to build a strong team and leverage everyone's strengths.

TIP

After reviewing your polces, processes, and procedures and considering whether you may be doing things that have a built-in bias toward either gender, here are a few tips for leveraging the strengths that both men and women bring to you team:

>> Give credit where credit is due.

>> Make sure that both genders get equal time for their ideas to be heard.

>> Use different approaches to problem solving that support both men's and women's natural tendencies.

>> Share leadership.

>> Engage in frequent team building and building bridges of trust, openness, and communication.

>> Make sure you assign low value, nonstrategic tasks on a rotating basis to ensure men and women share the load equally — for example, note taking, ordering lunch, planning happy hours, and such.

>> Establish a no-interrupting rule during meetings.

Connecting with the Generations on Your Team

Having generational diversity on your virtual team provides different perspectives and ways of looking at today's world. Many factors, including family of origin, early life experiences, community involvement, parental support, technology, and world events during adolescence, just to name a few, influence the way people present themselves and interact with others.

WARNING

Lumping a group of people together that were born during a specific time period and assigning them characteristics and behaviors that define who they are is entirely simplistic. Doing so doesn't take into account the ability to choose, which is still in everyone's control. However, having a deeper level of understanding of potential generational markers regarding their confidence and competence with technology, education level, working style, collaboration style, and communication style can be helpful information that positively influences your interaction from the start.

For example, Generation Z is more educated than any other generation with one out of two getting a college education. This heightened education level will certainly impact your training, mentoring, and onboarding process to ensure Generation Z employees are getting what they need and not wasting time on learning things they probably already know.

The following sections point out some general thoughts for working with different generations on your virtual team.

Working with all generations

People from every generation have significant life events, different modes of learning and connecting that shape who they are, and unique ways that they show up as a virtual team member. Here are a few tips for working with all the generations on your virtual team to create and nurture a productive team culture:

>> Team people up for projects with different perspectives, ages, and experiences.

>> Invite the younger generation to train the team on technology shortcuts, tips, tricks, and ways that team members can use technology to help the team connect.

>> Have a face-to-face meeting for team building at least once a year and more often if the team is new.

>> Practice flexibility and encourage others to do the same. Invite different perspectives and ways of doing things. You may discover something new.

>> Use style assessments to help team members get to know one another more personally. Find out how team members like to communicate and figure out what they need to be successful in their role from their team members.

Tapping the power of baby boomers

Baby boomers are the generation born from 1946–1964, typically characterized as ambitious, responsible, competitive, self-focused, and optimistic. Many baby boomers made their careers the priority over family obligations, so the growth of virtual teams and flexible work schedules are an exciting and welcome change. However, baby boomers, despite having flexibility, often still choose to work during traditional work hours. Depending on the boomers' work experience, they may need more time to adjust to a collaborative team environment, because they may be more accustomed to top-down, hierarchical management style. (See Chapter 10 where I discuss the different management styles.) You may find boomers more reserved than their younger colleagues when speaking up and offering opinions. As a rule, boomers are conscientious and, in general, complete tasks on time. After all, they're the generation that created the term "workaholic." Most importantly, don't assume that boomers are averse to technology. They may not have grown up with ubiquitous Wi-Fi and a smartphone in their hands, but research has proven that they adapt well to tech environments given the time to ramp up.

Baby boomers are also highly valuable on virtual teams because of their many years of work (and life) experience. Older team members have a greater perspective on issues and long-range insights into the ebb and flow of markets, consumer opinions, and product development. Respect their knowledge and experience.

Across the United States, baby boomers are delaying retirement. Virtual teams, tech-enabled flexible work schedules, and the gig economy are allowing this generation to continue to work. Many boomers are finding that virtual teams, where diversity is encouraged, is in some ways a better fit than a traditional office, where ageism is more likely.

Redirecting Generation X

Members of Generation X, those born between 1965–1980, are largely characterized by their independence, self-reliance, and skepticism. They question authority and are the pioneers of technology and the architects of the Information Age.

In large part, Gen Xers have rejected the baby boomers' philosophy of commitment to one company, one career, and long hours dedicated to the achievement of titles, perks, and salary.

As more and more Gen Xers enter C-level jobs, they're living up to their reputation by rewriting the rules for corporate policies and practices. They're open to working differently, are achieving high productivity with work-life balance, and aren't particularly interested in the frills of corporate success, like moving into the corner office. They're the most entrepreneurial generation and are leading some of the most innovative startups today. They also encourage autonomy and independent thinking. All these traits make them great fits for virtual teams, both as team leaders and team members.

Tuning in to the high-tech Millennial

Millennials, also known as Generation Y, were born between 1981 and 1997. They're the much-maligned generation that is now the largest employment group in the United States. Their noted characteristics are being self-expressive, diverse, globally minded, and tech dependent.

Millennials have a high level of comfort with technology; they're the first generation to grow up in a fully digital world. They welcome change and embrace innovation and creativity on a team. They're impatient with long-range planning, and they crave constant feedback and appreciate using technology to provide feedback to team members. Millennials thrive on new goals and challenges to keep them motivated, whether they're new products or a new organizational chart.

Across the board, Millennials are far more comfortable with openness, collaboration, and transparency. They're the drivers behind flat organizational structures and fewer titled roles, which helps virtual teams be more agile and sets up everyone to be seen as an equal. Millennials believe — and I agree — that you don't need a title to be a leader. Being a leader can come from heading up a project or stepping up to more responsibility on your team.

Millennials are business savvy. They absolutely care about the bottom line, but they care equally about their communities and the environment. They have a triple bottom line way of thinking: a strong belief in supporting people, planet, and profit, and they insist on including corporate social responsibility into strategic planning.

Although Generation X may have started the flexible work revolution, Millennials have changed the game completely. They believe that work and life events aren't separate and that they both occur around the clock. Because Millennials reject a command-and-control management style, they won't be looking over your shoulder. In other words, Millennials don't care where and when you work — or what you wear — as long as you get the job done.

Meeting the new kids on the block: Generation Z

Members of Generation Z, the newest generation to enter the workforce, were born since 1998 and are characterized by craving security and being more cautious than Millennials. Gen Zers are hard-working, technologically advanced, and fiercely entrepreneurial. Being the first majority nonwhite generation, they value working with people from different backgrounds and are curious and passionate about acquiring new skills. They're also skilled multitaskers, having grown up shifting from one screen or task to another. Many are opting out of traditional four-year college (and debt) and seeking education and work experience in other ways.

Gen Zers are extremely adept on global virtual teams, in part because of their comfort level with diversity and because they're an adaptive generation. Adaptive generations follow a disruptive generation, which has significantly changed society like the Millennials. Adaptive generations take the problems that surfaced by their predecessors and work on fixing them. In this way, Generation Zers are taking on diversity, global awareness, cultural sensitivity, inclusivity, and sexism in the workplace and exerting strong political influence over societal issues outside of the workplace.

They are extremely collaborative and flexible, value compromise, and embrace change in the workplace.

Building Your Cultural Intelligence

On a virtual team, differences in behavior, language, gestures, values, beliefs, levels of assertiveness, relationship-building techniques, emotional intelligence, and more creates an unbelievable opportunity for personal growth in an area called cultural intelligence. *Cultural intelligence (CQ)* is defined as the ability to adapt to the dynamic and complex variances of a multicultural workplace. A person with high levels of CQ can understand and appreciate cultural differences, leverage multiple perspectives and diversity on a team, and bridge relationships and knowledge gaps between people who have difficulty connecting.

As today's world becomes more of a global workforce, CQ isn't just nice to have on your team, but it's quickly becoming a need to have for many companies. In fact, 90 percent of executives from around the world have identified cross-cultural skills as one of the most important capabilities needed to remain competitive. The good news is that CQ can be cultivated and developed over time by focusing on increasing knowledge of other cultures and cultural norms and building your empathy and relational muscles so that you can relate and work effectively when in a culturally diverse situation.

TIP

Check out the Cheat Sheet at www.dummies.com and search for "virtual teams" to find some tips for practicing and meditating CQ.

This section provides you with ideas for helping build more CQ on your team by understanding cultural norms, building more cultural knowledge and sensitivity, and bringing to light any unconscious bias that may exist.

Getting to know your team members

Developing your awareness and understanding of what is important and valued in other cultures only can happen when you have a desire for more knowledge and a willingness to adapt. Approaching cultural diversity with an open mind and interest for identifying the unique differences between cultures, norms, values, and beliefs is the first step toward forging strong cross-cultural connections with other team members.

I don't know of anyone who has worked on a diverse team who hasn't had an experience of being offended, annoyed, or angry due to a team member's lack of awareness of what is culturally acceptable behavior. Speaking out of turn, hugging, shaking hands, using a loud voice, and even making direct eye contact are all examples of behaviors that can cause misunderstandings and confusion when you have a team of people from different cultures working together. But many of those examples are exclusive to teams working in the same office. On virtual teams specifically, interrupting, making certain hand gestures, displaying certain body language, or saying no can cause offense when on video or conference calls.

TIP

Here are a few tips to get to know your culturally diverse virtual team members and expand your world view:

>> **Share experiences.** Create one-on-one time with team members to hear stories about their upbringing, family values, or common cultural practices and why they exist. Host a virtual lunch where team members share an ethnic food dish while discovering more about the culture from another team member.

>> **Seek out more information.** Watch culturally diverse movies, read fictional books or biographies about different cultures, travel, or live or work outside your home country. You can even read newspapers that cater to a particular population.

>> **Attend cultural events.** Visit cultural events happening in your town or city and soak up the sights, sounds, and food, which are great ways to build more appreciation for diversity.

>> **Do a checkup from the neck up.** Catch yourself when you notice if you're stereotyping a particular group. Positive or negative stereotypes are never true for all people in a given population or culture, and most stereotypes aren't reliable. Developing your own opinion through interactions and relationships is much more important.

Understanding more about your team members and their culture increases your CQ or ability to be open to others viewpoints, thoughts, and beliefs. It helps you refrain from judgment, expands your point of view, and increases your ability to accept and value differences.

Sharing culture norms

Cultural norms are behaviors or beliefs shared by a group or society that are usually passed down from generation to generation. In the process of getting to know your diverse team, identify cultural norms that may be different from your own. These differences can easily be misunderstood and cause cross-cultural conflict unless you keep an open mind and willingness to understand them. Acknowledge the common cultural differences and norms in Table 9-2.

TABLE 9-2 **Common Cultural Differences**

Cultural Norms	American Culture	Other Cultures
Use of eye contact	Direct eye contact shows assertiveness and being present.	Avoiding eye contact can be seen as a sign of respect.
Time management	Time is limited and punctuality is important. Being late is a sign of disrespect. Time equals money.	It's normal to have someone wait all day or come back the next day. Time is spent on relationships.
Professional dress	Casual dress and athletic attire are acceptable in many workplaces.	Professional dress is a sign of position, wealth, or prestige.
Work relationships	Emphasis is on individual accomplishments.	Emphasis is on relationships.
Family	Focus is on immediate family. Value is on youth. Age is viewed as a negative.	Focus is on extended family. Age is respected and given status.
Communication	Prefer directness. Interrupting is considered rude. It's appropriate to ask questions if confused.	Interrupting and talking over one another is normal. In other cultures, there is a more cautious attitude toward expressing differing opinions that could lead to conflict or undermine the authority in the room.

Practicing cultural sensitivity

Practicing cultural sensitivity is another skill that helps develop your CQ. If you're culturally sensitive, you recognize that differences between you and other team members exist and those differences are neither right or wrong, good or bad. Rather, you respect different characteristics and believe that no one culture is better than another.

On a virtual team that crosses cultural boundaries, consider these several practices to help your team members become more culturally sensitive and build an environment of cultural appreciation, respect, and understanding. They include the following:

>> Discussing the benefits and recognizing the positive impacts of a cultural diverse team

>> Making a strong commitment to ensuring everyone is clear on the importance of each role

>> Focusing on creating a team environment where everyone has a voice and reining in any team members who have a tendency to control the discussion

>> Sharing beliefs and values and understanding how they can affect others on the team when they're demonstrated

>> Providing training and development to all team members on building cultural competence, awareness, and understanding

>> Sharing leadership on the team

>> Evaluating cultural competence regularly

>> Hiring a cultural competent leader on the team

>> Creating space for team members to share their personal stories, backgrounds, and cultural norms

>> Having agreements regarding appropriate communication methods in different situations

>> Providing cross-cultural training (see the next section)

>> Creating a zero-tolerance policy for culturally insensitive behavior

REMEMBER

Focusing on being culturally sensitive helps you move from an *ethnocentric* point of view, which is someone who avoids or denies cultural differences and believes that his culture is the only one that matters, to a *ethnorelative* point of view where you accept that people are different from you, you're open to understanding and adapting, and eventually you develop empathy for other cultures.

TIP

For more ways to practice cultural sensitivity, go to the Cheat Sheet at www. dummies.com and search for "virtual teams."

CULTURAL DIVIDE: PREDICTORS OF VIRTUAL TEAM SUCCESS

Multiculturalism and diversity on teams is nothing new. Working teams have always had differences in gender, ethnicity, religion, differently abilities, cultural diversity, and thought diversity, even if team members were co-located and lived in the same city. Of course, those teams had ample opportunity for informal connection and nonverbal cues like eye contact and body language to make communication easier.

What is different now is a more globalized workforce and the growth of virtual teams. The likelihood of cultural confusion is *so much greater* when time and space divides you, and your only connection is via a screen.

Virtual teams have a greater responsibility — and challenge — to be inclusive. To become a truly high-performing team, cultural diversity acceptance must be part of your virtual team charter.

Cultural training experts such as Nozomi Morgan, CEO of Michiki Morgan Worldwide, has seen all the mistakes teams have made. Morgan focused on developing leaders and teams that can work effectively beyond global borders and cultural barriers. According to her, three common cultural blunders make global teams:

- **Assuming you have similar values and follow the same rules of engagement because you work for the same company.**

  Here are a few examples:

  You're on a team call and you think everyone has agreed on an issue. The U.S. associates were certain there was consensus, but the Japanese team members actually only acknowledged that they *heard* you. The lesson is that you must over-communicate with as much clarity as possible and verbally ask for commitment.

  Tip: Always distribute an agenda prior to meetings that identify the key issues you'll discuss and set the expectation that you're seeking opinions from all. Certain cultures aren't accustomed to giving feedback, so give them time to prepare.

  Use a facilitator during meetings to gather responses from everyone. Immediately following the meeting, post a summary restating what was decided, who was assigned tasks, and what timelines are for completion, in order to catch any errors quickly. Basically, overdocument and overcommunicate all the time.

- **Thinking someone who is a high performer in the United States is the right person to lead a global team.**

    When companies send leaders overseas to lead multicultural teams, the decision should be based on a variety of factors. Oftentimes, companies send their top performers based on the U.S.-centric measures of success. These performance measures may not be a good fit in a different culture, and they're the reason for the high failure rate.

    Remember: Behaviors that may have led to success in the United States — aggressive, energetic, highly competitive, opinionated, loud, top-down style — won't be assets overseas. Instead, look for mature leaders with global awareness, cultural sensitivity, deep self-awareness, humility, curiosity, patience, empathy, and great communication skills.

- **Not prioritizing time to focus on communication, expectations, and agreements.**

    Just like with any team — virtual or otherwise — you need to create a team charter and agreements. Due to the team's cultural diversity, doing so is even more critical. Morgan recommends that a team conduct a cultural assessment early to discover and understand the team's diversity and establish cultural awareness right away. A cultural assessment can pick up on nuances that will impact team relationships and communication.

    Even after the cultural assessment, she recommends that team leaders make it a habit to overexplain and overcommunicate everything.

    With global teams, leaders often can't see the struggle, confusion, or hesitance people may have to ask clarifying questions. Leaders have to make the extra effort to draw out any confusion that people may have. Although it's not rocket science, Morgan has seen teams fail time and time again due to this.

Just discovering how to successfully navigate cultural diversity in the workplace isn't enough. Cultural diversity is something to be celebrated, and more importantly, leveraged. Embrace differences, new perspectives, and different ways of doing things. Having a cross-cultural team means more opportunities for creativity and innovation. Start thinking of cross-cultural teams as an asset, not as a liability.

Offering cross-cultural training

If you want a collaborative cross-cultural team, plan on investing in training to develop deeper levels of understanding about communication differences, cultural norms, and values, and then provide support that helps your team members adapt and actually adjust their behavior.

REMEMBER

Remaining open to different cultures is important, but it's not enough and doesn't help your team develop new ways of working together. Some of the most important training you can do focuses on adaptability strategies that can require an investment of time, coaching, and practice — not just an online training program or webinar. The key is to understand what your team needs and then customize the training accordingly. Don't waste time and money on training that doesn't make a difference.

The best training programs help your team members recognize and address their biases and provide them with tools and techniques for raising their comfort level in those situations. An example would be to provide an opportunity for team members who are accustomed to remaining quiet when the leader is presenting to practice speaking up in team meetings and then give feedback. Additional topics that may be helpful to consider for training are:

>> Cultural diversity issues

>> Cultural self-awareness tools

>> Knowledge of cross-cultural communication skills

>> Understanding cultural norms

>> Confidence building in dealing with people from different cultures

Be sure that training doesn't happen in a vacuum and that it's done together as a team, discussed as a team, and debriefed as a team to understand where you can apply it in day-to-day interactions. Then encourage all team members to recognize and provide feedback to each other when they notice cross-cultural sensitivity being practiced. Doing so builds a team with high levels of CQ that can achieve great levels of success and, more importantly, can increase the team's ability to adapt in any culturally diverse situation.

Chapter **10**

Transitioning from Old-School Manager to Virtual Team Leader

W hen leading a virtual team, using an old-school style of management isn't only out, it's outlandish to even think it could work.

If you try to use an old-school style of management with your virtual team, you'll be completely out of your depths in the new world reality of virtual team leadership. The ways of old-school management — which some business schools are still teaching — become a liability on a virtual team where adaptability, emotional intelligence, and a collaborative mindset are required.

More than likely you know what old-school management looks and feels like and feels. It's top-down, command and control. It's close-minded and bullying. It always knows best, never asks your opinion, and it fears change. It doesn't value diversity of people or ideas. It makes you feel like you just stepped into an episode of Mad Men, but no one offered you a scotch. If you use an old-school style of management, you'll likely fail miserably as a virtual team leader.

This chapter examines and compares leadership styles that can work most effectively in a virtual environment. If you've worked in a traditional environment up until now, I encourage you to adopt a new mindset and style of management that can serve you and your team in the best way possible. I also provide you with tips on building a team community and help you steer clear of common problems that virtual teams face.

Recognizing Which Leadership Style Works Best

What makes a virtual team effective includes building trust and connection, supporting self-directed work, setting clear expectations and goals, providing collaborative opportunities, and engaging in innovative thinking.

These are the skills of an authentic leader. They're also essential skills to adopt when you're the leader of a virtual team. The following sections explain the qualities that make virtual leaders successful as well as what leadership style and approach work best with a virtual team.

Examining what makes virtual team leaders succeed

Understanding the mindset of a leader who excels in a virtual environment can help you assess your current leadership style and where you have opportunity to grow. Here are common qualities that have helped virtual team leaders succeed:

» **Flexibility:** The nine-to-five model is dead, even for people who work in offices. On virtual teams, work happens at all times of the day (and night) to accommodate team members around the country and the world. More and more, people are working less traditional business hours. Effective leaders of virtual teams understand that their team has been hired to produce a specific outcome and are willing to adapt to members' various work schedules while keeping an eye on the big picture.

» **Trust:** Micromanaging from afar is a nuisance to team members and a waste of time for the team leader. Effective virtual team leaders know how to provide employees the resources they need to do the job and then trust them to get it done.

>> **Communication:** The idea that technology hinders communication is outdated. After all, technology *is* communication. Leaders of virtual teams who communicate most effectively, most often, and most efficiently with technology are the most successful. Effective leaders of virtual teams recognize the need for more communication, feedback, and guidance than onsite teams and step up their game in this area.

>> **Comfort with technology:** You don't need mad programming skills, but you need a general understanding of the technology that gets your team collaborating and communicating. Effective leaders choose their technology wisely and are quick to put it into practice and lead the way.

>> **Listener:** Effective leaders of virtual teams are empathetic and know when to talk and when to solicit feedback. They know when something is off with a team member and a face-to-face meeting is necessary. They also take time to listen deeply and with a sense of curiosity, so they can discover where to support their team members where they need it most.

>> **Collaborator:** Leaders must be able to lead people and teams through collaboration. Working with others when you're all under the same roof can be difficult. Adding distance and different time zones to the equation can further complicate things. The best virtual leaders know how to overcome these challenges and foster strong collaboration within their teams.

>> **Patience:** Some things will take more time when you aren't in close proximity. Effective virtual leaders are used to it and are patient with the process. And they're always looking for ways to streamline and improve.

>> **Diversity champion:** Leaders who get the best results from their virtual team appreciate diversity in all forms — gender, age, religious, cultural, ethnic, sexual orientation, sexual identity . . . and of course, diversity of thought. They adapt to their increasingly diverse employee base and demonstrate sensitivity to a variety of backgrounds, worldviews, and values on their teams.

>> **Results oriented:** All managers need to be results oriented, but effective virtual team leaders have clear individual accountability in place with agreed methods of monitoring and measuring performance. They worry less about how their team members are spending their time or when they actually do their work and focus on delivering results.

In addition to having the right mindset, virtual leader success requires that you're astute enough to recognize what style of leadership will work with different people and in different situations.

AN OLD-SCHOOL MANAGER'S MINDSET

Most managers aren't complete dinosaurs, but many do have some shades of old-school thinking. I know because I come across their path regularly in my work. Here are a few things I see that shape their mindset:

- **Seeing is believing.** Old-school managers equate time at your desk or at the office with productive work. If they can't see you doing the work, then obviously you're slacking off. Not only will they micromanage your time, as an added bonus, they'll constantly ask for updates.

- **Desiring work-life balance is soft.** If you want to attend your kid's school function in the middle of the day or leave work at 5 p.m. every day, then you're not committed to your job. Old-school managers see these type requests as outrageous and don't place any value on providing flexibility to their employees so that they can manage the increased demands of everyday life.

- **I'm in charge. Now let me beat my chest.** Old-school managers don't want to be challenged, and they rarely use collaboration skills. Their body language will almost always communicate superiority, whether they cut you off in a meeting, don't listen to your ideas, or take your good ideas and make them their own. They'll look for every opportunity to demonstrate they're in charge. These managers expect that you'll never challenge authority by asking questions, offering feedback, or voicing disagreement, rather they prefer to be surrounded by yes people that do as they're told.

- **I deserve reverence and respect.** Generational bias is a real thing, and old-school managers simply don't get it. They rarely tap into the breadth of new skills and new insights of their team. Because of experience or education, they believe they obviously know more than anyone at the table.

- **Stay the course. You'll hear from me when you mess up**. Old-school managers can go weeks or even months before they provide you with feedback. When they do, it's because you messed up. The once-a-year performance appraisal is their preferred method of letting you know what they think of your performance, which usually leads to a lot of unwelcomed surprises. Your only recognition for your good work is your paycheck.

You can quickly realize that none of these behaviors will make the cut in a virtual team environment. Your proverbial ship will sink fast. Successful remote workers are most likely more educated than you and want their ideas to be heard and considered. They value transparency, feedback, flexibility, and innovation. In addition, what's more important to them than a paycheck is contributing to a team goal that's meaningful.

Determining if you're a micromanager, coach, or hands-off manager

Managing and leadership are different, and both are necessary when leading a virtual team. Management requires you to plan, organize, monitor, and execute the work to be done, including:

>> Clarifying roles and goals

>> Communicating priorities

>> Organizing resources to get the work done

>> Putting in place measures to analyze success

>> Setting deadlines and holding others accountable

Meanwhile, leadership is establishing direction and influencing team members' behavior through recognition, coaching, support, and communication. As a virtual team leader, doing all of these things at one point or another is necessary. However, many virtual team leaders sometimes spend more time in one area or even neglect an area all together. Where a virtual team leader spends the majority of her time usually has to do with her style and what comes most naturally to her. Here I review three common styles of leadership and when they're appropriate.

REMEMBER

Each of these styles works in different situations, with different team members, at different times. Skilled virtual team leaders have a pulse on what is going on with each of their team members and will adapt their approach and style accordingly.

Directive style

A *directive style* comes naturally to you if you're most comfortable with having control over what gets done and how it gets done. This style is most appropriate when a team member is new, asks for help, needs to gain specific skills or knowledge to reach her goals, or is stuck in some way and needs you to walk them through a process step by step. A directive manager:

>> Provides very specific direction

>> Keeps close tabs on the work and the how it's being done

>> Gives immediate feedback when something doesn't meet her expectations

>> Sets goals and expectations for the team member

>> Defines process and procedures for getting work done

>> Closely monitors results

This style of leadership — which is more controlling and can come across as micromanaging — doesn't work well long term and can quickly demotivate your remote team members. In an emergency or high-risk situations, this style can extremely effective because it's fast and clear. But, if this happens to be your natural style, consider opportunities where you can use a more facilitative or hands-off approach with your virtual team.

Facilitative style

A *facilitative style* helps employees use their own internal resources to solve problems and develop skills and knowledge. This style of leader takes time to coach team members and is passionate about their growth. If this is your natural style, you most likely connect with your team directly on a regular basis and are always looking for ways to collaborate. You also do a good job at providing regular feedback and coaching.

By asking open-ended questions, listening closely, and guiding your team members where to look for answers, the facilitative approach relies on your team members' innate abilities and empowers their self-development. A facilitative manager uses questioning techniques to:

>> Encourage team members to identify what motivates them

>> Involve team members in problem solving and goal setting

>> Ask team members to develop a plan of action to address any performance issues

>> Provide coaching and support as needed

>> Work together with team members to agree on performance measures and deadlines

REMEMBER

A facilitative style of leadership can work well in a virtual environment but can also cramp the productivity and creativity of high performers on your team who prefer a hands-off approach.

Leaders who excel at using this style are experts at asking great questions. Here are some facilitative questions that you can use:

>> What do you want to have happen?

>> What's already working? What's not working?

- >> What has worked for you in the past?

- >> What have you already tried or done?

- >> What are the reasons this didn't work as well as you had hoped?

- >> What is the situation from your point of view?

- >> What is the situation from other perspectives?

- >> What's another way of looking at it?

- >> What needs to happen in order for you to . . .?

- >> What's getting in your way?

- >> What will you take away from this?

- >> If you had to do it over again, what would you do?

- >> What resources are available to you?

- >> What would be a courageous action?

- >> What support can I provide you?

Hands-off style

If the *hands-off style* is your natural approach, then you probably agree with the concept of hiring the best and then getting out of their way. You have a great deal of trust in your team members to complete the work. If they're experienced, they have a sense of fulfillment and foster higher levels of creativity.

This style can also work well in leading a virtual team when team members clearly know their role and can deliver results quickly. Collaborative technology and project management software can help you to stay abreast of progress and obstacles while still allowing team members to self-direct their work.

WARNING

Be careful of being too hands-off and becoming disconnected with your team or missing out on details that may indicate a team member is struggling or unhappy. Being hands-off has its benefits, but problems can also more easily hide until it's too late to correct them.

Comparing control-based and trust-based leadership

In a virtual team environment, leaders should focus not on making the team more stable but on making it more *flexible*. The essential difference between the traditional control–oriented team approach and a collaborative, trust–based team approach can be broken down like this:

>> **Control-based, traditional approach:** Maintaining control is a leader's most important job.

>> **Trust-based, collaborative approach:** Anticipating and preparing others for change is a leader's most important job.

When you approach leadership as a collaborative effort — as the person who helps your team foresee and prepare for continuous change — you strengthen your team, build high levels of trust, and demonstrate your value as a leader. Table 10-1 outlines the differences between the two approaches.

TABLE 10-1   **Control-Based versus Trust-Based Leadership**

Control-based leadership	Trust-based, collaborative leadership
Control-based leaders believe their power comes from their position.	Collaborative leaders believe that power comes from building trust and cohesion on a team.
Control-based leaders determine and plan the work.	Leaders and team members jointly determine and plan the work.
Roles and responsibilities are narrowly defined.	Roles and responsibilities are broad and evolve and shift, depending on need.
Control-based leaders view cross-training as inefficient and unnecessary.	Collaborative leaders consider cross-training the norm and an important part of team effectiveness.
Control-based leaders rarely solicit feedback and input from the team.	Feedback and input from the team is a pillar of team culture.
Important information is kept confidential and only between managers.	As much information as possible is freely shared at all levels.
Training focuses on technical skills and solving issues.	Training focuses on building emotional intelligence, leadership, communication, and technical skills.
Control-based leaders discourage and even punish risk taking.	Collaborative leaders encourage and support thoughtful risk taking in the spirit of innovation.
People work alone.	People work together.
Rewards are based on individual performance.	Rewards are based on individual performance contributions to team performance.
The leader determines the best methods.	The team collaborates to analyze and improve methods and processes.
Performance reviews happen once a year.	Performance feedback and coaching happens regularly and consistently.

On a virtual team, effective teamwork is your greatest strength and most valuable competitive advantage. Trust-based leadership is what to focus on to build and sustain a team environment that brings out the best in your people and garners the best results.

Playing in Your Sandbox

Companies that have been around for a while are struggling with making the shift to virtual teams and flexible working arrangements. Why? Because they have a traditional corporate culture with clear lines of authority, established communication methods, old-style performance management systems, a professional work environment, teams that work independently from one another, a keen focus on the bottom line, and a tendency toward being risk adverse.

If you've been managing in this type of culture, you most likely are used to the consistency of rules and roles, the way that decisions are made, and the methods that information is disseminated. It may even bring you a sense of calm and control that feels comfortable.

Due to technology, new forms of communication, and talent spread across the world, traditional cultures have seen a major shift in how they operate, which can be quite a struggle. However, it also presents a major opportunity for growth if managers embrace the innovations of technology and a new leadership philosophy.

So the question is how do you manage in this new team culture when you work for a traditional company? In my experience, it's about experimenting, being willing to take risks, trusting your team to make decisions, and pushing authority to the individuals who know the work the best. The following sections help you organize your approach for making the change to a virtual leader.

Pushing the boundaries of culture and C-level expectations

You may not know it yet, but you have the chance to be a trailblazer. You have the opportunity to shift how work gets done, goals are accomplished, and technology is used to communicate. And in some cases, ignoring corporate cultural norms that don't serve your virtual team is unquestionably an important part of the growth process. I guarantee you though that taking the leap to establish a new foundation won't be easy.

In fact, my research study on virtual team effectiveness in 2016 glaringly showed an obvious disconnect between how executives perceived the productivity of virtual teams and how the team perceived their results. More than half of all virtual team members reported that increased productivity was a benefit of virtual teams, compared to only 13 percent of executives who agreed. Why the disconnect? I can make some assumptions:

» Many executives haven't worked in a virtual team environment and come from a more traditional approach managing people and teams. If they can't see you doing the work, they don't believe that actual work is taking place. They may be holding onto a biased way of thinking about how work gets accomplished and what productivity looks like.

» Executives continue to measure results through traditional methods, such as sales revenue, earnings per share, and quality or service levels when other important ways can measure value that include innovation and collaboration.

» Virtual teams and remote work is new to the company culture and executives don't understand how to shift their mindset to embrace and support this new world of work.

REMEMBER

If you're leading a virtual team in a traditional culture, you may find that the cards are stacked against you. Success requires you to have a plan of action that includes the following:

» Push consistent communication pushed to the company, highlighting team projects, progress, and impact to the bottom line. Your job is to raise awareness about how awesome your team is doing and how it's having a positive impact on others.

» Share recognition frequently for innovative ideas that are moving forward and for projected financial results if they're implemented. This proves that your team is creating value.

» Introduce remote new hires to the company in a fun, engaging way and share what other teams they'll be supporting or working with. Generate excitement for the level of experience and knowledge that your new team members bring to the company.

Knowing when to manage up

No other relationship can impact your team as much as the relationship you have with your direct manager. Having a solid foundation of trust and openness creates an environment that supports your virtual team members in getting the resources they need to solve problems and address opportunities. If your manager doesn't understand the value your team brings to the table, she won't go to bat for you when issues come up or won't support the work your team is doing if ever questioned.

TIP

Getting your direct manager in your corner is something to take seriously and here are a few ideas to help you get started:

>> Be clear and aligned on your team's purpose. What value does your virtual team bring to the company?

>> Understand your manager's goals and what drives her. When you present progress updates or ask for additional resources, describe how your team can help your manager reach her goals.

>> Nurture the relationship. Get to know your manager as a person and build trust. Doing so helps you discover more about her style and what's important to her.

>> Be strategic and anticipate what she needs from you such as progress reports, stats on what's in the pipeline, error rates, and so on.

>> Keep your manager in the loop. Never let your manager get blindsided by a hiring or firing decision. Be sure she is up-to-date on team dynamics, changes, or resource requirements.

>> Ask your manager what you need and provide feedback. If you need more direction, clarity around goals, recognition for a job well done, ask. She can't read your mind.

>> Go above and beyond whenever possible. If your team frequently overdelivers, that creates real value that your manager can easily tout to others in the company.

Recognizing Common Virtual Team Issues

Virtual team issues are similar to in-person team issues, but they may look a bit different and require a different set of skills if you're a traditional manager. If you're used to managing employees you can see every day, you may be surprised at some issues that virtual teams face — and the skills you need to overcome them. In this section, I review the most common virtual team issues and how they differ on virtual teams to help your transition to managing virtual teams less rocky.

Poor communication

Communication quality and quantity is vital to virtual team success. Unfortunately, my research has proven that poor communication is one of the top fail points for virtual teams. Old-school one-way communication won't work.

My research proves good communication leads to good outcomes in new and old virtual teams. Experienced teams that communicate effectively were 19 times more likely to report that their members were highly engaged. Likewise, newly formed teams that communicate effectively are 12 times more likely to accomplish their goals and 55 times more likely to be responsive to customers.

When virtual team leaders and executives viewed communication within the team as strong, they were 31 times more likely to indicate the team accomplishes its goals and 21 times to view the team as effective in responding to customers. Be sure to spend the time setting up communication agreements with your virtual team members. Check out Chapter 13 to find out more about best practices in virtual team communication.

Lack of clarity, direction, and priorities

This issue is largely related to poor communication. Old-school managers may limit discussion of roles and responsibilities to an annual review or face-to-face meeting, which doesn't happen often. Virtual team leaders know that all team members need crystal-clear expectations to ensure productivity and reduce the incorrect assumptions that can fester when there is no regular dialog. And it's ongoing dialog, not just an annual event. My research shows that establishing clear rules of engagement early — and sticking to them — is the key to virtual team success. You're largely responsible to have this conversation and work collaboratively with your team members to establish how and when work will happen, hold them accountable to the agreements, and take corrective measures, if necessary. When virtual team leaders and executives indicated the team had high levels of accountability, they were:

>> Thirty-two times more likely to indicate the team accomplishes its goals

>> Forty-one times more likely to indicate the team meets deliverables on time and within budget

>> Twenty-four times more likely to view the team as effective in responding to customers

Loss of team spirit and morale

As a virtual team leader, you're responsible for creating a clear and compelling direction for the team and making sure each individual is connected to the team vision. Old-school managers may assume that team members already understand how they contribute and why they matter but that mindset and lack of communication can undermine team spirit. The key is to recognize that creating and nurturing strong morale on your virtual team won't happen overnight — it's created through hundreds of everyday interactions. That's why you need to encourage cohesiveness every time you communicate with team members. That could look like always asking for their opinion, making time for recognition on every team call, or explaining the impact of their work accomplishments on the business.

Lack of trust

You've never met them in person. You can't see what other people are doing. There is a delay in getting responses immediately, and you're rarely working (or in some cases awake) at the same time. It's easy to see why trust can be an issue for an old-school manager. To get up to speed with virtual teams, you must set the example and trust your team members to do the job that they're hired to. Establishing a culture of strong accountability, setting clear goals and expectations, and creating awareness of each other's contributions also helps to build trust. Chapter 12 examines ways that you can build trust as a virtual team leader.

Lack of social interaction

For all its perks, working remotely can be isolating. Old-school managers are used to relying on chatting and quick check-ins with team members around the office. Virtual team members miss out on the office banter and in-person friendships that enrich their work lives. In every study I've seen on virtual teams, getting together in real life is important.

More than 40 percent of the survey participants in my research on virtual team effectiveness got together in-person monthly. Teams that meet in person frequently had higher effectiveness ratings (defined as meeting goals, team productivity, and engagement) than those that meet two to three times a year. Make it a priority as a virtual team leader to budget for your team to get together and check in on each team member regularly for some nonwork conversations.

Tech issues

Not everyone is a technology expert, but people on virtual teams need to be competent at using the technology in place in order to connect with their team. Tech fails — or simply non-use or underusage of technology — is one of the biggest issues facing virtual teams and leaders. Old-school managers must quickly become fluent in using the team's technology or the entire team may suffer the consequences.

In fact, in a study I conducted with more than 150 remote workers at various Fortune 500 companies, one of the biggest challenges for newly formed virtual teams is figuring out how to effectively use technology. Mastering collaborative technology is imperative for the leader so that she can create efficiency, work-flow tracking, and connection within her team. The research showed teams that rate themselves as effective at using collaborative technology are:

>> Ninety-eight times more likely to come up with innovative solutions

>> Seventy-four times more likely to deliver on time and within budget

>> Thirty-seven times more likely to accomplish goals

Cultural clashes

Good communication on virtual teams is vital — even more so when teams cross cultures. Old-fashioned, narrow thinking about people and their backgrounds is dangerous on a virtual team. Virtual team leaders must practice openness and acceptance and encourage others on the team to do the same. Miscommunication on a virtual team can happen in so many different ways than what can happen on an in-house team. Examples include nonverbal cues, voice inflection, or cultural and language nuances that are misunderstood. Virtual teams have a greater responsibility — and challenge — to be inclusive. Refer to Chapter 9 where I discuss how to handle cultural differences on a virtual team.

4

Getting Your Team Rolling

Follow best practices that keep virtual team members engaged and improve retention.

Hold virtual team meetings that people actually want to attend and find a valuable connection opportunity with their teammates.

Utilize and respect the strengths of each team member and meet the diverse demands on your marketplace.

Create team connection that transcend space and time zones and provide personally fulfilling relationships.

Employ communication strategies and agreements as well as training methods and topics that set up your virtual team for success.

Find out how to measure the impact of your virtual team and hold team members accountable for results.

Know what essential technology tools your virtual team needs to stay connected and engaged to become a high performing team.

Adapt to changes in virtual team membership and leadership without disrupting team effectiveness.

» **Setting realistic goals and expectations**

» **Developing a virtual team community**

» **Building a team agreement**

» **Planning and conducting virtual team meetings**

Chapter **11**

Establishing Best Practices of Engagement

Worldwide engagement levels are at an all-time low with only one out of three employees reporting being fully engaged at work and 17 percent of all employees reporting they are completely disengaged. Engagement impacts customer satisfaction, profits, productivity, turnover, safety issues, absenteeism, quality, and more. Not surprising, engagement is also costing your company big time. The Gallup organization estimates that more than $300 billion a year is lost due to disengaged workers. It's obvious that engagement needs to be a strategic priority for every leader in every company.

What is known for sure is that engagement is one of the most important and challenging aspects of virtual teams. Numerous research studies, including the virtual team effectiveness study my company conducted in 2016, have proven this. As Figure 11-1 illustrates, my research revealed that on established virtual teams, keeping the team engaged and motivated was by far the biggest challenge, along with continuing to focus on effective communication. Correspondingly, communication had a big impact on engagement levels. In fact, established teams that reported that they were effective at communicating were 19 times more likely to say the members of their team were highly engaged.

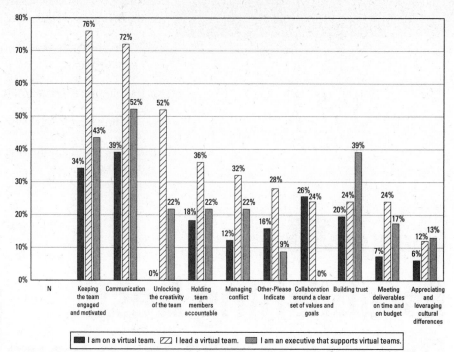

FIGURE 11-1:
Engagement is one of the biggest challenges on a virtual team.

© John Wiley & Sons, Inc.

Although communication and engagement are common challenges for any team, differences in time zones and lack of face-to-face interactions contribute to this challenge and are unique for virtual teams. Virtual team engagement is greatly influenced by team agreements, technology, communication guidelines, and the levels of trust that exist on a team.

This chapter discusses best practices that drive virtual team engagement, including clarifying team purpose, establishing collaborative goal setting, setting up a team charter, deciding how to communicate, and running your virtual meetings. I provide ideas, tips, and tools that you can put in place immediately with your team to improve engagement.

Addressing Personal Disengagement

Disengagement on a team spreads quickly, like a virus. It has immediate negative repercussions on team productivity, communication, collaboration, innovation, morale, service levels, you name it! You may find yourself in a situation where you need to address individual levels of personal disengagement on your team rather than how the whole team is engaging.

TIP

Here are some suggestions that may help you:

>> **Check for alignment with purpose and values.** Does the team member understand why his role is important? Does he feel like he is making a difference? If team members can't connect why the work they're doing matters, they can easily become disenchanted with their job. A second reason for disengagement may be that they don't agree with the team or company values and aren't willing to live those values on a day-to-day basis, which brings to the surface a cultural fit issue that needs to be discussed. Is there a way to recognize their individuality while still maintaining a sense of values on the team?

>> **Have a heart-to-heart discussion.** Do so in a face-to-face meeting either in person or via videoconferencing. Ask where the team member is right now and more importantly what he is missing from his work. Research has shown that unmet and unspoken expectations are large contributors to employee disengagement. However, after you speak those expectations— even if he can't meet them — engagement levels go up. You may also find out about personal issues outside of work that are taking up his focus, time, and energy.

>> **Reassess workload.** How much time is required to complete each task? Is it possible that your team member is completely overburdened due to being short staffed or the only person on the team with a particular skill set? Consider what low priority items could be delegated to another team member or let go of completely.

>> **Encourage the team member to volunteer for a challenging project.** Let him work on something he would find interesting, preferably something that would stretch his abilities and isn't directly tied to his role.

>> **Allow for more accountability.** What decisions could the team member make that you currently make? Talk with other team members about what this may look like if you delegated some decisions to them. Set clear expectations for success.

>> **Ask your team member to revisit his career path.** When is the last time the team member considered doing something new in the company? Is there another area in the organization that interests him? Are their opportunities to job shadow in the organization? Discuss these options with him.

Having a Meaningful Team Purpose

Most people are looking for more from their work than just a paycheck. They want to do something that has meaning and provides them the opportunity to contribute to something they believe in. Chapter 4 discusses the importance of defining a team purpose that aligns with your company vision and values and helps team members understand why the team matters to the company and every role is important. If purpose isn't clear, team members will feel disconnected to their roles and won't feel like they're making any progress. This feeling quickly gets old quickly and may cause team members to check out or even look for another job.

REMEMBER

As a leader, your task is to be sure that at every opportunity you're communicating and recognizing the team's purpose and values. Focus on it during weekly meetings and even in one-on-one meetings to let individual team members know the impact of their work on others in the company or community.

Years ago, I was a training manager at a company that manages 9-1-1 data-base systems. This company makes sure that your 9-1-1 call is routed and delivered to the right emergency services center and communicates your actual location. Even though my role was in a support function, the CEO and every leader in the company made it clear how every single employee was saving lives on a daily basis. That purpose was an engagement driver that meant something way beyond a paycheck and is why many people I worked with almost 20 years ago still work there today.

These sections identify several ideas that you can use to consistently clarify and communicate your team purpose as an important strategy for keeping people engaged.

Clarifying the why and how team members contribute

If people don't understand why their job exists, how the team contributes to the success of the larger organization, or why you're asking them to prioritize a task or project over another, then you're going to quickly be looking at a team of disengaged and demotivated employees who feel like they're wasting their time.

REMEMBER

Having a defined purpose for your team makes decisions easier. Your team can decide what work gets prioritized, what requests to say no to, or what customers are worth fighting for and which ones you're okay letting go.

A clear purpose at both the team and individual role level needs to be communicated and marketed by your team leader throughout your recruiting and hiring process. Why? Because you want to attract a team member to do the work who is in love with the purpose of the work. That's how you create engagement even before a team member starts on day one.

You may be thinking that it won't work for your virtual team because you need a team of remote workers who are flexible and adaptable and can handle anything that is thrown at them. Just because you're working with a team of chameleons who work on different things all the time doesn't mean that purpose is more difficult to define. It just means you have to spend more time clarifying it and talking about it. Table 11-1 lists some tips for when to clarify purpose with your team members.

TABLE 11-1 **Clarifying Team Purpose and Role Purpose**

When to clarify team purpose	When to clarify role purpose
At the start of every new project, discuss the purpose for the project and ask these questions: What will the outcome be of this work? What impact will it have on people, customers, community? Why are we the team to do it?	At the start of every new project, discuss the purpose for individual roles and ask these questions: What will the outcome be of your work? What impact will your work have on the team's success? Why are you the right person for this task/role?
When you notice in meetings that people are talking about goals, ideas, or accomplishments that don't seem to matter.	When a team member starts questioning why he's being asked to do certain work and it seems like it's a waste of his time.
When you notice your team is taking on a lot of pet projects for other teams or executives and you're not getting your actual work done that is alignment with your purpose.	When you notice a team member has difficulty saying no or prioritizing his work. You can use the purpose discussion to help him decide what gets done, how it's aligned, and why it matters.
When the team isn't moving closer to its vision of success or moving the needle on reaching its goals.	When a team member is off track and not meeting expectations.

Identifying values on your virtual team

Decide on team values together and make sure guidelines or expectations represent how team members will treat each other, work together, communicate, and even what the team stands for. Not only is defining the team values important but also identifying behaviors that represent the team values are essential for people to be able to demonstrate them.

Here is an example of behaviors that represent the value of collaboration:

>> Brainstorming new ideas and problem solving with other team members

>> Providing feedback to other team members on weekly calls

>> Gaining consensus on methods for completing projects or tasks

>> Giving recognition for others' contributions

Similar to purpose, values are important to attract the right people to your team. If a team member isn't in agreement with the team values or willing to live them on a day-to-day basis, then discuss whether and how the team member can honor his personal values while still working effectively with the team.

REMEMBER

Values drive engagement because they provide team members insight into what matters. Values also provide team members with the confidence to make better decisions and develop a deeper connection to the team and the company in accomplishing its goals. What's important to maintaining engagement is that the team recognizes and rewards others when you notice the values in action. In a virtual environment this means that everyone has to be on the lookout and pay attention for when team members are walking the talk. Read Chapter 7 where I take a deep dive on how to develop values as guideposts for your virtual team.

So how do you keep a pulse on what's happening with your virtual team so that you can recognize values in action? Doing so is more challenging when you're not face-to-face, so you have to do some investigating. Here are a few ideas when to seek out and celebrate your team values in action:

>> **Milestone accomplishment:** When a team member or the entire team hits a major milestone, reach out to others in the company they worked with and ask for their feedback. Specifically ask for story examples where they noticed your team member demonstrating the values. Then highlight that value in action with specific examples when you recognize the milestone success.

>> **One-on-one meetings:** In your virtual one-on-one meetings with your team members, ask them to describe how they worked through a problem with another team member or customer and what their approach was. This way gives you the opportunity to hear how they live the values out loud when no one is watching. With their permission, share these values in action stories with the team.

>> **Team meetings:** Ask team members to speak up during team meetings with an example of how they noticed another team member living the values. Encourage them to provide specific examples of behavior.

Recognizing virtual values

After you identify when a team member or the entire team has been living the values out loud, recognize the act! During the hundreds of teams and thousands of leaders I've worked with, I've noticed consistently that people aren't recognized enough. How can you expect people to continue to engage in behaviors you think are awesome if you've never told them so? Recognition is another major influencer of engagement. Be sure to set a goal to get better at recognizing your team members when they deserve it. Check out Chapter 19 for more information on using recognition as a powerful motivational technique.

Using Clear Goals and Expectations to Build Engagement

It's difficult for team members to be engaged and excited about their work if they aren't clear what they are heading toward or if they're doing it right. One of the most important things that you can do for your team members is to provide them with opportunities to grow by setting inspiring goals. Growth is a basic human need, and making progress toward meaningful goals has been researched and proven to create happy, engaged employees, as written about in the book *The Progress Principle* by Teresa Amabile.

TIP

The key is to involve your team members in the process of goal setting using the following tips:

>> Set goals collaboratively to ensure that team members have buy-in and feel that their goals are inspiring, fair, and challenging.

>> Discuss and agree on expectations of how the work gets accomplished and define standard levels of performance. In other words, express what needs to get done, when it needs to get done, how often they need to do something, and how much you expect.

>> Align the goals and expectations to their job purpose, team purpose, and company purpose.

>> Take into account their strengths, skills, and natural style when setting goals and expectations so that you're setting them up for success rather than failure.

>> Agree on what success looks like and how you'll assess progress. Measures could include quantitative, qualitative, or observable data.

>> Provide ongoing, consistent feedback on how they're doing.

>> Offer support and coaching as needed.

Depending on your team members' work styles, they'll require different levels of communication, coaching, and clarity from you. Working together with your team and each individual to set goals that are aligned, specific, realistic, and measurable has been proven to engage team members and help them to be more successful. See Chapter 4 for more information on criteria to consider when setting goals and how to set goals that are motivating and inspiring.

Building Your Road Map Together with Team Agreements

Your vision is to have a team that works well together and is engaged and happy in their jobs. But as a virtual team leader, you'll face moments when team members are being pulled in a million different directions and you may not even be aware of it. If you and your team don't have a road map to help everyone stay on track and engaged, you'll soon find that your team isn't focused on the right priorities, has developed a few bad habits, isn't getting along, and is failing to meet deadlines and goals. This certainly can and will destroy engagement in short order.

Enter, stage left, the virtual team agreement.

REMEMBER

Team agreements take everything that this chapter discusses and more and puts it into a working document. *Team agreements* state the team's purpose as well as team values, vision, roles, and goals. Agreements define communication guidelines, how the team will handle conflict, how the team will use technology, and what the team's decision-making and problem-solving processes are. This road map provides direction, spells out expectations, and helps to ensure that everyone on the team is focused on the right things, with the right people, to the right degree, in the right time.

WARNING

Don't overlook the importance of team agreements or think that you can't take the time to build them with your team. The process of building team agreements together helps to establish your team culture and is a key strategy for ensuring your virtual team achieves great results. Make the time the do it.

In the next few sections, I provide you with guidelines for what to include in your team agreements and how to build them when everyone is working virtually.

Understanding the top areas to cover in your team agreements

Although team agreements vary from team to team, I recommend key areas that every team agreement covers. They include

>> Team purpose and values: See Chapter 4 for more information.

>> Team vision and strategic goals: Check out Chapter 4 for more details.

>> Team organization, including roles, responsibilities, and authority levels: Refer to Chapter 7 for more information.

- » Budget and resources, including how projects get funded, what is top priority, and how resources get allocated.

- » Measure of success, including your teams' most important measures of success defined: See Chapter 14 for more details.

- » Cultural acceptance and understanding, including conducting a cultural mapping or assessment for your team that captures each team members' experience, expertise, cultural customs, and personal information: See Chapter 9 for insights on how to work with cultural nuances.

- » Operating guidelines, including

  - Communication methods: How often you communicate, what method of communication is appropriate, and how quickly you get back with one another. Refer to Chapter 13 for more information.

  - Technology guidelines: Technology you use and for what purpose. See Chapter 16 for more details.

  - Conflict resolution process: How you handle team conflict and individual conflicts. See Chapter 17 for more.

  - Team meeting guidelines: How often you meet, for what purpose, how and when to use an agenda, the importance of starting and ending on time, and participation. See Chapter 11 for more details.

  - Ethics and code of conduct: The ethics and code of conduct that the team agrees to follow. See Chapter 12 for more information.

After you complete your team agreements, you'll have a living, breathing document that clearly defines the expectations that team members have for one another. Be sure that your agreements are simple and supported by all and define specific behaviors that people can demonstrate.

Building your agreement virtually

When creating your agreements virtually, do it together with all team members present, face-to-face, using videoconferencing. Send communication about the purpose of the meeting ahead of time and include information on why team agreements are important, how they benefit the team, and even a few examples from other teams or companies to get their juices flowing. Set the expectation that everyone comes prepared to participate.

TIP

Here are a few simple steps to follow to build your agreements:

- » Gather important team information that's already set in stone, such as vision, values, purpose, and so on.

>> Brainstorm a list of agreements that the group thinks will make for an effective team and then combine common ideas.

>> Keep track of areas where there isn't alignment or agreement. You may want to revisit these items as a team in the future.

>> Finalize. Be sure that everyone virtually signs the agreements.

>> Have agreements accessible or visible in future meetings. Post the agreements on your team dashboard or team landing page to keep them visible.

>> Review agreements at least yearly or anytime someone joins or leaves the team. Update this flexible document as your team changes and grows.

REMEMBER

The key benefit of working on these agreements together and having each team member sign that they agree is their enforceability. When team members aren't upholding the agreements, calling them out or holding them accountable is less awkward.

Using the right technology can make building your team agreements virtually more fun in a collaborative online environment. One tool that works well for this purpose is Lino (`http://en.linoit.com/`), a free sticky note service to use in a virtual environment. The entire team can participate by adding sticky notes to the collaborative whiteboard as you gather ideas for your agreements.

MERGERS, ACQUISITIONS, AND THE IMPORTANCE OF A TEAM CHARTER

Virtual teams are complicated enough when you consider the need to establish trust, enforce accountability, and communicate with people you may never have met face-to-face.

Consider the additional complexity that a company merger or acquisition brings to the table. People who were formerly competitors now must work as a team. People who were peers now must accept a hierarchy. People are likely coming to the acquisition with their own biases, agendas, and resentment. Things can get ugly fast.

This situation faced Scott Gilbert, an executive at Monarch Landscape Holdings, a commercial landscape company. Following the acquisition of Terracare Associates by Monarch in 2017, Gilbert was named the leader of the newly assembled Central Services team. The team included people from both companies who were based all over the United States. In addition, he was named to the executive team of the newly merged company — also a dispersed team. For both of these virtual teams the first order of the day was establishing regular communications and accountability. I interviewed him to find out more about his approach.

- **Initially, what was the biggest challenge?** "We all came to these new teams via acquisition. We had no history of working together. No shared culture or language. We were from many different backgrounds and we had different approaches. We all travel constantly, and we didn't meet until after the acquisition was complete. Our CEO recognized that since we did not have the benefit of hallway catch-ups, we needed something to connect us."

- **What was the secret to your success?** "One very simple but powerful thing — every morning, we have a ten-minute video call. We call it the daily huddle. I first meet with my Central Services team, and then I meet with the executive team — both on video, and usually on mobile devices because we are always traveling. It's fast, informal, and we make quick connections on priority items of the day. And most important, it is consistent. It's the bedrock of our team charter.

  "Secondly, we established clear team agreements. Key elements include our daily huddle, clear direct communications, excellent service to our internal customers, accountability, and trust. I mean, we meet every day — if you commit to doing something, you will be held to it. We are all functional leaders who travel a ton. I'm never curious about where they are — just about broad strokes of what they are doing. But the details are up to them."

- **Was there any resistance?** "Oh yeah, there were some skeptics about the daily huddles. They have since come around. They basically went from reluctant to *all in* over the course of six weeks. It really flattened the curve on rapport and relationship building. We get so much done. It fast-forwarded our team culture."

- **Any words of wisdom for new virtual team leaders?** "If you hire good people who are smart and conscientious, the kind of people who know what they are doing, then you are gold. This is so important on a virtual team. It doesn't work with people who need a lot of direction or require a lot of supervision. You want to be in a role where you consult with team members on strategy but leave the tactics to them.

  "We established fundamental expectations for everyone on the team very early on. It didn't allow for a whole lot of interpretation. We were very clear about how to be a successful virtual team member. Plus, it's not my nature to micromanage. As a team leader, hire great people and let them do what they do best."

Conducting Virtual Meetings That Have an Impact

Virtual meetings are as much a part of virtual teams as a remote employee working in their pajamas. They're how virtual teams connect on an hourly, daily, or weekly basis. They reduce social isolation, unite far-flung teams, and drive relationship building. Virtual meetings are an absolute critical part of how work gets done.

The key to having a great virtual meeting is to focus on participation and engagement and limit issues that come up from glitchy technology, distracted attendees, and lack of preparation. Here I walk you through the steps to having virtual team meetings that are worth team members' time and have an impact.

Ensuring full participation and engagement

In every team meeting you have an opportunity to build trust and connection between remote workers to enhance your team's engagement. Don't squander that opportunity by being unprepared or leaving everything to change. Have a plan to effectively use your technology and build in lots of engagement points to the meeting agenda.

TIP

Here are several best practices that help you to ensure participation and engagement in your virtual meetings:

>> **Insist on video.** Body language is crucial for interpreting whether or not your audience is engaged. Video makes people feel more engaged because it allows team members to see each other's emotions and reactions, which immediately humanizes the room. They are no longer just voices on a phone line; they're the faces of your coworkers. *Tip:* Turn the video camera on early before the meeting starts so people can chat casually prior to the meeting.

>> **Don't underestimate the icebreaker.** *Icebreakers* are discussion questions or activities to help participants relax and ease them into a group meeting. Icebreakers can create a positive group atmosphere, break down social barriers, and help people become more familiar and trust one each other. Have some fun with virtual icebreakers, such as sharing a meme that you like or a picture of your workspace or the view outside your window. *Remember:* Keep icebreakers quick and positive, not too personal.

>> **Send out agenda in advance.** Sending an agenda to all meeting attendees is the best practice for any meeting, but doing it is extremely important for virtual meeting engagement. Ask your attendees to think ahead about the content, formulate ideas, and prepare content as assigned. Encourage collaborative problem solving in your agenda, which is when the leader raises a topic for group discussion and the team works together to generate fresh ideas in response to a business challenge. Incorporating collaboration is a vast improvement over the standard status reports, which most likely your team can do using your project tracking software rather than wasting time on the call.

>> **Make engagement a part of the agenda.** In face-to-face meetings, engagement occurs during brainstorming breakouts in small groups voting with sticky notes. In virtual meetings, you have the same options — and more.

Many videoconferencing apps have sticky note and brainstorming capabilities. You can also use whiteboards for drawing and sketching, instant polling to collect feedback, and emoji to create engagement and interactivity. If the meeting is long and the energy is dropping, link to a video with some simple stretching exercises to get the blood moving again.

>> **Assign roles within agenda.** Go out of your way to address individuals by name and ask specific questions. Don't let one or two people dominate the discussion. Pay attention to the team members that you haven't heard from and call on them for their opinions. By verbally engaging your meeting participants, you can ensure that everyone feels included, and they aren't multitasking by messing around on Facebook or doing other work.

>> **Choose time of meeting wisely.** When planning your virtual meetings, be mindful of the various time zones of your meeting participants. If you're forcing your meeting participants to meet late at night or early in the morning, chances are that they aren't going to be engaged. If it's unavoidable, make sure you rotate the meeting time so all participants take turns meeting at inconvenient times.

>> **Make sure you follow-up.** You know that informal gathering that occurs immediately after a meeting has ended? That time when attendees have side conversations about how they really feel? Make the water-cooler conversation the formal ending of the virtual meeting, instead. Five to ten minutes before the meeting ends, do what everybody would've done after the physical meeting — but do it *in* the meeting and make sure it's transparent and conscious, processing people's real feelings. Keep it informal, and the team members will respond with less guarded conversations about what they really care about. Include these final-thoughts moments in your meeting notes.

Managing tech issues

For all the technological advances, virtual meetings still have issues. Granted today's options are so much better than they were even five years ago, but nearly everyone you talk to has a story about a virtual meeting gone bad with technical issues or people issues so distracting that they completely overshadow the purpose of the meeting.

For example, the list of technical problems are endless — lagging audio that clips the end of every speaker, distracting background noise, awkward and unnatural speaking delays when you're not sure if you can jump in, the faux pas that occur when the mute was not on (but should have been). The list goes on.

Many of the tech issues that arise are completely avoidable. Because virtual meetings are essential to the success of virtual teams, I put together this list to provide you with best practices for conducting highly effective virtual meetings:

- ❑ **Check the technology.** It isn't a matter of whether or not technical problems will happen — because they will. Don't let your meeting get derailed because you chose to experiment with a new tool, and it doesn't go as planned. Get ahead of all issues by thoroughly testing your videoconferencing program and all the tools you want to use within it (brainstorming, polling, and so on). The good news is that a lot of great options are available, and all you need is an Internet connection and computers with cameras and a mic.

  Attendees don't want to spend much time setting up cameras and microphones, downloading software, and uploading docs. In your meeting invite, include all the information about the program you're using, including the correct links, apps, and troubleshooting tips. Tell attendees to log in a few minutes early to ensure you're all set to start on time.

- ❑ **Have a back-up plan.** Mid-meeting, your platform drops callers. An attendee can't share his screen. There is too much background noise to hear. The video buffers for too long. Despite your testing, you have a tech fail. You need to roll with the punches and have a back-up plan, which could look like having IT on standby to resolve the issue, stepping in and sharing your screen, or quickly switching to an audio call and asking attendees follow along with the presentation attached to their invite. Try to anticipate problems and have a plan. Also, don't waste a ton of time trying to resolve the issue. If your meeting is losing steam, switch to Plan B or reschedule.

- ❑ **Know who is doing what.** Do you need IT on standby? Who is taking notes? Who is watching the clock to make sure you're not going over on time? Who is keeping everyone on task and on the agenda? Depending on the size of your meeting, you can't do it all. As the facilitator, you may need to act like a master of ceremonies, which means you need to clarify your role and prepare everyone else. Make these decisions ahead of time and bring the right people on board prior to the meeting.

- ❑ **Have the right people in the virtual room.** No one wants to attend a meeting they don't need to. Double-check the attendee list. Make sure everyone you're inviting is essential to the meeting. You can even designate attendees as mandatory or an optional attendee. People will thank you for it.

- ❑ **Send out an agenda.** This best practice applies to any meeting. But for a virtual meeting, the invite should also include everything attendees need to know about joining the meeting. Is there a link? Is there a download or testing that needs to happen prior to meeting? Do attendees need more than Internet access, a web cam, and microphone? Who is the facilitator? Time keeper? Do team members need to prepare to present information?

Practicing Virtual Meeting Etiquette

Just because you work from home doesn't mean you can slack on professionalism. You can easily fall into a too-casual trap when your commute is a short walk from your kitchen to your home office. I know this temptation well because I work from home most days.

I include this list of videoconference etiquette best practices that I compiled with the help of Michelle Greene Chessler, a Boulder, Colorado–based marketing executive and veteran virtual team leader. When she joined Polycom in 2007, she inherited a virtual team of eight people and she switched to a 100 percent virtual model, using Polycom voice/video collaboration technology. In fact, she didn't meet her boss face-to-face for 18 months ("You're so tall!," was her first reaction), and then she only met him face-to-face three times in five years. But for Chessler, leading her first virtual team was a smooth transition. "I was lucky. I had a really good boss, and I inherited good people, all very high performers."

More than a decade later, her first virtual teammates remain very good friends — and she's still never met them face-to-face. As for the early days of their video calls, no etiquette guidebook was available so they wrote their own rules. Keep these tips in mind as you write yours:

» **Beware of your background.** Your coworkers won't take you seriously if you have a pile of dirty clothes or an unmade bed in the corner behind you. Make sure your background is professional, distraction free, and work appropriate, and that the lighting is good. "My team struggled with this at the beginning," she said. "We were even sent background screens to set up behind us so that we looked more professional, even though we were all calling in from our homes."

» **Make sure you are screen ready.** One of the best things about working remotely is the freedom to wear anything to work. However, when you're in a virtual video meeting, your coworkers don't need to see your sweats and bedhead. Put on a clean shirt, brush your hair, and set up your webcam at eye level. "We used to joke that we were like news anchors. From the waist up," we looked very professional, but behind the desk were pajama pants and slippers.

» **Minimize distractions.** Video meetings have enough background noise, so don't add to it. Make sure you're in a quiet room; turn off stereos, cell phones, and TVs; relocate pets; and make sure the nanny has the kiddos settled somewhere. Also, minimize use of your keyboard because the sound is distracting.

» **Speak clearly, concisely, slowly, and don't interrupt.** The technology has improved greatly for videoconferencing, but it's still smart to speak clearly, concisely and slowly. If you have a decent mic, you don't need to yell. Your normal speaking volume should be fine. As much as possible, stick to your natural speaking cadence. "When I led international teams, we had some team members with heavy accents who were not native English speakers," said Chessler. "After frequently asking people to repeat themselves, we learned to really slow down and enunciate to make sure everyone could follow the conversation."

» **Make eye contact.** During your video call, your screen probably has the presentation open, a window to type comments, and multiple video screens with your colleagues' faces. When it's your turn to speak, remember to look into your camera, not at the multiple distractions on your computer screen. It takes a while to grasp this, but it looks more natural and connects to people much more effectively.

» **Don't eat.** Even if the meeting falls during your normal mealtime, don't eat during your video call. Just because people can't smell it doesn't mean they can't hear or see you chewing. Trust me, no one wants to see you stuff your face while discussing important business matters.

» **Don't multitask.** According to a survey by Raindance Communications, 70 percent of people do unrelated work, 50 percent read or send emails, and 36 percent mute the call to talk to someone else while on a video call. All of these are no-nos. Give the meeting your full attention. It's more productive and more respectful. "We worked in a high-demand company, so naturally people tried to multitask during our video meetings," said Chessler. "We had to nip it in the bud early on."

» **Keep the mute button handy.** Nothing is more frustrating than hearing that alien echo noise or high pitch screech from conflicting microphones. If you're working in a noisy cafe, an airport, or anywhere that has a lot of background noise, make sure to keep your microphone muted when you're not speaking. It gives everyone else the ability to chime in without distraction.

» **Be patient.** If someone doesn't respond immediately, give him a few seconds. The slow response may be an audio delay or people may be desperately trying to unmute themselves.

» **Practicing cultural appreciation on global teams**

» **Using retreats and off sites to provide sacred face time**

» **Creating connection**

Chapter **12**

Building Trust and Rapport

"Trust is the denominator of efficiency." I heard this quote from a company leader who I worked with as we discussed the impact of trust on manager–employee relationships and relationships with customers. Trust creates efficiency, and this quote hits the nail on the head when considering all of the skills, behaviors, and actions that make a team successful. In my experience working with thousands of team members, you have no chance of long-term team success if trust doesn't exist. It's the foundation of a healthy team. On a virtual team, trust is even more important because high levels of trust and social capital are established upfront. In fact, lack of trust on a virtual team will derail productivity, engagement, and results faster than you can say Usain Bolt.

Everyone knows that building trust isn't easy, but destroying it is extremely easy. Trust creates a virtual team where people hold themselves accountable, where information is shared freely and openly, where silos are nonexistent, and where people are involved in designing their own jobs and creating systems to do their jobs to the best of their ability. It's about caring about each other, encouraging constructive feedback, communicating with integrity, asking for what you need, and providing support even when it's not your job.

If your team trust and rapport levels are slipping — or just need to be strengthened — you can take key steps to help. This chapter explains several ideas to build or repair trust on your virtual team.

Getting Started: What You Can Do to Build (or Repair) Trust

Building (or repairing) trust is an inside job and starts with the leader setting the example, leading the way, and building trustworthy habits into the team culture.

TIP

Use these ideas to build or repair trust on your virtual team:

» **Encourage team members to build social capital.** This tip is especially helpful on a global team. Simple strategies for doing this include

- Ask about their culture or family traditions.

- Spend time early on sharing personal interests or hobbies.

- Put together a global team map to share that highlights each team member's professional background, languages spoken, and career aspirations.

- Develop a fun facts sheet that each team member contributes to and is accessible by all. This sheet can include information about special talents, family makeup, pets, surprising life experiences, and so on. Tie these facts into relevant conversations when appropriate.

» **Ask team members to share the personal vision they have for their role.** Each team member has individual goals he or she wants to achieve and reasons why. Asking your team members to share their vision of their contribution to the team is empowering.

» **Spend more time on mentoring and coaching and less time micro-managing tasks.** By focusing on the personal growth and development of team members, you demonstrate care and that you trust them to get their work done without being a task master.

» **Share and rotate leadership on team projects or during team meetings to create opportunities for growth.** Putting team members in leadership roles is a great confidence booster. Plus you can reveal hidden leadership skills.

>> **Use technology to make feedback on virtual team progress ongoing and easily accessible to all.** On virtual teams, technology must be leveraged to connect team members. Put systems in place where you and team members can post updates and feedback.

>> **Adjust your team meeting agenda.** That way, you can create opportunities for open discussion, feedback, and creative thinking.

>> **Let people step up.** When something needs to done, share ideas with the team and then ask for voluntary participation to make it happen.

>> **Encourage team members to share mistakes and lessons learned.** You discover more from failures than from wins. Start at the top and share your mistakes to create a culture of vulnerability-based trust.

>> **Collectively decide on agreements and frameworks that support a quality process around the following:**
- Problem solving
- Decision-making
- Communication
- Recognition
- Onboarding

>> **Build emotional intelligence on your team through the use of assessment tools.** Raise awareness around different needs and help members discover how to adjust their approach and style accordingly.

>> **Discuss how people like to be recognized and appreciated for their contribution.** People like to be recognized in different ways: publicly, privately, during a meeting, with a gift card, and so on. Find out what works for each teammate.

>> **Schedule time for building personal connection and not always just about business.** Trust levels are higher when you know and understand people as individuals. Allow time for nonwork connection virtually or in person.

As you review this list, consider if you have a healthy virtual team culture and what shifts need to happen to create an atmosphere of trust.

In these sections, I look closer at leadership-based trust and provide you a way to assess your current trust levels as well as define the behaviors that impact trust in a positive way.

Tallying the Leadership Trust Scorecard

The Leadership Trust Scorecard (see Table 12-1) can help you identify opportunities for building more trust on your team. Focus on one idea each month with your team to improve levels of trust and continually be on the lookout for ways to build cohesiveness and leverage team member strengths.

TABLE 12-1   Leadership Trust Scorecard

	As a leader, how often do you:	Never	Once in a while	Ongoing
1.	Explain to your team members how they're making a difference and adding value for your customers, community, culture, company, or team?			
2.	Take the time to understand your team members' values and motivators and how they show up in their daily work?			
3.	Communicate a vision of the future that excites the team members and aligns with what's important to them?			
4.	Collaboratively discuss specific, measurable goals and expectations with your team members?			
5.	Discuss your team members' career development goals and help them consider a plan to reach them?			
6.	Check in with your team members to discuss progress toward goals and offer mentoring and coaching when they need it?			
7.	Give team members honest feedback about their performance, both positive and corrective?			
8.	Communicate candidly about problems or issues with the team and empower the team to develop solutions together?			
9.	Appreciate and recognize your team members throughout the year that connects to what they care about?			
10.	Adapt your approach and communication style to best meet my team members' needs?			
11.	Provide opportunities for team members to discover how to challenge themselves in a way that is exciting to them (for example, lead a meeting or innovative project, attend specialized training, be a mentor/coach)?			
12.	Engage in activities and conversations during virtual meetings that focus on building team trust and cohesion?			
13.	Invite debate into decision-making as a necessity for growth and momentum and work through it together to come up with the best solution?			

As a leader, how often do you:	Never	Once in a while	Ongoing
14. Make it a habit to personally connect with each team member?			
15. Make sure that everyone has a chance to contribute during virtual meetings?			
16. Set aside budget to get your team together in person?			
17. Ask for suggestions and feedback on how to be a better leader?			

As you work through the scorecard, ask whether your leaders are currently using best practices to build trust with virtual team members and creating an environment where they're motivated to give their very best. Check the box that best describes current trust-building initiatives on your virtual team.

TIP

Share this scorecard with your team members and ask for their feedback to discover essential areas of opportunity for building more trust.

Setting the stage for trust to exist

When assembling your team and getting it rolling, consider implementing these ideas from the get-go to build trust on your team right away:

>> **Share your vision.** Encourage team members to share their personal vision for their role.

>> **Practice the golden rule.** Ask team members to serve their customers they way they want to be treated. Then trust them to do the right thing.

>> **Define what a connection culture looks like.** Have frequent discussions as a team what it would look like to appreciate one another, put others first, openly communicate, and care for each other.

>> **Act more as a mentor and coach rather than a taskmaster.** When leading virtually, you have to come into it with a high level of trust and let go of the process of how things get done.

>> **Share leadership on the team.** Take time to allow others on the team to share the leadership role by allowing them to lead meetings or discussions.

>> **Provide ongoing feedback on progress.** Specify meetings or ways to connect and communicate that consistently keep your team updated on progress.

>> **Readjust your virtual meetings.** Focus a portion of your team meetings on creating more openness, sharing feedback, thinking creatively, and taking risks.

» **Ask for volunteers.** Share ideas with your team members on what tasks and projects need to get done. Then ask for voluntary participation to take responsibility over those tasks and projects. Doing so creates an opportunity for people to rise to the occasion, stretch themselves, and try something new if they're interested. You'll also get a high level of commitment when you approach problems or new opportunities with a deep level of trust that your team can get the work done.

» **Encourage risk taking.** Innovation only happens if you trust your team members to take risks, knowing that occasionally they'll fail. However, the greatest growth takes place when they share their mistakes and lessons so that everyone can grow from them.

» **Use a problem-solving and decision-making process.** Consistency creates quality outcomes. Quality outcomes create a level of safety and trust in knowing that the team will eventually achieve the best result. Here is an example of a nine step decision-making process I recommend with my clients:

1. **Clarify the decision to make or problem to be solved.**

2. **Gather data.**

3. **Analyze data.**

4. **Identify issues, obstacles, and opportunities.**

5. **Decide on possible solutions.**

6. **Narrow down solutions based on risk versus reward, time, money, level of difficulty, and so on.**

7. **Implement a solution.**

8. **Analyze and evaluate the result.**

9. **Start the process over with improvement tweaks, if necessary.**

As you review this list, consider if your current team culture imposes more authority and control or operates from a high level of trust where people are free to do their jobs to the best of their ability. Consider what it would take to begin trusting your team to do the right thing and what mindset shifts you may need to make to move in this direction.

Practicing behaviors that build cohesiveness

I hope that you've had the chance to work with a team of people where you felt such as strong bond with your team members that there would be no amount of money that someone could pay you to leave. If you have, then you experienced group cohesion — a sense of unity among team members — where everyone resisted leaving the group primarily because they really liked each other and found the work to be personally rewarding and valuable.

You may not know how your team got to this place of nirvana or you may think it was the perfect storm of the right people, doing inspiring work, with a strong leader. That may be the case. However, research has shown that if you have a virtual team of people with psychological similarities such as similar opinions, beliefs, likes, or dislikes and that the team engages in social activities that aren't work related, members can quickly break down social barriers and build strong levels of cohesiveness. This research reaches two important conclusions:

>> Hire for culture fit first for your virtual team.

>> Build opportunities for your team to connect outside of work-related activities.

In addition to these important recommendations for building cohesiveness, it's helpful to understand the natural stages of development that teams go through. Figure 12-1 illustrates the Tuckman Team Development model, one of the most referenced and well-known models for teams ever used. By understanding where you team is on this model at any given time, you can use the right approach and tactics to build cohesiveness. The following sections delve deeper into the five stages.

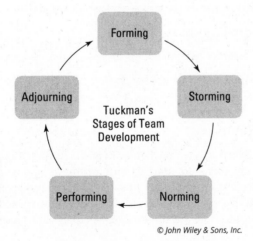

FIGURE 12-1:
The Tuckman Team Development model.

Forming stage

Any time a team comes together for the first time, or a team experiences any shift in membership, the forming stage takes place. The *forming stage* is where team members get to know one another and make contact for the first time. Team members identify similarities, agree on goals, and establish expectations about the work and each other. Tactics you can use to build cohesiveness at this stage include the following:

>> Communicate team purpose.

>> Establish team values together.

>> Clarify goals and expectations.

>> Explain the importance of each role.

>> Make everyone feel included.

Storming stage

The *storming stage* is where people start to feel comfortable enough to disagree with each other, question tactics and authority, and express differences in ideas and feelings. Communication is usually lacking and team members aren't clear on who to go to for support or how to get the resources they need. Here are some tactics to build cohesiveness at this stage:

>> Build communication agreements and expectations.

>> Train the team on communication technology.

>> Develop guidelines together on how to manage conflict and decision-making.

>> Clarify roles and responsibilities.

>> Create opportunities for team members to give and receive feedback.

>> Make time for sharing and team building.

Norming stage

The *norming stage* occurs on a team when everyone is in agreement about how the team works and team members start to form strong relationships. Things just start to flow and team members daily practice sharing, transparency, patience, and appreciation. At this stage the team is becoming cohesive, and your goal is to keep up the momentum. Here are some strategies to use at this stage:

>> Provide recognition and encourage team members to practice appreciation.

>> Continue to provide clarity about goals, roles, and processes as needed.

>> Involve team members in decision-making, innovation, and problem solving.

>> Share leadership.

>> Get the team together in person.

Performing stage

In the *performing stage* cohesiveness stands out and members deeply care about one another and achieve outstanding results. Team members know what to do and how to do it, and the team leader can take on the role of coach and mentor. The important focus here is to look for opportunities to celebrate success and keep up the good work.

Adjourning stage

If a team was brought together for a specific project and has achieved its goal, it's ready to move on or *adjourn*. This stage provides an opportunity for celebration and recognition and allows team members to reflect on best practices and improvement opportunities. This stage may not happen if you have a full-time team that continues to work on future projects together.

Leveraging Team Member Strengths

Experts in human behavior know that when people are able to use their strengths at work they are happier and have higher levels of performance and overall satisfaction with their job. Strengths represent the things you do that are easy or natural for you, motivate you, and give you energy. Another way to think about it is when you're able to use your strengths you're able to bring your best self to the party. Unfortunately, on many teams I work with, my focus is to fix behavioral problems, issues, and struggles and to overlook what people are good at. When the focus is on areas of weakness, people are diverted from their areas of strength and more often than not, they are set up to fail. Working from a place of weakness is a losing battle. It's like swimming upstream without a paddle.

REMEMBER

An important mindset shift is to spend more time focusing on identifying when team members are engaged, passionate, and excited about what they're doing. Helping your team members figure how to spot and appreciate strengths in others that are different from their own may take some time, but doing so is an important way to build trust and cohesiveness on your virtual team.

Here are three important tips to leveraging team member strengths and using them to build more cohesiveness on your virtual team.

Discover your own strengths first

Before you can begin to recognize strengths in others, you need to understand what you're good at first. Helping someone discover and embrace what she is good at is so rewarding because surprisingly, most people don't know. One of the best ways to do this is through the use of a strengths-based assessment tool or a *360 process* where people you work with closely provide you with feedback regarding your performance. You can also explore a few of the following simple questions:

>> What do you love doing at work?

>> When are you most engaged and productive?

>> What is something you look forward to doing?

>> When's the last time you were working on something and lost track of time because you were so engaged in the work?

Recognize the strengths of team members

Find out what strengths your team members have by paying attention to when they're most engaged and what gives them a sense of meaning in their work. Be sure to point out their strengths when you notice them and compliment them on what you see. Encourage team members to do the same. Bring up strengths at work during team progress updates, after the team meets a goal, or when the team discusses performance. Ask team members where opportunities exist to use their strengths more often and encourage discussions with the team on how you can leverage the strengths of all team members on an upcoming project.

Create opportunity for people to work on a project together

Innovation occurs when people come at a problem or idea from different angles or strengths. Pair people on special projects who have strengths that are different and would complement each other. You'll be amazed at the results.

By focusing on the strengths of each team member and collectively discussing how the team can leverage those strengths on projects, with customers, or with other internal teams, you're building confidence. You're also making it glaringly obvious to all team members the importance of collaboration.

Making Respect a Nonnegotiable

When your remote team represents different ages, genders, styles, strengths, cultures, social preferences, races, backgrounds, religions, and experiences, you're bound to have moments when someone feels disrespected. But the more you keep these instances to an absolute minimum, the better off your team will be. Make "showing respect for team members" one of your team agreements and collectively agree on what respectful behaviors look like. Chapter 11 provides helpful information on building team agreements.

Here are a few additional ideas for how your team members can demonstrate respect and build a strong foundation of trust and care for each other whether they're spread out in the same city or across the globe.

Act as if you're all virtual

When you have geographically dispersed team members and team members in a home office, undeniably, virtual team members feel left out of the playful office banter, the conversation that happens before the meeting gets started, the inside jokes, and all the other chitchat that takes place at the coffee station in the conference room. One of the best ways to show respect for your virtual team members and ensure everyone gets the chance to participate equally is to act as if you're all virtual. That means everyone uses Skype to call in or everyone is on their own conference line rather than half the team sitting together in a conference room and the other half the team trying to get a word in edgewise.

Gain understanding from each other

Be a lifelong learner. Get excited to discover as much as you can about cultures that are different — that is what brings richness and diversity into your work and your life. Seek first to understand rather than pushing to be understood. Practicing the art of asking great questions on a virtual team is the fastest way to build bridges. Ask about the expectations of different cultures, generations, or genders. Then share a little bit of your history with team members so that they can establish a connection with you that goes beyond the work. Refer to Chapter 9 for more tips.

Discourage cliques

On a diverse team, relationships can easily form when people share common interests, tasks, or locations. However, if those relationships start to make others feel isolated, left out, and disrespected, they can damage team relationships and undermine trust. If cliques are forming on your team or there is a good chance they may, openly discuss the topic with all team members and the impact that cliques can have on team trust.

Address mistakes together

A team is a team not just when you're winning but also when you're losing. Mistakes happen, and if team members quickly start pointing fingers and people feel disrespected in front of their peers, recovering can be difficult. Always approach mistakes as an opportunity to grow. Discuss how the team can make changes to avoid the mistake in the future. Discuss problems and solutions as *one* team, rather than singling out individuals.

Practicing Cultural Appreciation on Global Teams

A global virtual team can have several unique situations that can erode trust, including the following:

>> **Geographic dispersion of team members:** Having a majority of the team located in the same country or city and other team members sprinkled through the world can create a power struggle on a team. You may notice that the majority group tends to dominate conversations, push the team to adopt their decisions, and act as if their input is more valued and important. Having the team leader in the same location as the majority of team members can further exacerbate this. In this situation, global team members may feel ignored and that their opinions don't matter. Eventually they'll begin to withdraw and limit their contributions.

>> **Language differences:** If not approached thoughtfully and with care, language differences can quickly derail a global team. Those team members who don't fluently speak the native language may find themselves taking a back seat to decision-making, problem solving, and generating innovative ideas.

>> **Cultural differences:** Across the world, people build respect and trust differently. If your global team hasn't created time and space to discover the cultural norms and expectations of each team member, invariably someone will engage in disrespectful behaviors without even knowing it. Misinterpretations and misunderstandings can quickly cause high levels of distrust on a team.

>> **Communication habits:** Communication habits on a global team frequently get in the way of ensuring that the intention of communication is received in the intended way. Obviously with email and texting, you lose the ability to

decipher tone, body language, and emotion behind the message. When you have a variety of languages and cultural norms on a team, relying heavily on a communication method like email can cause the true meaning of the message to get lost and incorrect assumptions to be made. That's why using a balance of direct communication methods like a phone or video call, as well as written communication, is best. See Chapter 13 where I discuss ways to improve communication with your virtual team.

Chapter 9 discusses other important pointers when working with differences in gender, generation, and culture.

Giving Team Members Face Time

No matter how well a virtual team works in a dispersed environment, sometimes team members need to get together in the same physical location. In fact, all the research — including mine — supports getting together face-to-face occasionally to drive relationship building, trust, productivity, and overall team success.

REMEMBER

In my research, 41 percent of virtual teams meet in-person monthly. Teams that meet in person very frequently (weekly or monthly) had higher effectiveness ratings (defined as meeting goals, team productivity, and engagement) than those teams that meet two to three times a year.

What are the best times to get together? As often as your budget will allow! But seriously, if you're looking for a good reason to pitch to your manager, here are a few great reasons to get your virtual team together:

>> To introduce everyone when your team is first assembled.

>> To build commitment to a new vision.

>> To launch a new project.

>> To discuss when a major change occurs (acquisition, merger, new executive leadership, change in team or company direction, and so on).

>> To onboard new team members.

>> To explore significant business issues or concerns.

>> To leapfrog innovation for new products, services, or processes.

>> To celebrate a milestone (team and company) or accomplishments.

>> To connect everyone when the team is feeling disconnecting and you're noticing bad habits starting to surface.

Although logistical and budgetary restrictions can play a big role in limiting the possibility of team face time, make this budget line item a nonnegotiable if you want to set up your virtual teams for success. You're saving a ton of money on real estate costs, so be smart and set a portion of that savings aside to fund your company retreats.

You can connect face-to-face with your team in many creative and fun ways. The following sections give you some great ideas for building team trust, rapport, and connection when your team is together in person.

Recognizing the importance of "in real life" (IRL) meetings

Savvy companies already understand the benefits of getting their remote workers together. They often bring their global teams together at least twice a year somewhere amazing for both a little bit of work and a lot of fun as an opportunity to build culture, trust, and engagement. Some companies are even including family members in the team getaway, and they're reaping the rewards.

So, if you can get your teams together IRL (in real life, per the text abbreviation), the benefits are plentiful. Here are many proven benefits of getting your virtual team together in person:

>> **Increased productivity:** Retreats build trust and put people in touch in the company who may not be communicating as frequently as they should be. Undoubtedly, making connections with people who impact your success can improve efficiency and results.

>> **Better communication:** Without screens or chat windows to come between you, people connect on a deeper level when face-to-face.

>> **Improved morale and motivation:** Nothing is better to create esprit de corps, boost morale, and align behind your team goals than spending quality time together.

>> **Stronger commitment to the company:** A team that plays together stays together. Retreats that send colleagues to bucket list locations inevitably create memories that aren't easily forgotten and many employees will remain committed to your organization if they feel genuinely cared for.

>> **Deepened relationships:** Getting together humanizes your colleagues and fosters real bonding. It's also a powerful introduction for new team members.

- **Creativity and new ideas encouraged:** The simple shift to being together in the same room can breathe fresh life into a stagnating team, encourage problem solving, and help inspire new ideas and thinking.

- **Barriers broken through:** Maybe there's a teammate you never really clicked with or there are some contentious issues to work through. IRL meetings are the best way to go when dealing with sensitive or emotional issues.

- **An employee benefit:** When considering a new job on a remote team, make sure people understand how often they'll get to meet their team in person. More than likely, they'll ask this question in their hiring interview, and it's quickly becoming recognized an important employee benefit.

- **Recruiting and marketing tool:** With the competition for remote talent continuing to grow, companies are looking for opportunities to add benefits and perks that employees care about and would attract talent. Meeting IRL in a team retreat happens to be one of them.

Getting up to speed on IRL best practices

Trust falls. Drum circles. Horse whispering. Purging ceremonies. People probably think of these activities when they hear the words "team building" or "team retreat."

Face it. Team building has gotten a bad rap. It's been associated with frivolous time off that doesn't accomplish anything or worse-case scenario, it's been known to damage working relationships by unearthing problems and resentments in an unhealthy, unconstructive way. However, despite its reputation, team building is the most important investment you can make for your virtual workforce. If done with care, thoughtfulness, and clear outcomes, it can build trust, mitigate conflict, encourage communication, and increase collaboration. Effective team building results in more engaged employees, which is good for company culture and boosting the bottom line.

TIP

I've led many team retreats and team building events in my career with transformational results. If you want to get your team together IRL and make it memorable time well spent, I recommend the following strategies:

- **State the reason.** What's the point of bringing the team together? Be sure that you clearly state the outcomes and positive benefits you hope team members receive from their in-person time together. Set the stage for openness, collaboration, sharing, and laughter.

>> **Establish ground rules.** If you're doing more structured team building like working together to solve a hypothetical problem or trying to escape a locked room, you must establish rules of conduct. Listening respectfully, mutually respecting each other, not interrupting each other, and showing basic courtesy toward all members go a long way toward making the team building work.

>> **Focus on the debrief.** Activities that are too heavy-handed in pushing practical takeaways are less powerful. But spending time together, sharing an experience, or working toward a common goal allows bonding to happen. It's also valuable to discuss what people got out of doing an activity together. Here are some questions that I use:

- What did you find out about your team members that you didn't know before?

- What did you notice about your reactions when under stress or time pressure?

- Did you have ideas but didn't feel comfortable speaking up?

- Did you take over and not let others have a chance to lead?

- How do some of these same behaviors show up with the team? What's the impact?

Having these debrief conversations after an activity allows for organic learning to occur.

>> **Think beyond the company picnic.** Don't invite your team to the company picnic and think that's team building. Trying new things with your team members can generate good vibes among them, which in turn benefits the business itself. Choosing something unique and slightly outside of people's comfort zones can encourage them to come together in new ways. Here are a few unique ideas for you to consider:

- Flash mob training and performing

- Master chef team competition

- Treasure hunt or scavenger hunt through a fun city

- Improv workshop

- Volunteer event

- Escape room

- Mystery dinner

- Cultural event

- Sporting event

- Outdoor activity such as hiking, biking, sailing, kayaking, and so on

>> **Get reflective.** Although you're recognizing individual contributions and celebrating team success, also offer time for honest reflection. Allow team members the opportunity and space to look back at what they have done and what they're excited about moving forward. Doing so is essential for personal development and the progress of the team.

>> **Make it fun, not terrifying.** Sure, you want to have a little adventure and get people to try something new, but people can't find out new things about themselves and the team if they're anxious over the height of the zip line or getting pummeled with paintballs. Know your staff and choose your adventure thoughtfully.

>> **Keep it going.** Most team building falls flat because it's one and done. All the good vides evaporate when everyone goes back to their virtual office and its business as usual. The key is to find ways to keep the connection going. Build off the connections made at the retreat so that people can continue to develop their relationships and interact in meaningful ways, outside of regular meetings or presentations.

Creating a Connection Culture That Transforms Trust

I recently facilitated a virtual executive roundtable on the topic of virtual teams for a group of ten Chief Human Resource Officers (CHROs). When I asked the group members to share their best strategies for building connection, they most commonly answered making videoconferencing the standard method for holding team meetings. I couldn't agree more. You're doing a disservice to your team, engagement levels, connection, trust, and relationship building if you're not making it a requirement to connect face-to-face using video technology. It establishes a human connection.

REMEMBER

Fighting isolationism is a real issue for remote workers, which is why you need to prioritize creating a connection culture and ensuring all virtual team members feel included. One of the easiest ways to do this is to make it a common practice to do a personal check-in at the start of team meetings and allow for personal sharing before you get down to business. Team members get a chance to share a personal story about a recent accomplishment, family adventure, or upcoming road trip. If you've had the opportunity to share something that you care about with others who listen deeply, you know it feels good.

Here is a compilation of the best connection ideas that I've collected from the virtual teams I've worked with. Pick five that you'll use with your virtual team starting next month.

>> Dedicate time to develop interpersonal relationships and share virtual coffee breaks, lunches, or breakfasts together once a week.

>> Use polls during virtual meetings to engage members.

>> Hold monthly forums on topics of interest using technology as a development opportunity.

>> Kick off each meeting with a quick social or team-building activity.

>> Give dedicated time to a new person with each team member for get-to-know-you calls.

>> Check in after meetings with a colleague if you think there may be a conversation after the conversation. (Have conference room number or separate line for post call.)

>> Allow time on calls for peer-to-peer recognition.

>> Go through a virtual team or leadership program together.

>> Have virtual walking meetings.

>> Stand up against "elephants in the room," which are issues or problems that no one is talking about. Give team members an elephant stuffie when they join the team. During team meetings, ask, "If there's an elephant in the room we can't see, but we need to address."

>> Send everyone a basket of goodies to make their favorite sundae and host an annual ice cream social.

>> Hold team leader office hours where the team can instant message you and ask questions.

>> Send out recognition every Monday morning with some interesting note or family recipe and provide the family history behind it.

>> Host a monthly book club.

>> Rotate meeting times for different time zones on your team.

IN THIS CHAPTER

» **Grasping why good communication is essential**

» **Recognizing the limitations of text only communication**

» **Giving consistent and frequent feedback**

» **Discovering and using different communication styles**

» **Creating best practices with communication agreements**

Chapter **13**

Adopting Best Practices in Communication

Communication is everything for your virtual team.

If done effectively, it can influence, build trust, empower, and energize your team members. And, of course, if done haphazardly and without thoughtful consideration and collaborative agreement, it can create frustration, confusion, detachment, rework, and even conflict for everyone involved.

Simple, positive approaches in how you and your team communicate can initiate personal shifts in attitude, behavior, style, and focus that have a positive ripple effect throughout your team. The end result is establishing powerful communication habits that create happier and more productive, engaged employees, higher levels of respect and trust, as well as improved customer service levels.

In this chapter, you consider important communication practices to implement with your virtual team. You discover how to recognize and adjust when communication isn't working and what communication method is appropriate when. I provide you with practical strategies for providing consistent feedback, working with different communication styles and establishing communication agreements. By reading this chapter, you can walk away with ideas that you can implement with your virtual team immediately.

Identifying Four Components to Transform Your Communications

Good communication doesn't just happen all by itself. It requires a commitment to engaging in practices that make it successful. When I work with teams to instill better communication habits, I initially focus on four key components that people should quickly ponder before they engage with others. Getting in the habit of using these mindful and thoughtful communication techniques can positively transform your virtual team relationships.

>> **Consider purpose and intent.** You communicate in everything you do. You don't even need to think about it. But you should. Before you speak, write an email, or turn on our laptop camera, consider the purpose and intent of your communication. These questions can help you:

- Why am I sending this? What do I want them to do with it?

- What is their communication style, pace, and knowledge level? How should I adjust?

- What content do they need?

- How much information do they need?

- What is the chance of a misunderstanding?

- What is our relationship like?

Based on the answers to these questions, you can determine how to frame your communication, how much information to share, and what communication method to use.

>> **Consider assumptions.** You know the old adage about making assumptions – everyone makes them and sometimes they're wrong. That's why you need to consider the expectations and beliefs of both the sender and the receiver of

any communication before you assume anything. If you're the sender, ask yourself these questions:

- What do I know and believe about this person?

- What assumptions might he make that could impact how he interprets my communication?

- How can I provide more clarity?

As the receiver, ask yourself these questions:

- What do I know and believe about this person?

- What assumptions could impact how I alter this communication?

- How can I get more clarity?

Based on how you answer these questions, you'll have a greater understanding about the questions you should ask, the level of detail you should provide, and the communication method that will work best.

» **Make use of body language.** By choosing to communicate using a method where your body language is visible such as video, you have a higher chance of ensuring that your intention behind the message is understood correctly. Body language is the natural way people broadcast their true thoughts and feelings even if the words they use don't match. For example, someone may say, "Yes, I understand," but if their body language says something different, you may stop and ask more questions to ensure understanding. When you solely rely on words alone, getting your feelings and attitude across is difficult, if not impossible, which is a valuable and intricate part of communicating. Make sure you talk about the importance of body language and how you'll use video technology with your virtual team to limit misunderstandings, confusion, and conflict.

» **Incorporate a feedback loop.** A *feedback loop* (see Figure 13-1) ensures that the message sent is the message received. By having the receiver of the communication repeat back to the sender of the communication what he heard and understood in his own words, it ensures clarity and understanding.

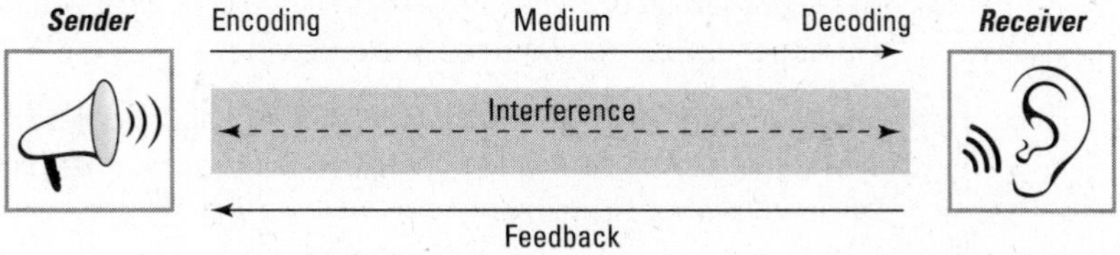

FIGURE 13-1: The feedback loop.

Sender   Encoding   Medium   Decoding   *Receiver*

Interference

Feedback

© *John Wiley & Sons, Inc.*

Looking Closer at Text-Only Communication

Not that long ago cell phones just made phone calls. No text, no apps, no calendars, no games, no emoji. Just a phone that was a complete marvel because it wasn't tethered by a cord to a wall. But enough of the nostalgia. Studies show that texting has replaced voice calls and even emails as the primary form of communication. In fact, in a recent poll by *Time*, 32 percent of respondents said they'd rather communicate by text than phone, even with people they know very well. This shift to text isn't just for personal communication. It's even truer in the business world where people prefer to email or text with colleagues.

Even though more and more people are using text-only communication (IM, phone text, and chat functions) in the workplace, it does have its pros and cons, which the following sections discuss. I also point out how you can effectively utilize text-only discussions in your virtual teams.

Examining the pros

The following are the pros to using text-only communication, which includes phone text, instant messaging, and chat functions:

» **Response time:** When you text, you can expect an immediate answer. Of the 6 billion daily text messages in the United States, the average response time is three minutes. Email response times are getting slower in the wonderful world of spam, and voice calls often aren't answered due to inconvenience or intentional avoidance.

» **Easy:** Text messages, unlike emails, appear instantly on your screen, demanding a response. Sending and receiving texts is a breeze. You don't even need to open an app.

» **On your time:** No need to worry about time zones. Similar to email, you can send, read, and respond to texts at your convenience — not someone else's.

» **Message managed:** The text message says exactly what you want it to say and it's sent to specific, targeted audiences.

» **On the record:** When you send a text message and receive a response, there is an accurate, written — and printable — proof of what was sent, when it was sent, and to whom it was sent.

Considering the cons

Here are the cons of using text-only communication:

>> **Overwhelming feeling:** Although texts are immediate, people can become overwhelmed by them popping up and interrupting their work, so they may not jump and respond or possibly ignore it all together.

>> **Loss of interpersonal skills:** Developmental psychologists have been studying the impact of texting, and they're especially concerned about younger adults because their interpersonal skills haven't yet fully formed. Most older adults already had fixed social skills before the era of smartphones, although these skills have eroded recently with high text usage.

>> **Miscommunication:** Without body language, facial expressions, or vocal tone, text messages can be misinterpreted or misunderstood. It's far too easy for a sarcastic comment to be misconstrued as genuinely hurtful. The real meaning of your message gets lost through the medium.

Your message can be miscommunicated in the following ways:

- **Unspoken feelings:** With text-only communication, you can miss out on the opportunity to discover feelings behind a message or a person's general attitude and understanding about the message that you're conveying. Your intent can easily get lost in translation when you only use words to communicate.

- **Tone of voice:** Tone of voice is an important aspect of communication when working virtually. By using text-only communication, you lose the opportunity to build your personal brand, trust, and influence with team members. Using your voice you can come across technical, verbose, factual, direct, enthusiastic, friendly, funny, or informal. If you're concerned with building team culture, consider choosing another communication method other than text-only communication.

>> **Diminished language:** Texting creates poor grammar habits. An entire vocabulary of shortened (misspelled) words, acronyms, and emoji not only can lead to confusion and misunderstanding, but it also makes communication much less formal and even can make genuine statements seem insincere. Most importantly, using poor grammar is highly unprofessional.

>> **Impersonal communication:** When people communicate primarily via text, they're much less likely to have meaningful conversations. For highly sensitive or emotional conversations, such as an apology or a contentious issue, people are avoiding having real conversations and instead taking the easy way out and using text.

Using text-only communication effectively

The big question is how to use text, chat, and IM effectively while still encouraging meaningful communication on your virtual team. It boils down to choosing the right medium for the right message. Ponder two important questions when considering your communication purpose and intent:

>> **What's the chance that the message could be misunderstood?** Consider if the message is highly technical or contains a lot of details. Ask yourself if the receiver of the message has the knowledge and skills to understand or comprehend it.

>> **What is the risk to the relationship?** Think about your current relationship with this person or group. Have you had a recent conflict or issue that may have damaged trust? If so, then you need to consider the risk to the relationship if the receiver(s) misread and make any assumptions about your message's intent. Do you know the receiver(s) well to whom you're sending the message? Do they trust you and believe that you have their best interest in mind?

Depending on your answer to these questions, you can choose the right method of communication. Figure 13-2 shows my virtual team communication method matrix that can help you determine what method of communication is best to use, ranging from impersonal to more personal methods of communication.

Virtual team communication method matrix

	Low	**Medium**	**High**
High	Voice mail or Phone conversation	Videoconference	In person
Medium	Email Chat rooms Voice mail	Phone conversation or Videoconference	Videoconference or In person
Low	IM Text Email	Phone conversation Videoconference	Videoconference In person

Chance of misunderstanding (vertical axis)

Relationship risk (horizontal axis)

FIGURE 13-2:
The virtual team communication method matrix.

© John Wiley & Sons, Inc.

If you want your team to become better communicators, build communication agreements that incorporate different methods of communicating for different situations and reasons. A *communication agreement* basically defines how your team will communicate, by what method, and for what purpose. The later section, "Establishing Best Practices with Communication Agreements" discusses how to set up and what to include in your agreements. Be sure to discuss the communication method matrix and agree on when texting is and is not appropriate.

Providing Consistent and Frequent Feedback

Feedback is a gift. And on a virtual team, it's the gift that keeps on giving. Feedback is an opportunity to help others grow and develop on your team, including you. Creating a team culture where constructive feedback is given freely and accepted with care and thoughtfulness is a vital part of building trust. Also, if you've done a good job providing regular feedback to your employees, there should never be any surprises during performance discussions. Employees should have a clear understanding of how they performed toward achieving goals and meeting expectations as well as what areas they need to work on improving.

One aspect of giving feedback is taking the initiative to have a clear dialog with each team member. Providing regular feedback keeps the lines of communication open between you and your virtual team members and creates an environment where everyone can succeed. Taking the time to discuss, clarify, and agree on role expectations will enable you to provide feedback that's meaningful down the road. It also helps set up an environment that encourages all of your virtual team members to do their very best.

These sections examine the importance of setting clear expectations and providing frequent, effective feedback to create a strong virtual team relationship with each team member.

Establishing clear expectations

In order to provide valuable feedback, you need to be sure of what you expect from your team members and discuss it with them. This is the best way to make feedback meaningful and in the spirit of helping your team members improve or supporting them in continuing to perform at a high level. To establish expectations, keep the following in mind:

>> Designate an expected standard level of performance for each team member.

>> Discuss these agreements or expectations with your virtual team members when they're hired and ongoing. You can discuss expectations by expressing the what, when, how often, or how much. Here are two examples:

- "Complete your weekly progress update by Friday at 3 p.m. using the team progress update form on Google Drive. Provide information on your wins/accomplishments and obstacles/solutions as well as your plan for the following week."

- "Respond to all customer complaints via the website within one hour and be sure that their issue was handled to their satisfaction at the end of each interaction. Provide a follow-up call within 24 hours to thank them for their business and for bringing the problem to our attention."

WARNING

When your feedback blindsides your team members, it usually means that you didn't establish clear expectations from the beginning.

Recognizing the importance of two-way feedback and performance discussions

When providing feedback to the team, keeping the following key elements in mind is important so that the feedback is clear and understandable and achieves the desired results.

>> **Choose the right communication method.** Depending on what the feedback is for, be sure to choose the right communication method using the matrix provided earlier in the "Using text-only communication effectively" section.

>> **Make it specific.** Craft your communication using clear, objective examples of the behavior or performance that you observed (positive or negative)

>> **Remember that timing is everything.** Feedback needs to take place as close as possible to the performance event or behavior that you observed or heard.

>> **Keep it positive and corrective.** Regularly give feedback for performance that needs to be adjusted or for performance that you want to see continue.

>> **Share the impact.** Effective feedback lets the team members know how their behavior or performance affects the team, department, or company. Taking time to explain the impact of the behavior or action removes the feeling of it being a personal opinion.

>> **Allow for team member input.** Your team members should always have an opportunity to share their perceptions. There may be additional information that you need to know.

>> **Turn it into an opportunity.** Feedback is an excellent opportunity to work together to establish an action plan for improvement to redefine expectations or goals or to put developmental plans in place if necessary.

By using these feedback strategies consistently, you can create a culture of transparency and openness that can help your virtual team experience the greatest levels of success.

Giving feedback: The how-to

Most team leaders aren't experts at giving feedback. Most virtual leaders usually don't have a good template for providing feedback that is simple, to the point, clear, and offers an opportunity for collaboration. For more than 15 years, I have used the following five-step feedback model that walks both leaders and team members through the feedback delivery process to ensure is the feedback is clear, effective, and respectful:

1. **Describe the facts.**

   Express and explain the specific concrete behaviors or actions that you noticed, heard about, or witnessed firsthand. Discuss facts only, no judgment, which means no adjectives or general traits.

2. **Focus on the impact of the behavior or action.**

   State how the behavior or action impacted the result and/or the individual, team, organization, or customers in a positive or negative. By focusing on the impact and not the person, you help to keep the conversation from getting defensive.

3. **Offer some time for reflection.**

   Provide an opportunity for your team member to reflect on the feedback and provide insight about the situation. Involve him in considering the impacts and what may happen if it continues.

4. **Work together to come up with a solution or reinforcement.**

   Collaborate to gain commitment to specific future actions or changes in behaviors, or reinforce the positive behavior that you want to see continue.

5. **Follow up to chat about progress or questions.**

   Plan a time to follow up in the near future to discuss any progress or questions team members may have. Follow-up also provides the opportunity to offer recognition if they quickly were able to turn around a particular behavior.

In a virtual environment, all types of communication are vital to success. However, giving feedback to your virtual team members is one of the most critical as well as most often overlooked components of effective communication.

Shifting focus from individual accountability to team accountability

If your virtual team is truly a team and not a bunch of individuals working as lone rangers in remote places around the globe, then creating team accountability for results is the way to go. Although your virtual team consists of unique individuals with distinctive skills, the team as a whole needs to understand what it is responsible for accomplishing collectively. Here are seven tips for creating team accountability:

» **Define a common purpose and goal.** Be sure to provide feedback on the team's purpose and what the team is meant to accomplish. Discuss how important each role is to the team's success and have all team members provide feedback on how they impact the goal.

» **Discuss role expectations and what success looks like.** Clarify what team member is responsible for and where people need to collaborate and why. Gather feedback from the team to create a story of what success for the team looks like.

» **Measure and track.** Use technology to measure and track team progress. This tip should be visible to all and improves accountability when it's obvious that one team member isn't pulling his weight.

» **Collaborate and coach.** Look for opportunities in team meetings to ask questions, encourage insight and participation with problem solving, and offer coaching and support when necessary.

» **Hold each other accountable.** Agree upfront how team members will hold each other accountable. Practice how to provide feedback to each other.

» **Communicate and recognize.** Constantly communicate progress and provide feedback on successes. Explain how certain behaviors or skills have helped the team move forward. Generously share recognition and feedback when things are working to keep the team moving in the same direction.

» **Continually discuss improvement opportunities.** Create space for reflection as an approach to continuous improvement where the team provides feedback on what is working well and where improvements need to be made. Work together on formulating new solutions.

Establishing Best Practices with Communication Agreements

Every virtual team needs to agree on guidelines about how you'll communicate, the technology and methods you'll use, and what is acceptable and unacceptable concerning response times, participation levels, and more. Taking a mindful approach to communication is the best strategy to steer clear of accidental communication that can quickly wreak havoc on your virtual team.

REMEMBER

Mindful communication involves planning and coordination between team members to agree on communication expectations for a variety of situations. It supports transparency, helps to address difficult situations such as conflict or problem solving, and increases team and personal engagement.

On the other hand, accidental communication is when your team has no plan in place for communication, which creates a reactive culture. There is a lack of coordination and alignment of goals and usually an avoidance and fear of dealing with conflict and difficulty solving common team issues. Here I discuss a few mindful communication agreements to discuss with your team.

Choosing appropriate communication methods

Agreeing when to pick up the phone, scheduling a video call, or even getting the team together in person is important. Talking through what communication methods are appropriate and when to use them is important for building team trust. Furthermore, understanding the level of comfort different team members may have for using different methods is also helpful. Some team members may prefer to text whereas others may prefer to email. Individual team members or the team as a whole can make agreements and may choose a preferred method of communication as a group. Table 13-1 explains in detail when to use different modes of communication and the best practices when you do use them.

Agreeing on expected response times

Every virtual team should discuss and agree on a timeframe for answering an email or text. You also want to agree on if an acknowledgement is necessary every time and when others should be copied. Make this more of a guideline for people to follow rather than a hard-and-fast rule.

TABLE 13-1   **What Communication Modes to Use and When**

Communication mode	When to use	Best practices
Instant Messaging	When the issue is fast and easy to resolve.	Use to clarify information.
	When you can keep it simple, to the point, and complete the conversation in a few minutes.	Use to inquire about information or resources.
	When the information isn't confidential, sensitive, or highly technical.	Use for checking availability.
	When you don't have to share personal information or company information.	Be brief and to the point.
		Check for spelling errors and use correct grammar.
		End the IM conversation appropriately.
		Limit the use of acronyms and emoticons.
		Give people the time to respond.
		Ask Yes or No questions.
		Set your IM appropriately.
		Consider your IM audience.
		Turn on IM when working remotely.
Email	When the information needs to be delivered to more than one person.	Use your subject line as your headline. State the level of importance or action required in subject line and use URGENT or IMPORTANT sparingly.
	You want to be sure it was received and/or you want a record.	Only carbon copy (cc) people who need a record of the email. Limit the use of reply all. Don't spray messages.
	You want to be able to easily retrieve it at a later date.	Know when to bail on email and pick up the phone or have a face-to-face meeting.
	When providing an outline or list to help organize your information.	If you need a particular response, decision, or action taken, clearly state it in the email and be specific. Set clear expectations so the receiver can meet them.
	You want time to compose your thoughts and information and revise your message if needed.	Don't use email for sensitive or emotional topics or if you believe your intentions have a high probability of being misunderstood. Never send an inflammatory email; instead take a break.

Communication mode	When to use	Best practices
	When it's not personal or emotional.	Avoid reading between the lines about the sender's intent. Assume good intent. If you have questions about the meaning, pick up the phone and ask.
		Handle important topics/decisions or bad news regarding a customer over the phone or in person.
		Check for spelling, punctuation, and grammar errors. Use spell check every time.
		Don't use all caps; it reads like you're yelling.
		Limit emails to a single topic.
		Don't use acronyms or company jargon that the receiver may misunderstood.
		Get back to people in a timely manner or let them know when to expect a response.
		Always have a proper signature line in your emails that includes your contact information.
		Track and easily search ongoing communication on an important topic by limiting your email to a single topic.
		Remember that your email communication represents you. Is it making the right impression?
		Appropriately use blind carbon copy (Bcc).
Phone or voice mail	When it's personal.	Be clear and have your ideas outlined.
	When you want to make sure your message is understood.	Let people know how much time you think the phone call will take and agree on an ending time.
	When you want an immediate response.	Set expectations for the call and what you want to accomplish.
	When you want to build the relationship.	Engage in active listening techniques during the call.
	When you want to be able to interpret the other person's reaction.	Ask questions to clarify understanding and eliminate any confusion.

(continued)

TABLE 13-1 *(continued)*

Communication mode	When to use	Best practices
	When it's a complicated message that would be too difficult to communicate via email.	Plan for a follow-up call if appropriate.
	When you have several questions or topics to discuss.	Review your voice mail before hitting send.
		Proactively provide information to internal and external clients (for example, "I wanted to let you know, you just were approved. . .").

REMEMBER

Recognize that different time zones that may impact response times. If you're working on a global team, having every team member agree to using status notifications to help set expectations for response times is helpful.

Setting the rules for handling conflicts

Conflict on your virtual team is inevitable, so you need to have a formal process or agreement for managing it. For conflicts that escalate beyond the team's ability to resolve them, you'll need an escalation path for assistance within the larger organization and HR. Team members should discuss the following questions:

>> Who do you involve when they need to resolve a conflict?

>> When is it appropriate to bring in a third party to help mediate or coach?

>> Who makes a final decision in the case of a deadlock where the conflict can't be resolved?

>> What method of communication is appropriate when conflict exists?

TIP

Don't let conflict fester and agree on expectations that help the team deal with the conflict productively.

Choosing a problem-solving model

Understanding some basic techniques for idea generation and decision-making is vital when bringing your virtual team together to problem solve. Having these tools in your back pocket can help to ensure that your communication stays on track and moves forward. Here are a few problem-solving models to consider:

>> **Brainstorming:** This method is common for a group of people to creatively generate a high volume of ideas on any topic; it encourages open thinking when a team or group is stuck.

>> **Fishbone diagram:** Also referred to as an *Ishikawa diagram* or the *cause and effect diagram,* this model allows a team to identify, explore, and display all of the possible causes related to a problem and discover its root cause.

>> **Five whys:** With this model, you ask why again and again until the root cause of an issue becomes obvious.

>> **Pareto chart:** To focus your efforts on the problems that offer the greatest potential for improvement by showing their relative frequency or size in a descending bar graph, use this model. It's based on the proven Pareto principle that 20 percent of the sources cause 80 percent of the problems.

>> **Flowchart:** This model identifies the various steps in a process or components within a workflow to understand the steps, duration, and costs.

Agreeing on a process for communicating outside the team

Effective communication on any team has three distinct directions: Downward, upward and horizontal. Figure 13-3 represents this cascade of information.

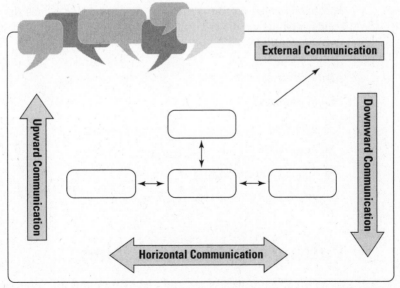

FIGURE 13-3: Communication channels.

© John Wiley & Sons, Inc.

Downward communication represents the flow of information from leadership through the team. Examples include:

>> Purpose and vision

>> Goals, strategy, and objectives

>> New organizational rules, regulations, and guidelines

>> Organization wide procedures/practices

>> Role definition and job instructions

>> Performance feedback and recognition

>> Talking points from executive leadership meetings

Upward communication represents the flow of information from your virtual teammates to leadership. Examples include:

>> Problems (working conditions and working relationships)

>> Suggestions for improvement

>> Customer feedback or trends

>> Complaints

>> Information gathered from meetings with other team members

Horizontal communication is the flow of information across the team or to other teams laterally or diagonally, which supports collaboration and coordination. Examples include:

>> Problem solving

>> Joint projects

>> Innovation

>> Recognition

>> Support and education

>> Information gathered from team meetings

Putting together your plan

On a virtual team, discuss and agree on a communication plan so that information is shared with the right people at the right time. Here are eight areas to focus on with your team members and questions to answer when building an effective communication plan:

>> **Sources:** Where or who are you receiving information from that needs to be cascaded through your internal network? If you aren't receiving information, where do you go to get it?

>> **Stakeholders/audience:** Who needs to know this information that you're receiving?

>> **Objectives:** Why do they need to know it? What should they be able to do with it?

>> **Methods:** What are the ways that you can communicate to them?

>> **Role:** Who is responsible for communication?

>> **Frequency:** How often does communication happen (daily, monthly, quarterly)?

>> **Alignment:** What are the ways you can align your message to important goals or strategies to create value?

>> **Feedback:** How will you incorporate a feedback loop?

To help you build your virtual team communication plan, download my communication plan job aid with video instructions on how to use it at www.team communicationplan.com.

Establishing standards for meeting participation

Agreeing on how your remote team wants your meetings to run establishes a sense of trust and openness and creates a climate where people are more willing to share. Helpful agreements may include the following:

>> Everyone participates and comes prepared to discuss agenda items.

>> All ideas will be respected and can be questioned for more specifics or deeper understanding.

>> Everyone shares what they know.

>> The focus of the meeting will be on the set objective and creating a strategy or solution to accomplish the objective.

>> If you don't speak up, we'll assume you agree.

>> We will start and end on time. Everyone is responsible for getting the information they need if they arrived late, left early, or missed the meeting all together.

>> Team members will agree on next steps and action plans together and hold each other accountable for follow-through.

>> Confidentiality will be maintained.

Utilizing the DISC Assessment Tool

Influential and successful communicators understand themselves and how their communication affects others. They also understand their reactions to other people and know how to adapt their communication approach based on the situation.

One of the most effective ways to help your team members understand their communication style and the style of others is through an assessment tool called DISC. DISC is a simple and practical assessment I've used with more than 15,000 team members to help them leverage the various styles on their team. Table 13-2 describes each communication style and strategies for effective communication.

TABLE 13-2   **The DISC Assessment Tool**

DISC styles	Style descriptions
D = Dominance style	Tends to take an active, assertive, direct approach to obtaining results. Likes communication to be direct, to the point, and focused on the bottom line.
I = Influence style	Tends to approach others in an outgoing, gregarious, socially assertive manner and can be impulsive, emotional, and reactive. Likes communication to be positive and inspiring and appreciates the opportunity to brainstorm and persuade others.
S = Steadiness style	Tends to prefer a more controlled, predictable environment and is steady, stable, sincere, deliberate, patient, and group oriented. Prefers communication is two-way and is a great listener that provides empathetic feedback when prompted.
C = Conscientiousness style	Tends to have high standards and prefers that things are done the right way. Tends to be conscientious, controlled, complex, cautious, precise, courteous, and tactful. Wants communication to be professional and include details. Makes a decision after gathering all the facts.

PRACTICING THE COMMUNICATION INTELLIGENCE MODEL

After working with hundreds of teams on improving communication, I noticed that a few strategies make communication work. Access my Communication Intelligence Model infographic, video training program, and team effectiveness questions at www. powersresourcecenter.com/communication–intelligence–team–program that helps you and your team to:

- Discover where your communication falls short
- Assess the effectiveness of your current communication behaviors and strategies
- Reveal the gaps that are preventing you and your team from getting the results you want
- Develop a plan to address the gaps so you can move forward on your vision and more

The best part about this video training program is that no matter how pressed for time you are, you can use it to improve communications across the board. In fact, I've designed it so that you can work through each step with your team in less than 30 minutes. Each video session includes a six to eight minutes of video and questions to guide your discussion.

Your team can walk away from this training with a deeper understanding of how well you're communicating, the gaps that are preventing you from achieving a higher level of success, and the steps you need to take to eliminate the gaps.

Chapter **14**

Measuring Virtual Team and Team Member Success

Y ou can't manage what you can't measure, as the saying goes. Tracking and measurement is even more important for managing virtual teams where you don't have the benefit of daily face-to-face check-ins or seeing how much someone is actually working. With remote workers, measures should focus on output and results. In order to do so, rely on good technology tools to measure your team's success as a whole and keep track of individual team members.

Successful virtual team members must be able to work autonomously with little supervision for their work. They must be able to self-motivate, self-direct, and make decisions independently. But that doesn't mean that they're excused from keeping the team — and you, their leader — updated on their progress by using project management and tracking tools. If you're not using these tools that I discuss in greater detail in Chapter 16, then most likely you're struggling to keep a handle on what your team members are up to and whether they're hitting the goals and milestones you expect them to.

In this chapter I discuss ideas for tracking your team's progress and what data to pay attention to that may indicate time to course correct. I also share common measures for virtual teams to pay attention to that are signposts of success. Finally, I talk about the importance of observable measures and how a quick emotional check-in can point out where your team members are and who needs coaching and support.

Tracking Virtual Team Success

With remote workers, tracking progress matters a lot — even more so than teams who are located in the same office. Why? Because using the proper technology and collaborative platform can improve collaboration, team trust, accountability, profitability, and most importantly, results. Here's how:

>> It keeps your team on track.

>> It improves billing accuracy.

>> It helps with prioritization.

>> It's transparent so team members know each other's contributions to the project.

>> It helps you celebrate milestones and successes.

>> It identifies areas that need improvement.

>> It answers big questions, such as the following:

- Which projects, tasks, and meetings are the most profitable?

- Which projects, tasks, and meetings are the most time consuming?

- Which activities should have a higher priority because they contribute the most to reaching team's goals?

Keep in mind that your tracking methods will only be as good as the tools you use. Slow, difficult, or distracting systems mean that workflow and productivity suffers. At the same time, not being able to easily compare your team's progress with outcomes will make capturing accurate data that helps you hone in on where to make adjustments and who needs coaching or support challenging.

TIP

When you introduce tracking to your team members, let them know how important it is. Find a case study from within your company where tracking revealed insightful key lessons, uncovered additional opportunities for revenue or costs savings, or helped a team member understand where she needed more focused training.

These sections help you identify what data to measure, how tools can help, and how data can improve your team's performance.

Knowing what to track

Keep in mind that your tracking is only as good as your organizational skills. The better organized your project, subprojects, tasks, and billing/cost centers are, the better and easier your tracking will be. I recommend that you only gather data on things that are actionable. In other words, if you aren't billing for it or coaching team members on it or have an identifiable action plan for it, then don't track it.

REMEMBER

When you determine what data to track, stay simple. Some leaders want to have data for every part of their project plan, but sometimes you can overengineer your project planning into so many subprojects that you're spending more time tracking the minutia than getting things done. Try to resist thinking about all the possibilities and future reporting options. Here are some common performance-related metrics to ensure virtual team success:

>> On time and on budget

>> Quality outcomes

>> Meeting goals

>> Participation, engagement, and communication

Recognizing the importance of tools when tracking

Having a project management tool that all virtual team members use is absolutely essential to your team's success. Your team uses this tool to organize a project, including outlining goals, strategies, milestones, and deadlines, and assigning work tasks. Everyone can see what everyone else is doing, and the tool shows virtual team members how they fit into the overall picture. More importantly, the tool establishes accountability by indicating how team members' tasks impact other's deliverables. Refer to Chapter 16 for some of the most popular project management tools for virtual teams.

In addition, time-tracking tools are also important for project billing and tracking work time. Many options are available, some of which are bundled into project management or collaboration software. Again, flip to Chapter 16 for a few popular time-tracking tools and how to figure out which one is right for your team.

Use time-tracking tools for the right reasons and not because you don't trust your team members. If that's the case, then you didn't do a good job hiring, setting expectations and goals, and building a strong relationship with your team.

Measuring participation and engagement is something that is observable. Are team members attending meetings, participating in brainstorming, connecting with employees via your collaboration tools like Slack or Workplace by Facebook?

Pay attention to engagement and collaboration levels on a virtual team because almost always, engagement will slip before performance slips. Chapter 11 discusses in greater depth how to keep your team members engaged.

Using data to coach your team members

Your measurement tools and the data that you collect can provide you with quick insight regarding where a process may be broken, where training or coaching needs exist, or when a team member may need more challenging work to remain engaged.

The best coaching is driven by data. And some of the best data available for virtual team effectiveness comes from tracking. When team members aren't hitting goals, engaging with the group, or turning in quality work, coaching may be the best strategy to help them identify behaviors that are hindering their performance, analyze the situation, and consider alternate solutions. With your guidance, team members can discover how to make their own decisions in order to become more effective.

When coaching team members, here are four simple things to keep in mind:

>> **Answer the why.** Share the data and compare it to the expectations or goals you already discussed with your team member. Clearly describe why something needs to change. Answering the why question is a key motivator. Explain where the team is going, how you're going to get there, and how the team member's role contributes.

>> **Open a dialog.** Analyze the data and discuss ideas for potential solutions and approaches. Focus on performance and data, not the person. Engage in a collaborative conversation about solutions.

>> **Confirm understanding.** Listening is key. Make sure that both you and your team member confirm understanding and walk away with a clear plan that everyone feels good about.

>> **Show appreciation.** Recognize the progress she has already made and show appreciation for her commitment moving forward.

Measuring Data That Matters

All measures aren't valued the same. You'll be more concerned with some data more than other data, depending on your job role in the company. I noticed this distinction in my research on virtual teams. I divided the results into three distinct audiences:

>> Executives that support virtual teams

>> Virtual team leaders

>> Virtual team members

All three of these roles have different perspectives about the measures that matter most for virtual teams.

Looking at the results from an executive point of view

Executives who oversee virtual teams have their own unique perspective on the measures that are important. As executives, their role is more strategic with a focus on aligning virtual team goals with the larger company goals. They want to be champions of virtual teams, but they need data to support it.

In my research, I discovered that executives who oversee virtual teams overwhelmingly view them as a means to getting the right people to work together regardless of location. They also see cost savings and a means to leverage talent as key benefits of virtual teams. To that end, executives are most interested in big-picture measures around:

>> **Hard cost savings:** Reducing travel expenses, operational expenses, and so on

>> **Soft cost savings:** Reduced turnover rates due to better recruiting and retaining, improved work/life balance, and so on

>> **Productivity rates:** Improved response time, higher revenue, leveraging talents throughout the organization, and so forth.

Interpreting performance from a virtual team leader perspective

Virtual team leaders have one foot in the virtual team and one foot on the management team, so they have to consider the needs of both. Their job is to lead their virtual team, align its activities with the larger organization, and communicate the success of their virtual team up the chain and across the organization.

My research showed that virtual team leaders, more than any other group, see virtual teams as a means to improving work–life balance and are strong advocates for effective communication supporting results. In fact, when virtual team leaders and executives viewed communication within the team as strong, they were 31 times more likely to indicate that the team accomplishes its goals and 21 times more likely to view the team as effective in responding to customers. Virtual team leaders are interested in the following measures:

>> **Work-life balance:** Measures related to flexibility, engagement, satisfaction, job retention.

>> **Communication:** Measures on daily team check-ins, one-on-one meetings, project updates, conflict resolution, and so forth.

>> **Accountability:** When virtual team leaders and executives indicated the team had high levels of accountability, they were

- 32 times more likely to indicate the team accomplishes its goals.

- 41 times more likely to indicate the team meets deliverables on time and within budget.

- 24 times to view the team as effective in responding to customers.

>> **Productivity:** Team goals reached, technology leveraged for more efficient processes, ability to meet external customers and internal customers' needs, and so on.

Evaluating performance as a virtual team member

Virtual team members are primarily interested in supporting the team, making progress toward team goals, and having the support and tools necessary to do their job effectively.

In my research, I've discovered that team members strongly relate to the benefits of work–life balance on virtual teams, and they're also big believers in the increased productivity of virtual teams. The measures of most interest to virtual team members are:

>> **Work-life balance:** Great job satisfaction, flexibility, engagement

>> **Communication:** Any measure on usage rates across team communications channels — chat, IM, videoconference, text, email, project status updates, and so on

>> **Technology:** A measure of the effective use of technology to do their jobs effectively

>> **Productivity:** Any measure that validates the strongly held belief of increased productivity in virtual teams

Recognizing the Engagement Levels of Your Team Members

Engagement and accountability can occur as people move through changes they face every day. A few years ago, my friend and colleague Wendy Boyer of Boyer Consulting and I collaborated on a process that would help leaders use observable measures to understand levels of engagement and accountability on their team and where team members get stuck. This process highlights common phases that team members must move through during small or substantial change to get to a place where people are engaged. And it never happens step by step. In fact, people can fluctuate from phase to phase at any time. It's also important to note that the amount of time people stay in a phase plays an important role in determining their mindset and whether they're stuck in the past or looking toward the future.

REMEMBER

Based on what phase someone is in, it impacts her engagement levels and the emotions you'll notice, which are considered *observable data.* By observing emotions in team members, you can determine the best approach to offering support and coaching and keeping your team on track. Here are explanations of the different phases team members experience and tips to help you identify your team members' engagement levels:

>> **Disbelief:** In this phase, your team member has experienced a change that is a shock to her system, which can be a change of job title, project focus, reorganization in the company, or a new leader. Your team member doesn't fully accept that this change has happened and operates from a state of disbelief or that it's not real. Emotions you may notice include fear, denial, anger, sadness, disorientation, frustration, uncertainly, and a sense of loss. Behaviors include zero to minimum productivity, silence, and hiding.

>> **Opposition:** If a team member is in a place of opposition, she opposes whatever change has occurred or decision has been made, and she'll let you know through a full range of emotions ranging from anger, resentment to fear, stress and depression. Behaviors include sabotage, refusal to work or move forward, withholding information and resources, low productivity, gossip, asking questions to keep things stuck, and more.

>> **Inquiry and solutions:** In this phase, team members emotions shift toward optimism and curiosity as they begin to ask, "What's possible?" Behaviors include giving something a try, learning proactively, asking questions, and problem solving to move ideas forward and offering solutions. While they still may be fearful or anxious about the decision or change, they begin to search out ways to support it.

>> **Investment:** Team members who are fully invested in the decision or change will be your advocates and deliver results. Trust is high, and behaviors include a willingness to mentor others, celebrate success, and tolerate ambiguity and risk taking. They demonstrate an openness to reevaluate their direction and lead innovation efforts to minimize complacency and maximize future opportunities and growth.

>> **Innovation zone:** Innovation occurs when creative tension is present between the phases of opposition and inquiry and solutions. Without innovation, teams and organizations cease to exist over time. This zone is a critical opportunity for leaders to leverage and use as a mechanism to learn from the past and move toward the future. Teams must be willing to encourage healthy debate, brainstorming, and risk discomfort and exploration for the sake of innovation and sustainable results.

It's normal for team members to fear change or resist decisions that they believe aren't good for them. This response can often trigger an emotional process that is necessary in order for the teammate to move through the framework toward investment. However, if team members get stuck in disbelief and opposition, they often feel as though they're victims to their circumstances with no way out and no control. By recognizing the observable data and understanding the normal emotional process that people go through, you can support and coach your team in the most effective way possible. For more strategies on how to communicate and engage with team members during each of these phases, see Chapter 17.

Chapter **15**

Training Your Virtual Team

Professional sports teams, rock bands, dance troupes and musicians practice for months — and sometimes years — before they ever do any public events. Virtual teams, however, are rarely given adequate time or support to thoroughly prepare for their big debut. Team members often don't have the opportunity to get to know one another and each other's strengths. And most of the time, in almost all the companies I work with, this group of virtual strangers is expected to become a high-performing team without proper training.

You may not be surprised, and in fact, you probably have experienced this lack of preparation yourself if you've ever been on a virtual team. But consider that research proves that virtual teams who spend time in the early forming stages getting trained properly, experience greater levels of confidence and trust down the road, which drives their overall effectiveness and productivity levels.

Workplace training encompasses a broad spectrum of topics like onboarding, compliance training, workplace harassment prevention, administrative training on how to submit expense reports, training on new software, and skills training on topics like products, process, ways to be more service-minded, or strategic thinking. Most companies have mandatory training that all employees must take, but the very best organizations invest in training leaders and teams on an ongoing basis.

Training does matter. I certainly can attest to the transformational changes and improvements that I've witnessed firsthand from working with teams using training, facilitation, and coaching. Ongoing training for your virtual team is just as important as training for your in-office teams — and even more.

I hope that you work in an organization where there is a learning culture, and where improving performance, team cohesion, and strong leadership are a focus and commitment. If not, then change begins with you. This chapter provides you with ways to build a virtual team culture that invests in ongoing learning as a strategic priority for success, whether your team is brand new or has been together for a while. You gain insights into where your greatest opportunities for learning exist with your team members and how to immediately implement strategies to guide your virtual team on the path to success.

Training during the First 90 Days

Many companies struggle to properly train remote employees, and many times they're left trying to figure out processes, platforms, and technology on their own. Companies who are missing a successful training program for new hires can expect lower levels of engagement and employee retention to suffer. But by having a solid training process outlined for the first 90 days that includes technology, communication, and collaboration tools, as well as important company policies and procedures, the process of getting your virtual new hire up to speed will be much easier and will yield a happy, engaged, contributing employee in no time. See Chapter 7 for additional details on building a solid onboarding process for new hires.

REMEMBER

New hire training for each company will differ, but the principles are the same: get to know company policies procedures and culture, get comfortable with internal systems and technology, and shorten the learning curve as much as possible. As a best practice, many companies have all remote employees attend orientation in person at the company headquarters. However, if your entire company is remote, then much of the training will happen virtually via one-on-one meetings with the manager, assigning a mentor or providing online courses. Table 15-1 shows a sample 90-day new hire training schedule.

The following sections help you to consider some of the most important methods for training your new hire in the early stages of their employment.

TABLE 15-1   **90-Day New Hire Training Schedule**

	30 Days	60 Days	90 Days
People Training	Perform manager and team orientation Assign and set up mentoring relationship Schedule regular check-ins with manager and mentor	Evaluate comfort level Answer questions Address concerns Perform cross-functional team orientation Introduce to customers	Evaluate comfort level Answer questions Address concerns Evaluate mentoring relationship
Process Training	Clarify roles, responsibilities, and goals (short term and long term) Discuss expectations and team values Introduce company culture, policies, and procedures	Recognize progress and demonstrate values Schedule product and services orientation Dive deeper into company culture, policies, and procedures Check in on short-term goals	Recognize progress and demonstrate values Have performance evaluation progress check-in Retrain where appropriate Set long-term goals
Technology Training	Train on technology Train on collaboration tools	Continue training on technology and collaboration tools	Customize tech tools

Assigning a mentor to instill culture

Just because a virtual employee may never step foot in the corporate office, you can't underestimate the importance of instilling culture in new remote employees. You can do this through coaching, mentoring, and technology. Making just one strong connection with another team member can make all the difference in the world.

TIP

If your company is mostly virtual, assign a mentor from another team to all new hires so that they have a source to better understand how the company operates and can build cross-functional relationships. You may also assign a mentor from your own team to help the new hire quickly understand your team culture and values. The mentor can also promote connection opportunities with other team members more quickly.

Utilizing communication tools for training

Virtual teams rely on a variety of communication tools to keep them connected. When new team members are added, make sure everyone on the team utilizes all these tools to connect with them. Equipping your team with the right communication tools facilitates constant communication between team members — something that's critical to making remote employees feel connected to their colleagues.

The newbie should also understand the channels to use for formal communication (email, project updates, shared calendars) and what to use for informal communication (chat, IM, text). As the team leader, make sure you connect frequently with the new team member by using all available methods. Refer to Chapter 16 for more discussion about what technology is important.

Sharing information about your company

New employees must understand how to align their day-to-day tasks and behaviors around the company goals. In order to do this, they must develop a basic knowledge about the company, its values and goals, as well as products, competitors, locations, and so on. Here is a sample list of company-related topics that are important for your virtual new hires:

>> Company overview and history

>> Business industry

>> Organizational structure and reporting relationships

>> Company policies including ethics, safety, HR procedures

>> Welcome message from the CEO

TIP

You can use technology to share company information with new team members. I recommend the following ideas:

>> Recorded webinars lead by subject matter experts on company process, products, or intellectual property

>> Online courses about company history, competitors, or industry

>> Online topics and research via the company website with a follow-up quiz to assess understanding

Being organized and following up

When onboarding a virtual employee, you can easily lose track of what you must do. Hence, being extremely organized and having a detailed plan of everything you need from your new employees — and the things you need to do for them — is essential. One-on-one follow-up meetings between you, the team leader, and your new employees offer a chance for the employees to share any concerns or ask more detailed questions. As the team leader, you can gauge how well the new hires are picking up company lingo and culture.

REMEMBER

When onboarding new team members, be prepared to constantly make adjustments. Your goal is to give every remote team member a great introduction to your team and your company, so regularly collect feedback from remote new hires so you can improve and adjust the onboarding process and training strategy as needed. When collecting feedback about the effectiveness of your onboarding program, assess if your virtual team members:

>> Feel welcomed and connected to the company and team

>> Are clear about their role and expectations

>> Can discuss company culture and team values

>> Are knowledgeable about company history, competition, products, and services

>> Understand the company structure and where they fit in

>> Know important policies and procedures to follow

>> Are clear on where to go to for help if needed

>> Believe they made a right choice to join your team

REMEMBER

Keep in mind that your work isn't done after 30, 60, or 90 days. Stay in touch with new team members and review any concerns they may have at regular intervals. Schedule these check-in meetings on their calendar for the first 90 days using collaborative technology. Remember, technology is your friend and can support the onboarding process and help remote employees feel welcomed and included on your team from Day 1.

Keeping Your Team Members on Top of Their Game with Ongoing Training

Training may not always be the answer when something isn't working on your team. The answer may be that you need to fix a process issue, provide more clarity around roles and responsibilities, engage in more virtual team collaboration, or something else. Perform a needs analysis to validate that training is required. Be sure any training that you offer has goals and outcomes associated with it and a clear reason why you're offering the training.

REMEMBER

Training can be knowledge based, skill based, or behavior based, so keep track whether the training is effective in reaching your goals. Questions to establish your goals include the following:

» What's the gap between the current and desired behaviors or skills?

» What do you want your team member to be able to do after the training?

» How will you know the training was successful? What new behaviors will you see? What new knowledge will team members have?

» Is baseline data (such as turnover, revenue, sales, timing of deliverables, engagement scores, and so on) available to measure progress?

» What support and resources do you have for the training?

Keep whatever training you offer interesting and engaging, ensuring people can contribute and participate even if it's an online self-directed course. The time that people will invest in training needs to be worth the outcome or benefit they'll receive. Furthermore, make sure the training is focused on meeting your team or organization's goals and outcomes. Ensure the new team member can immediately notice how it's applicable to his virtual role.

When considering what training to offer and how to offer it to your virtual workforce, take into consideration different points, such as when it's appropriate to use online training, when to engage the team in collaborative learning, how to evaluate if training is effective, and what to do if someone is struggling. This section provides you with some food for thought around each of these topics to build into your training for your remote workers.

Using online training

The good news is that many options are available. You already connect with your colleagues everyday using a variety of tech-enabled tools — videoconference, file sharing, and chat — so use these same tools for training. Here are a few best practices for online training:

» **Don't forget to test.** All training is designed to get your team to perform certain tasks in a certain way, so make sure team members understand the training goals and how you're going to measure what they learn. Include tests and quizzes to ensure they meet your training objectives.

» **Keep it relevant.** So often workplace training feels pointless and boring. You can overcome this negative stereotype by making sure your training is relevant to the individual, the team, and the company at large. Keep reinforcing why this training is meaningful in terms of skills, improvement process, safety, and so on. Regardless of training topic, make sure the training is consistent with the company's vision and values and why you're offering it. When you take valuable time away from projects for training, focus on making it relevant and meaningful.

» **Ensure your training program is accessible across all platforms.** Your online training needs to be available across various devices, operating systems, and browser. Make sure different devices can be used for the training and that the screen is optimized for mobile.

» **Allow independent learning.** Due to the global nature of your team, double-check that team members can complete some of the training modules independently, which is sometimes called *asynchronous training,* or training that can be accessed at any time by your team. You may want to do some aspects of training as a group, but because your team more than likely works in different time zones, allow the greatest flexibility to complete the training.

» **Review the training for cultural sensitivity.** Whether the training is an off-the-shelf online program or a live trainer facilitates it, verify that you take into account your team's cultural differences. Some words have different meanings in other cultures, so you want to avoid misunderstandings. Chapter 8 addresses important cultural accommodations.

» **Consider blended training.** If possible for your team (and your budget), consider a blended approach that combines face-to-face training with online-based training.

» **Give and get feedback.** Before, during, and after your training, solicit feedback from your team. Asking questions, doing surveys, and getting individual team member's thoughts about the training materials helps you to revise and improve your training program. Make sure your online training system integrates surveys and feedback along with the nuts-and-bolts content.

» **Leverage the visuals.** Everyone is connecting via screens, so take advantage of it. Emphasize visual training through videos, instant polling, dynamic images, screen sharing, and whiteboards to create an overall interactive presentation.

Paying attention to trends and practicing innovation: VR and AR

Virtual reality (VR) and augmented reality (AR) are the biggest areas of innovation, and they're quickly becoming real components of training and e-learning, delivering an incredible depth of knowledge in a fully immersive environment.

VR is a computer-generated representation of an environment that allows for user interaction through a digital simulation. *AR* differs from VR in that it superimposes a digital image, sound, data, or other sensory input over something real world, in real time, blending the simulated and the tangible.

For example, doctors in training can make surgical incisions to explore human anatomy or try new techniques without physical harm to a patient, airline and auto mechanics can navigate new engines and find out how to repair and replace parts, first responders can be trained on a variety of crisis scenarios, customer service reps can access subject matter experts in real time for live guidance, and the list goes on.

Experts agree that VR and AR will become more and more a part of the workplace, especially for dispersed teams. The question is how you'll use it.

Using teach-backs to build cohesion and advance understanding and mastery

The *teach-back method* is commonly used in the healthcare field where patients teach back the information that they heard and received in order to make sure they understand what's being explained to them and to help the provider evaluate if her communication skills are meeting the needs of the patient. This method has been successful in improving health literacy between patients and providers.

TIP

You can utilize this method to help your team members deepen their understanding of a topic by teaching it to others and answering questions. In a virtual environment, this method connects team members through building a common knowledge of a topic, technology, or method. It provides the opportunity for feedback and insight from other team members, and collectively they master and design a best practice or method together. In fact, research shows the practice of reassessing and teaching back to validate comprehension improves knowledge retention and advance mastery.

Evaluating training effectiveness

If you aren't evaluating whether the training you're doing to see whether it's meeting the goals and outcomes and people are using the training, then you're probably offering training that isn't of value. Stop doing the training if it's not working. It's really that simple. No one has time to waste.

REMEMBER

When evaluating training, focus on measuring the following:

>> **Likeability:** Did people enjoy the training? Was it engaging, innovative, and interesting? Were they satisfied with the content and the way it was presented?

>> **Improvement in skill, knowledge, or attitude:** Did the training actually achieve the desired outcome? Can you measure an increase in skills or knowledge?

>> **Application:** Are people actually doing something differently as a result of the training?

>> **Return on investment:** What are the impacts of this new training to the business and bottom line?

REMEMBER

You can accomplish training effectiveness in a variety of ways, including evaluations, surveys, before-and-after training assessments, observable changes, quantifiable data, and more. Just be sure to use an evaluation process to determine if the training you're doing is worth it. Training doesn't amount a squat if your team members aren't doing anything with it.

Here are ways to ensure that you're supporting your team's training efforts and that your team members are applying the training back to the job:

>> Conduct a thorough needs assessment before recommending training.

>> Coach leaders on how to support the training.

>> Provide leaders with coaching tips to use during follow-up.

>> Provide pre-training projects or tasks.

>> Offer real-world application exercises.

>> Use real company case studies.

>> Involve internal subject matter experts as teachers.

>> Build in practice time with other team members who provide the trainee with feedback.

>> Answer how to transfer to the job in training debriefs between the leader and trainee.

>> Build in-action planning throughout the training.

>> Provide training aids and reminders.

>> Send follow-up activities or check-ins via email.

>> Schedule a meeting with the leader after each training session to share the action plan.

>> Provide recognition by the team or executives.

>> Continue to share training effectiveness and evaluation data with the team over time.

Supporting team members who are struggling

If a team member is struggling to follow training and she isn't changing behavior or her skill set hasn't improved, the first step is to reach out and connect with a face-to-face meeting. Having a true pulse on what's happening with a team member is difficult when she is virtual. A multitude of things can cause a lack of follow-through after training has been implemented, such as:

>> Cultural misunderstandings

>> Communication styles

>> Lack of knowledge or skills

>> Lack of clarity on the contribution and value to the team

>> Role confusion

>> Lack of time management skills

>> Unclear goals or expectations

>> Conflict with other team members

>> Discomfort with technology

>> Personal situations

>> Overall job dissatisfaction

If you're the team leader, track the progress of each team member, so you can easily identify when someone is struggling or disengaging. Many times more training isn't the right answer, which is why having a face-to-face meeting (or one-on-one videoconference meeting) is the best approach to discover what's the best next step.

If you decide that additional training is necessary, then I recommend discussing the results you expect to see from training and then create a follow-up plan for after the training is completed. Good tracking practices can tell you whether or not your team members are keeping up with required training modules or if they aren't doing well mastering the new information.

REMEMBER

Team members who are struggling will benefit by having a mentor on the team in which they don't report. The mentor acts as a role model and can pass on her experiences and model the behaviors or skills that you're working to develop in others.

Tackling technology issues

Technical issues can crop up on any day, with any user. Even the most tech-savvy worker can struggle to get a program up and running. Hence, you can largely avoid issues by ensuring that your hardware, equipment, operating systems, firewalls, and browsers can handle the training program on the front end and then by conducting thorough testing before launch. Make sure you have a plan in place for tech issues that arise during a training session. Have technical support on speed dial, or better yet, monitor system performance during the training, so that you can address tech issues immediately.

Training Your Veteran Team Members

Veteran team members can easily disappear into the virtual ether because they know what they're responsible for and they know how to do it well. Unless you, the team leader, consistently focus on fostering team collaboration, frequent communication, and connection, team members will naturally disengage. No doubt these team members will accomplish their tasks efficiently and meet the goals assigned to them, but keeping them engaged and involved as valuable team members is important.

REMEMBER

Your veteran team members have institutional knowledge on your process, clients, and business history, so make sure they pass down this knowledge to new team members through mentoring, sharing of stories, and training. The best way to keep them engaged is to involve them in the training process. Consider them subject matter experts and rely on them consistently to develop others.

My top two suggestions for keeping your veteran employees engaged in the learning process include the following:

>> **Invite them to conduct the training.** Sure, they've been around the block, so have them suggest, develop, and conduct a training session for your team. The topic could be an area where they're subject matter experts or a functionality of a program you use. Another great idea is to ask them to share key trends they're noticing in the industry and insights or opportunities these trends create for your team.

>> **Create social learning opportunities.** *Social learning* is when team members learn either formally or informally from each other as they share an experience. For example, at your next team meeting, ask a veteran team member to lead a discussion about lessons learned when dealing with a certain client. You can also keep the team engaged by making training fun. For example, create an activity where everyone shares a funny meme on the benefits of your product, service, or team cohesion. Humor can go a long way to connecting teammates and keeping veterans engaged.

Chapter **16**

Checking All Things Technology: What You Need to Know

C an virtual teams exist without technology? Sure. I would argue that highly coordinated — and very effective — virtual teams have existed since Roman times, but this point is fair. The availability of reliable, high-speed Internet along with significant advances in hardware, software, mobile phones, smart-phones, and cloud-based storage have all fueled the rapid rise of dispersed teams across the world.

Not all technology is created equal. What works for one organization may not work for yours. Your team may not need the latest suite of collaborative software tools. Rather you may require just a solid video chat program and cloud-based document storage.

Understanding, identifying, and ultimately choosing the right technology for your virtual team is a significant challenge. The ever-expanding universe of platforms, options, applications, features, and functions can make your head spin. The main thing to keep in mind when choosing the right technology to connect your virtual team is functionality. When making any decision, always examine what you need the technology to do.

In this chapter, I provide some helpful definitions, categories, and guidelines for selecting the best collaborative tools for your virtual team.

Assessing the Right Fit for Your Team

Think about the story of Goldilocks and the three bears. She went for a walk in the woods, came across a house, and when she realized no one was home, she walked right in. She was hungry and tired. She methodically determined her needs related to chairs, porridge, and beds, and then eliminated what was too big, small, hot, cold, hard, and soft before finally settling on what was just right and promptly took a nap. Your quest to find just-right technology will be more complex than Goldilocks, but you still need to find a solution to fit your current needs with the scale and flexibility to meet your future needs. In most cases, the investment is significant, so you need to do your due diligence.

REMEMBER

Being thoughtful about team technology needs requires looking at several things such as the work you do, how big your team is, where your team members are located, your team members' skill set, and other technology the company is already using, just to name a few.

WARNING

Choosing the wrong technology for team can quickly result in a disconnected, frustrated, disengaged virtual team, not to mention a huge waste of money and resources. Deciding on the right technology upfront and being willing to continually assess what's working and what's not working for your team is something to make a normal part of assessing team performance.

These sections help you determine how to choose the best technology for your team by focusing on the functions you need and not being dazzled by the functions you don't.

Focus on the problem, not the technology

Have you heard of the expression "form follows function?" It's a modernist architecture philosophy that says that the shape of a building or object should reflect its function or purpose. Likewise, your technology decisions should be guided by the functions the technology offers — or problems you need to solve.

Start with an assessment of your organization and your team and ask yourself these questions:

>> How tech savvy are you and your team members?

>> How large is your team?

>> How dispersed is the team? Are the team members all in the same city, the same country, or all over the world?

>> What are you currently using to connect teams? Is your current technology limited to email and conference calls?

>> Do you have access to enterprise software currently being used by other teams?

>> Consider organizational compatibility — what can your operations and IT teams support with training, servicing, and troubleshooting?

>> What hardware do you already have?

>> Do all team members have a laptop with a camera and a mic?

>> Do all team members have consistent, reliable high-speed Internet access?

After you complete this initial assessment, think about what problems you need the technology to solve. Ask yourself these questions:

>> What are your team's pain points?

>> What is holding your team back from achieving peak performance?

>> What is creating obstacles in working efficiently?

>> Are you struggling with project management and keeping track of all the small moving parts, including time spent, status, deadlines, and progress?

>> Are you challenged by team communication and staying connected because it takes too much time or seems clunky?

>> Does a lack of knowledge sharing and training exist?

>> Is it difficult to find documents and where they are located?

>> Has the team struggled with task management and progress updates?

These questions can help you start the process; you know your team's problems better than anyone. Thinking through these questions can help you think about what features you need. Document and prioritize these needs and obstacles together as a team and let the technology decision-making flow from there.

Avoid jumping on the latest trendy tool

Today's workplace has new technology solutions popping up every day. It's both a blessing and curse that so many great options are available. Staying up-to-date with current trends is good, but be careful about jumping on the bandwagon too soon. Stick to your due diligence plan. Not every new tool may be appropriate for your team. Understand what problems you are solving or the competitive advantage you hope to gain.

With new, trendy applications, asking for references from companies in your industry and with teams that look like yours (size, locations, and so on) is even more important. The software may truly be the holy grail for certain companies in certain industries, but not for yours.

Also, consider that if the software is brand new, the company may not have a long track record and all the kinks may not be worked out. In addition, the company may not have all the backend operations you need to rely on, such as training, implementation, and customer support. Do your homework and make sure the company has a sizeable client base and will be available for the extended period of time.

Make a checklist of features

Look at the features and functionality you need to address the issues. Use Table 16-1 as a grid to help jump-start your thinking on the features you need to solve your problems.

TABLE 16-1 **Your Problem-Solution Checklist of Tech Features**

Sample issue/problem for your virtual team	Tool categories to solve it
My team never knows the status of projects. Deadlines/milestones keep slipping because my team never has clarity about the timeline and due dates.	Complete collaboration program with project management, workflow management, time tracking, and communication tools
My team is always unclear about who is assigned to what task and small details are falling through the cracks.	Project management, task management
The review and approval process for each step of a project keeps changing.	Project management, workflow management
My team needs a way to communicate quickly and informally throughout the day.	Chat or instant messaging
My team never knows where people are when they travel and when people are available or on vacation.	Shared calendars
My team has issues with version control on documents: Which is the most current? Which is accurate?	Document library
My team needs to improve its overall productivity and efficiency.	Complete collaboration program with project management, time tracking, and communication tools

Sample issue/problem for your virtual team	Tool categories to solve it
My team needs to have accurate data on the time it takes to complete all the tasks in the project plan.	Time-tracker incorporated into project planner
My team needs to have more opportunities to actually *see* each other to connect in a visual way.	Videoconferencing
My team is having an issue with documents. Team members need to be able to find them quickly and easily; the documents need to be stored in a clear, organized manner, and in one place.	Document library with shared document creation, editing, and sharing
Team members travel constantly and can't be tied to laptops.	Mobile applications for all tools (communication, collaboration, shared calendar, and more)
My team needs a place where team members can meet on projects, share ideas, and collect all notes.	Team discussion boards, brainstorming tools
Sometimes I want to get a quick read in real time on where all team members stand on an issue.	Instant messaging, flash polling, or brainstorming tools
Team members want to connect informally in a virtual way so they can know each other better outside of work.	Work-specific social media

Go with tools that your team loves

Choosing tech tools that are fun and intuitive to use is an obvious factor, but is the fun factor is often overlooked. When you get down to several great options, go with the one that your team members seem to love. Likability and usability are relevant factors in selecting collaboration tools. You want a 100 percent adoption rate, so make your job easy and involve your team in the final decision and let the popular vote win.

Collaboration tools are deeply ingrained in human behavior and team culture. Throwing something new and complicated at a bunch of people and telling them to start using it doesn't work. You want all team members to buy-in and embrace the collaboration tools that you choose so that they completely abandon the old methods and enthusiastically embrace the new ones so that the tools become a part of your team culture. After you're up and running and everything is clicking, you'll be amazed by the boost in productivity and organization your team will enjoy.

Include your IT department or tech guru in your decision

Be sure to loop in your company's internal IT department in any new technology or upgrade decision that you make. Don't get too far down the road in your research and selection before checking with your IT department. The IT department has a better handle on what the rest of the company is using, what's compatible, what features you may not have thought of or didn't even know existed, what bugs still need to be worked out, and more. Here's a quick checklist of factors to discuss with the IT folks when you have a tool you want:

>> **Compatibility:** First and foremost, you need to know if the tools you want for your virtual team are compatible with the overall technology in the organization.

- What are the minimum hardware requirements for installing and running the tools on servers and individual workstations?

- What are the minimum operating systems requirements for the server and workstations?

- Is IT already looking to launch an enterprise-wide collaboration tool?

- What software/tools already exists in the organization?

- Is there another team somewhere in the organization that is already using collaborative software successfully?

- What are the minimum high-speed Internet requirements for optimal performance?

- How fast are the connections of individual team members?

>> **Support:** Even the best technology needs service and support occasionally. Verify who will provide that support for your team.

- What happens if the technology goes down? What is the backup plan? In a virtual team, this question is especially important.

- What is the plan for scheduled maintenance updates that don't interfere with your team's productivity?

- Who is providing the technical support and troubleshooting?

- What is the maintenance and update requirements for the technology?

>> **Training:** Sure, a lot of new technology is intuitive, but your team still needs to be taught how to use the tool effectively.

- What's the word on the street about this vendor's level of training, support, and customer service?

- How long do you think the team will need to set aside for training?

- What is the normal ramp-up time on this type of technology before people become fully comfortable using it?

>> **Policy:** You don't want to be the team who violates a corporate policy. Do your due diligence and find out the rules.

- Do any purchasing agreements with certain vendors exist?

- What are the policies related to using programs on company hardware?

- What are the considerations needed to take into account regarding customers? Both internal and external?

>> **Security:** Don't go rogue with company data. Find out how your program handles security and privacy.

- What are the security regulations and compliance requirements of the organization?

- How will the app manage highly proprietary company content? Customer data?

- If necessary, how will any mobile apps manage secure login?

- What is the backup and disaster recovery options?

- What kind of networking equipment (routers, switches, firewalls) considerations are available?

>> **Reputation:** Do research on this new program. Find out what current users are saying about the technology.

- What reputation does this technology have in the industry? Is it proven?

- What problems does it solve?

- What results have other teams experienced?

- Is this software or platform known for having bugs that need many updates and fixes?

- Is there a better option?

Choosing Only the Essential Tools Your Team Needs

To make the selection on what technology to buy easier, the following categories can help you organize your decision-making around technology tools. These groups aren't distinct, but rather general. Features and functionality can overlap. For example, some collaboration programs include tools for time tracking and project management.

REMEMBER

Tech companies launch new products and tools daily, so be aware that new technology has been released that I didn't even know about when I wrote this chapter. However, the tools and products I recommend are the most relevant and most widely used available on the market today. Some have been around a while, whereas some are newbies. Do your own research and choose what fits your team's needs the best.

Collaboration suites

This category is extremely significant. Collaboration tools are at the heart of teams, because they boost productivity and help teams work together more efficiently. These tools help you collaborate with your team through a central hub for sharing information. They save you from emailing, knocking on doors, or leaving voicemails. They alert team members to tasks and deadlines that pertain to them. They ensure that the right people have access to the assets they need. They should be flexible and multipurpose and may include a menu of options, including project management, resource management, time tracking, task management, and communication tools. Popular applications include:

>> Asana

>> Podio

>> Slack

>> Spark

>> Trello

>> Workflow

Project management tracking

Project management tools help you manage and plan your projects with your team through task assignments and scheduling. These programs should be able to handle both project and resource management, workflow, task management, time tracking, and approval processes. Top brands include:

>> Basecamp

>> LiquidPlanner

>> Zoho Projects

Here are a few important questions to consider when deciding on your project management tools:

>> Do they have a free version or a free trial version for testing?

>> Are they compatible with your project management function?

>> Can they meet the needs of your independent contractors and your entire team?

>> Can they integrate with your billing system?

>> Do they come in a mobile version?

Workflow management and time tracking

These services focus on helping teams track what needs to get done, who is supposed to do it, what stage the work is in, and what stage it must go to next. Top brands include Asana and Airtable.

Shared calendars

With a dispersed team, you need to be able to manage your time as well as see whether your colleagues' are available, particularly if your team is scattered around the world. The best calendars aren't just functional, they're actually fun to use and make you more productive. This is definitely a case where you want your calendar available to you on a mobile device. Top shared calendar tools include:

>> Apple calendar

>> Blotter

>> Doodle

>> Google calendar

>> Microsoft calendar

>> Sunrise

TIP

If your team is spread out or travels a lot, use www.worldtimebuddy.com, so you always know what time zone your colleagues are in.

Meeting tools

Virtual teams obviously need meeting tools, and sometimes you just need to connect via voice with no video. Many include screen sharing, chat, meeting recording, and transcript services. Great options include:

>> AdobeConnect

>> Google Hangout

>> GoTo Meeting

>> WebEx

>> Zoho Meeting

Flash polling

Polling your team members is a great tool to use during presentations or as a stand-alone, check-the-pulse information gathering. Many collaboration and presentation tools have this feature. It's a great engagement tool however you use it. Popular options are:

>> Participoll

>> PollEverywhere

>> Swipe

Brainstorming

Sharing ideas and brainstorming are essential to collaboration. For virtual teams, you need to create a time and space for brainstorming due to the lack of available conference rooms and whiteboards right down the hall. Some virtual teams use sticky notes, highlighter, whiteboards, videos, pictures and documents, and the ability to post text, draw freehand, and erase. Great options include:

>> ezTalks Meetings

>> Stormboard

>> Trello

Social media

You know what they say about all work and no play, right? Social media use is ubiquitous, so bring your team in the fold with its own social media page. Here team members can be informal, share their nonwork interests, and connect on a personal level. Popular options are:

>> Chatter

>> Facebook Workplace

>> Yammer

File sharing

These tools help you store and share your files securely among team members. They should allow you to share, store, and create documents and make them accessible in one central location. Popular brands include:

>> Dropbox

>> Google Docs

>> Prezi

Cloud collaboration

Cloud collaboration is a way of sharing and co-authoring computer files through the use of cloud computing, where documents are uploaded to a central cloud for storage, where other team members can access them. The advantages to virtual teams is obvious — documents are stored in a central, cloud-accessible location, team members have easy access to large files, and they can make real-time updates. The cloud does create security concerns related to data privacy policies, snooping, and hacking, so check with your IT department. Examples include:

>> Dropbox

>> Google Drive

>> Microsoft Azure

Mobile options

If you have a team of road warriors, you want to be sure you choose collaboration tools that work flawlessly on a mobile platform. Most of the top collaboration programs do function on mobile devices, but make sure they're equally robust on your laptop and your mobile phone.

Videoconferencing

Video meetings are critical to keeping team members connected, whether it's your daily huddle or an impromptu video call that pops up throughout the day. It's vital to see your team in their workspace while you get to know their nonverbal communications ques and their household pets. The leading videoconferencing tools in this space are:

>> HipChat

>> Join Me

>> Polycom

>> Skype

>> Zoom

Chat and instant messaging

Team messaging apps allow groups of people to chat with one another in a setting that allows for both open and private conversations. When conversations are open, anyone on the team can read them and participate in them at will. When they're private, they're by invitation only. Popular brands include:

>> Glip by RingCentral

>> Jabber

Training Team Members for Success

Getting your team trained on your tech tools may be your biggest and most important hurdle. Don't be surprised by some feet dragging and resistance. New technology naturally has bumps as you introduce it to your team, and it may require that people change habits and ways of doing things or absorb something completely new. Team members may have a steep learning curve, and all team members will adopt to your new technology at different a speed. So be patient . . . to an extent.

Being able to connect everyday with your team members by using the same tools and speaking the same collaborative software language is essential. You don't have the luxury of connecting face-to-face, and you can't tolerate rebels who don't get on board. In fact, incorporate the adoption and usage of team collaboration tools into your team charter and agreements (see Chapter 11 for more info on the importance of collaboration).

Getting on board with your new tech tools is mandatory, and with proper training and leveraging team mentors and early adopters, you'll get your team members up to speed as quickly as possible.

Using mentoring to help virtual team members get up to speed

Every team has *early adopters,* those team members who embrace change and are tech savvy. And most importantly, they love helping others discover how to use new software. These team members are key assets when you roll out new technology, so be sure to leverage their leadership and spirit by naming them ambassadors or training leads and designating them as the go-to people for questions about the technology. Utilizing these people is such a powerful way to build team relationships and trust across a virtual team.

Depending on your team's size, you can even create a subteam of early adopters to master the new technology thoroughly, create real-world cases for each application, and then train the rest of the team. Everyone wins!

Or, bring the biggest naysayer or tech-averse team member into the fold. Keep an eye out for the team member most likely to resist change and have her join your team of early adopters. If you can turn that team member into a cheerleader, you can create significant excitement for the rest of the team.

Introducing tools strategically

Rome wasn't built in a day, so don't enforce complete 100 percent conversion to *every aspect* of your new technology overnight. Start by addressing the biggest pain points first and sell the benefits of incorporating the new tool and how it will make life for your virtual team easier or more effective. For example, if the absence of a shared calendar is causing disconnect on the team, adopt that functionality first. And so on.

If you've done a good job performing your upfront assessment, then you should have a clear understanding of the training and resources that accompany your new technology. I encourage you to have a plan for using them. Any program you purchase ideally will have extensive and highly detailed training resources, including videos, walk-throughs, information guides, and downloadable manuals. Take advantage of this material and train together as a team.

TIP

Schedule *learning labs* for your virtual team that the team members do together. You may train on a particular functionality of your new technology, practice using it together, and then agree on some standards about adoption. Here is a quick process you can follow to set up your learning lab.

1. **Choose your topic and a facilitator who knows the technology and how the team will use it.**

2. **Schedule a 30 to 60 minute meeting with the team to study a new functionality that the team can immediately start using.**

3. **Introduce the new functionality by watching a how-to video together, and have your internal subject matter expert or technology vendor explain what it does and why it will benefit the team.**

4. **At the close of the meeting, set expectations that everyone agrees on about when to use the technology and standards for using it.**

   Keep in mind that if team members only use a portion of what's available or they don't use the technology in the way that it was intended, the team won't experience the greatest level of benefit.

5. **Following your learning lab meeting, ask team members to practice and provide feedback as they use it.**

   This hands-on approach is how most adults learn.

6. **If appropriate, plan a few check-in sessions or Q&A meetings early in the adoption phase.**

   Continue to sell the benefits and agree on what successful adoption of this technology looks like. For example, how will team members know they are using the new technology effectively?

REMEMBER

You'll eventually experience setbacks when introducing new technology to your team. Someone will go rogue and fall back into her habits and begin using the old method. The only way to overcome these challenges is to constantly communicate with your team members and to create conversion deadlines — and then use coaching and mentoring to help enforce them. For more great ideas on training your team, see Chapter 15.

Use your new collaborative tools to review progress and share tips on the rollout with teammates. After all, the whole point of these tools is to bring your team together to achieve its goals, so use the tools to share tips about using the tools.

THE DANGERS OF COMPANYWIDE, VIRTUAL TRAINING

I've worked with many teams that were told they were going to start using a new technology by a certain date, and they were given one or two options for attending companywide, virtual training, which isn't aligned with how adults learn and doesn't provide the opportunity to ask questions, practice, and get feedback.

When companies have trained their teams on technology this way, I've seen results that were understandably poor. Here are some examples:

- A small percentage of the workforce adopted the new technology, usually the demographic population that was more tech savvy.

- A majority of the workforce didn't understand how to use it effectively and only used what they felt comfortable with, not what was most efficient and effective for the team.

- Technology and collaboration tools quickly became a sore subject and created a lot of frustration and conflict on teams.

- Teams were more divided because of technology, rather than more engaged and collaborative, which is in direct opposition to the goal.

Recovering from these situations is extremely difficult. You're in an uphill battle trying to get them to adopt it as soon as they make up their mind that the technology is doing more harm than good. This chapter offers plenty of hands-on advice to help you in your technology review, selection, and adoption process to make sure you don't find yourself the captain of a proverbial sinking ship.

» **Adapting as a new leader**

» **Adjusting to a new team goal**

» **Finding your footing after an organizational restructuring**

Chapter **17**

Rolling with the Changes

Imagine that you've assembled a powerhouse of virtual team members who can leap tall buildings in a single bound and continually exceed your expectations at every turn. And then a team member quits and convinces another team member to join him. Or the innovative project that your team was working on gets squashed unexpectedly. Or your team gets restructured and a new boss is now leading the group. Your team can quickly be in a position of being understaffed, concerned, and confused.

In this chapter, I talk about how to help your team adjust to shifts in team membership and goals as well as best practices for onboarding a new team leader. I also discuss several ways to keep your team grounded and focused after a company restructure.

Adjusting to Shifts in Team Membership

Inevitably, your team membership will change. People find different work, transfer to another team, or move to a new city and want to work virtually but close to their office. Or maybe they weren't a good fit to begin with. Whatever the reason, understanding why team members leave and how to keep the team cohesive in the midst of staff changes is important.

When a team member leaves, everyone on the team feels the impact, regardless if the team member was an asset to the team or a liability. Your team members usually have to pick up additional projects or do the work of two people until you can find that next great hire. It can cause additional workload, stress, and even a drop in morale when good team members walk away. Hence, you want to build a resiliency mindset on your team so that sudden changes don't throw the team into a tailspin that can be cognitively exhausting. Read on to find how to emotionally prepare your team for change.

Boosting emotional resilience

Resiliency isn't a quality that your team has or doesn't; rather it's a skill and attitude that your team can master. You can assist your team in developing certain skills to help in the face of chronic stress and increasing demands. Here are some important qualities to discuss and even practice with your team that experts agree will help to boost their emotional resilience:

>> **Mindfulness:** Mindfulness is a state of active, open attention on the present. When you're mindful, you observe your thoughts and feelings from a distance, without judging them good or bad. During change, allow team members to share how they're feeling without judgment.

>> **Empathy:** Empathy helps build your own self-worth when you see yourself and everyone around you as having value. Practicing empathy is the happy effect of oxytocin, the hormone that is released when you care for others. Consider how to have compassion for the person that left the team and the impact it has on others.

>> **Acceptance:** When a problem arises, own what is happening to you. Resilient people understand that stress or pain is a part of living that ebbs and flows. As hard as it is in the moment, it's better to come to terms with it rather than ignore it, repress it, or deny it. Engage the team in critical thinking, reasoning, and problem-solving techniques. Resist blame. Acceptance helps the team learn from mistakes and find meaning in life's challenges.

>> **Internal control:** Resilient people believe that they are in control of their own lives. They are realistic, proactive, and solution oriented, which give them a greater sense of personal control rather than feeling they are victim to their circumstances. This helps team members feel empowered and less stressed. Focus on what the team has control over such as attitude, personal decisions, and work ethic and where they have opportunities to exert influence during change.

>> **Optimism:** Resilient people see the positives in most situations and believe in their own strength, which can shift how they handle problems from a victim mentality to an empowered one. Discuss the opportunities ahead and what's possible.

>> **Support:** Resilient people tend to be strong individuals, but they know the value of social support and they surround themselves with people who give them the space to work through emotions. Encourage your team members to listen to one another and offer encouragement without trying to solve the problem.

>> **Sense of humor:** People with emotional resilience are able to laugh at life's difficulties. This trait is a huge asset because they have a greater perspective on the challenges. They also have the ability to perceive issues as a challenge, rather than as a threat. Laughter reduces stress hormones and increases health-enhancing hormones like endorphins. What lightness can you bring to the situation?

>> **Self-care:** Self-care can mean different things. For some, it's resting, reading, journal writing, or meditating. For others, it's exercising, listening to music, taking a bath, or relaxing with friends. Self-care is any activity that inspires you, nourishes your soul, helps you recharge your batteries, and fills your cup. Resilient people know what works for them, and they make it a priority. Encourage team members to practice and share their self-care strategies.

Using consistent communication to get on track quickly

When a team member leaves, make it a habit to take stock of lessons discovered. Consider the following questions and then engage your team members in a collaborative discussion before hiring your next team member. Here are questions for you to consider and even a few questions that you may want to ask the outgoing team member:

>> Did you appropriately define the role, responsibilities, and expectations clearly during the interviewing process?

>> Were there any red flags during the interviewing process that may have led you to believe the exiting team member may not be a good fit?

>> How well did the team member connect with others on the team?

>> Did he willingly support others on the team when they needed help? Did he get support from other team members?

>> Did you provide support and training to set him up for success in his role?

>> Was communication clear and consistent?

>> Was he challenged and excited by the work?

Quickly informing the team when someone leaves is also important. Hold a videoconference meeting so everyone can share how they feel, capture their feedback, and discuss next steps. Here are a few questions to discuss:

>> What are your concerns now that this team member is leaving?

>> How can we support each other through this transition? What does each person need?

>> Should we hire for the same role, adapt the position for the future, or distribute the work to the current team?

>> Who will be most impacted by his departure? What can the team do?

>> What opportunities does this present to our team? What can we do differently or better moving forward?

The answers to these questions can help your team come together, reflect, grow, and move forward as a cohesive group. Having these discussions consistently when a team member departs is an important practice in building trust and collaboration.

Regrouping around team goals, values, and priorities

Anytime a team experiences transition, you need to bring the team together to regroup and confirm that the goals, priorities, and values of the team are still the same. You may also discover that goals or timelines need to be adjusted. This consistent practice creates a sense of safety, predictability, and calm for virtual team members and can keep their morale up and the momentum moving forward.

Building Relationships as a New Leader

How teams adapt to a new virtual team leader isn't that different than adapting to a new team leader on an in-house team. Many of the same best practices are the same, but with a few nuances. For the purposes of this section, I assume that the new leader has the necessary skills for leading a virtual team — a great communicator and collaborator who is trusting, flexible, empathetic, and tech savvy.

REMEMBER

Virtual employees need more than just new marching orders from their new leader. They also need to establish trust, rapport, and a genuine understanding of their role during the transition. Trying to accomplish the work without building relationships first with the team is a major no-no. These sections talk about what you can do to build a strong relationship with a new team.

Onboarding strategies for a new leader

Meet the new boss. Yikes! Team members are apprehensive when a new leader is coming on board. Here are several best practices a new leader can use to reduce the tension in the first 30 days:

>> **Overcommunicate.** Everyone wants to know what you're going to change and where you're going to take the direction of the team. Be as open and transparent as you can. You may not know your strategy, but you can certainly talk about your values, priorities, and observations. Use every communication method available to you and push for getting the team together face-to-face.

>> **Keep an open mind.** You may have heard other's opinions on who is strong and who is weak on your team. Make sure you keep an open mind, make your own observations, and draw your own conclusions.

>> **Demonstrate your skills.** Show that you're comfortable managing a virtual team. Demonstrate your willingness to collaborate and value everyone's opinions. Prove your flexibility and trust in team members by being a hands-off manager.

>> **Get comfortable with the tech.** A virtual team leader doesn't get to slowly ramp up on the technology that connects the team. You have to hit the ground running and demonstrate comfort in using all the technology the team uses for communication, collaboration, and project management.

>> **Ask questions . . . and listen to the answers.** Be open. Be curious. Being genuinely excited about the opportunity to listen and understand what's going on within the company builds credibility and generally makes you more approachable and builds trust.

>> **Meet with team members separately.** Get to know their communication style and approach. Ask them to share a story about a leader they admired, which can help you understand what's important to them.

>> **Balance the quick fix with real change.** New leaders usually favor chasing quick, surface-level wins over implementing long-term, sustainable change. As a new leader, the first task you must undertake is accurately gauging the change readiness on your team. Being able to fix a significant pain point shows that you can listen and get things done.

Sharing cultural norms and styles

As the new leader, one of the first things to notice and understand is your team's culture. To do so, ask a few insightful questions. Broadly pose these questions to the whole team, but have team members respond separately so you understand their personal insights:

>> What are the best ways this team likes to learn?

>> What are the key ways you stay connected?

>> What are examples of how you live the team values in your day-to-day work?

>> How does the team like to be recognized?

By asking these deeper level questions, you can begin to uncover what's important to the team and what the relationships are like. In addition, I always recommend that new teams use an assessment tool like Everything DISC (http://powersre sourcecenter.com/everything-disc/). DISC uncovers individual strengths and styles and helps team members to discover strategies for working together and leveraging differences to build a stronger team.

Getting on Board with a New Team Goal

More often than having personnel changes on your team, a major team project goal will change, or your team's entire focus will shift to a new business priority and your team will be required to change course midstream. Doing so isn't easy, especially when the team members are collaboratively working toward a goal that inspires them.

As soon as you hear that the change may be coming, start socializing the change, share what you know, including any data to support the change, and highlight any key benefits. Most of all, be a role model by staying positive and being open to feedback. During change, team leadership really matters. Remember that your team members are looking to you to help them understand the changes, see the benefits, and set a new course.

Discussing the why

A company or team can change direction for different reasons. No matter the reasons, make sure that you share them with your team in full transparency. Sometimes companies make decisions that don't seem to be in the best interest of the team, so sharing the why really matters. Confront the facts, share what is changing, why it's changing, and what the outcome expected is. This clear and open communication will validate the trust and faith you have in your team to be able to make the shift.

Acknowledging successes and letting go

Most people have difficulty not seeing a goal through to completion. If your team is asked to completely shift direction and drop what it's doing, a mental transition needs to take place. Take a time-out to acknowledge how far the team members have come, the growth and accomplishment they've experienced, and what they'll have to give up by shifting goals. You can collaborate visually using tools like Mural.co to celebrate your successes and move on to the next challenge.

Grounding Your Team after a Reorganization

Restructuring in your company can impact your team at any time, and in my experience it's never pretty. As a best practice, your company should communicate as much as possible to prepare employees for the change. However, you can take a few actions to help your team members before, during, and after a reorganization to guide them through this typically difficult evolution.

Before any changes take place, keep these tips in mind:

>> Overcommunicate and allow for open conversations during meetings.

>> Touch base with each virtual team member more frequently.

>> Discuss support options for anyone who may be impacted.

During the transition, do the following:

>> Focus on providing as much clarity as possible.

>> Practice empathy and understanding.

>> Support employees impacted in the most caring way possible.

After the reorganization, touch base with your team in these ways:

>> Work on restoring trust.

>> Provide training.

>> Get the team together in person.

>> Find opportunities for quick wins.

>> Discuss the value of each team member and role.

>> Seek out opportunities to recognize and build team engagement.

Even after providing all the support and communication you can, recognize that certain team members may need more. Be prepared to assist team members through the emotional roller coaster they are riding.

Recognizing the stages of change

Experienced leaders know that people go through change in different ways and at different paces. You can't force people to immediately get on board and buy in to change. Humans go through emotional stages whenever they face change, and these emotions compare to the stages of grief, researched and documented by Dr. Elizabeth Kubler-Ross. They include:

>> Shock and disbelief

>> Anger and negotiation

>> Depression

>> Exploration

>> Acceptance

Meet your employees where they are emotionally. Use compassion and consideration to shepherd your team successfully through change.

Practicing empathy and understanding

Emotional reflective listening, also called *empathetic listening,* is reflecting back the feelings content of what your team member has communicated to you in a way that demonstrates understanding and acceptance. Practicing empathy is important during change because it builds relationships, encourages discussion about feelings, and reduces tension and defensiveness when the conversation is emotionally charged.

When practicing empathy, follow these simple rules:

>> Search for the core message.

>> State your understanding of the message.

- It appears you feel frustrated because . . .

- You seem excited about . . .

- My sense is that you're hesitant . . .

- » Stay focused on the other person's content.
- » Be brief and use your own words.
- » Don't interpret, evaluate, or give advice.

You can also show your team members that you care and understand what they're going through by communicating thoughtfully. Here are some tips:

- » Let me try to paint a picture of where we are heading and why it will be good for us.
- » I know change is difficult. I'm here to answer any questions and concerns you have to the best of my ability.
- » As a team, we have gone through a lot of changes. Change can cause stress and uncertainty, but it can also bring us new opportunities.
- » We have a lot of talent on this team. Let's focus on our past accomplishments and go forward to repeat them.
- » How are you feeling about this change?
- » What do you think is ending for you or for the team as a result of this change?
- » What impact will this change have on your work?
- » How has your experience of this change differed from what you expected?

WARNING

Don't think you can manage change via email. Your virtual team needs to connect more than you think is reasonable during times of major change. Use every channel at your disposal — calls, video calls, message boards, FAQs, and more. Have no fear of overcommunicating. Don't assume that just because everyone is virtual, change won't impact them significantly. Doing so is a mistake that can be difficult to recover from, and you could end up losing more great virtual team members in the process.

USING ON-DEMAND VIRTUAL TALENT TO CLOSE THE GAP

On virtual teams, the one thing you can count on is change. That change can come in the form of a new direction for the project, a change in the timeline, added product features or functionality, budget cuts, expanded scope on the client side, an acquisition or a merger. Personnel changes are the most disruptive changes that can occur on your virtual team, projects can easily lose momentum, and it can take a while to find your

(continued)

(continued)

footing again. Whatever the reason for the change to your team, you can bet that the work still needs to get done.

Trish Thomas is the CEO of TEEM, an innovative marketing and advertising agency that leverages the power and flexibility of the new independent workforce. TEEM is ideally suited to weigh in on dynamic virtual teams — it's the basis of what the marketing agency does. With a large Colorado-based team of co-officed talent and hundreds more on-demand virtual talent, TEEM assembles and deploys high-performing teams of specialists — writers, programmers, researchers, and designers — for clients all around the world. The idea that changes in personnel create highly disruptive events for teams isn't a part of TEEM's reality

"We have team members constantly moving on and off projects," said Thomas. "We are able to ensure that these changes are seamless because of two things: a philosophy of embracing change and a daily practice of thorough documentation and overcommunication."

It starts with every team member having a mindset that welcomes new ideas, new people, new direction, and a basic trust that changes are what's best for the project, followed by preparedness that is backed up with meticulous project documentation. Every discovery conversation and project launch is recorded and saved, as well as all project updates and meeting minutes. This commitment to documentation means that when new leadership or new team members come on board, everything is available. The ramp-up is quick.

But the real success factor for TEEM is the mindset of momentum, productivity, and the cultural intolerance for stalling out when changes occur.

"We work in an environment of impermanence," said Thomas. "If you have that spirit of collaboration and trust, you can weather any change that comes your way."

The experience of assembling and deploying highly productive, nimble teams all around the world has taught Thomas a few things about thriving through change. Here are the fundamental principles that guide TEEM's ability to keep its teams humming along for clients:

- **We are all human.** "At TEEM we understand that we run on human relationships. There will always be technology, but you have to know how to utilize technology to enable human connectivity — and not just to achieve team goals. Get to know your teammates as people, what makes them tick, how they process information, and what they enjoy outside of work. We get together for happy hours, learning boot camps, and lunches to engage with people on a personal level."

- **We are all on virtual teams.** "This notion that virtual teams are somehow still a novelty or something up for debate is baffling to me. It's the way of the world today. Job mobility within organizations is near constant. We are all project people, and it's the technology that connects us."

- **Change is constant.** "Virtual team or not, there will be change on your team. You've got to be able to roll with it, embrace the change, lean in to the new direction, and quickly reassemble your mindset to move forward. We don't have the luxury of dragging our feet. This is the gig economy, and you'll be left behind if you can't adapt quickly."

- **No one is an island.** "High-performing teams are no place for someone who needs to go off and work alone in a silo. Yes, you are allowed to have focused time to do creative and specialized individual work, but you are still part of a team. Your individual contributions support the overall goal. You must have a collaborative mindset, you must be able to communicate with your teammates, and you have to be open to feedback and that includes criticism. Working in isolation doesn't work."

5

Best Practices in Managing Your Virtual Team

IN THIS PART . . .

Explore ideas for getting to know each of your team members personally so you can build strong levels of trust and open communication.

Understand the importance of maintaining health and balance on a virtual team and how to lead the way.

Create a passionate team of virtual employees that love their work and your company.

Build clear processes to manage and track workflow to help your team efficiently achieve its goals.

Chapter **18**

Leading by Example

You may be leading remotely, but your employees pay attention to what you do and how you lead every single day. You're the role model who sets the tone for how the team will handle conflict, build relationships, and support one another. As a leader, if you don't walk the talk, you can be sure that you won't have a high performing, cohesive team. Why would your team trust you if you say one thing, but you do something different?

In this chapter, I focus on how you can lead by example and set the stage for a connected team culture that is healthy and productive. As you lead, consider your legacy and the impact you want to leave behind.

Building a Connection Culture

Building meaningful relationships starts with you. When remote employees join your team, what you do in the first 48 hours to welcome them to the group sets the standard for how the rest of the team will connect. Valuing the unique skills, abilities, and backgrounds of all your team members helps them feel appreciated and cared for. Openly encouraging dialogue, debate, and feedback provides the opportunity for contribution. All of these examples can help you to build a culture of connection and create a team of high performing, happy remote workers.

The following sections help you understand what you need to do to step up as a virtual leader and how you can be an inspiration to your team.

Being a leader your team wants to follow

Chances are, you've had both good bosses and bad bosses, and you can probably easily explain the differences in approach, credibility, and style. I encourage you to make the decision to be a leader that people choose to follow. Here are a few tips to help you:

>> **Don't ask anyone to do anything that you wouldn't do yourself.** Don't reinforce common hierarchy standards. If you want the team to believe that you have their backs and aren't above any type of work, prove it by stepping in when needed.

>> **Lead in alignment with a strong sense of purpose and values.** Make sure your team knows what you stand for.

>> **Be vulnerable and courageous.** It's okay to acknowledge failure and show your team that learning from mistakes is an opportunity to grow.

>> **Share information with your virtual team early and often.** When you have new information, share it. Be as transparent as possible.

>> **Create space for innovative solutions to be considered.** Be open to trying something that hasn't been done before. Give people license to present new ways of doing things. Encourage creative thinking by using brainstorming in meetings.

>> **Be a skillful listener.** Practice effective listening. Acknowledge what is being said by repeating back in your own words what you believe was the meaning behind the message.

>> **Practice self-care.** Role model healthy behaviors working from home. Exercise, don't text or email after 6 p.m., and check out when you take vacation.

Getting to know your team members

The challenge for the virtual leader is to transcend the boundaries of space and develop a supportive, collaborative connection with your team. Many of the best ways to establish a personal connection are also fun and sometimes even a little silly. I share some of my favorite connection activities in this section. Check out

Chapter 12 for why building trust and connection with your team members is essential.

Remember that humor and laughter put people at ease and help you to open up, so don't brush these ideas aside immediately. Instead, figure out which ones you can try with your own team over the next few weeks:

>> **My Window:** Ask team members to take a picture of what's outside their window and upload it ahead of your virtual meeting. Team members share a story about what's outside their window.

>> **Highs and Lows:** Have team members share a high and low from their past week.

>> **Table Topics:** Invest in a card deck of table topics and ask questions where people share their insights and opinions on different topics.

>> **Two Truths and a Lie:** Use this activity to get people to share three things that the team wouldn't know about them. Two of the facts are true and one is a lie. Your team members have to guess the lie. This activity always leads to some amazing discoveries about your team members. Here are the three that I share:

- I had dinner with President Obama at the White House.

- I was a cheerleader on stage with the Beach Boys.

- I was a regional organist champion.

Any guesses which one of my facts is a lie? (Unfortunately, I've never had the opportunity to have dinner with any president at the White House — yet!)

>> **Our Global Team Map:** Have a map of the world and a virtual pin in each location you have an employee. Ask your team members to share something unique about their country, city, or hometown.

>> **A Day in the Life:** If your team is coming together for the first time, have your team members put together a collage about their life that includes their family, hobbies, pets, favorite movies, books, and so on.

>> **Dine Together:** This is another great idea to get to know more about someone's heritage or ethnicity. Have each team member share a favorite family dinner recipe. Once a quarter, send a grocery list and gift card to each team member to buy the ingredients and cook the recipe. Have a virtual dinner together while your team member shares information and interesting facts about her family recipe.

Reaching out and building rapport

A key reason to take the time to connect with your virtual team members is to build rapport. Building a sense of camaraderie on your virtual team or increasing accountability and engagement is impossible if you don't have a plan for reaching out and staying connected.

Effective virtual team leaders create time for relationship management and rapport building into their schedule. They put a conscious effort in each day to build more effective relationships. If you want to know how you're doing, rate yourself on how well can you answer these questions:

>> How effectively are your team members meeting expected results and performance measures?

>> What performance will be needed from them in three to six months given their role and where the business is headed? Are they prepared?

>> What are their aspirations at work this year and in the future?

>> What makes their work (and their objectives) meaningful and satisfying to them?

>> Why are they here? What motivates them? What stresses them?

>> How do they like to be recognized, acknowledged, and rewarded for a job well done?

>> What limits them from delivering their best? What are their derailers?

>> What support, tools, resources, skills, or empowerment do they need from you as their manager to be more effective?

In my virtual leadership training programs, I encourage clients to adopt a reach-out strategy with their team to keep their finger on the pulse of what's happening with each team member and make sure they're getting the support and feedback they need to achieve their very best. I don't recommend using a rigid schedule, but rather I recommend reaching out as needed in 10-, 20-, or 30-minute sessions. Table 18-1 shows my reach-out recommendations.

TABLE 18-1   **Reach-Out Recommendations**

Reach-Out Timing	Purpose	How Often	Questions
30 minutes	Talent development/ career advancement discussion. This reach-out needs an analysis conversation with a *future focus*.	Quarterly	Where are you? Where would you like to be?
			What do you love to do? When are you in the zone? How does this fit with our strategy?
			What is needed in the department and from your role to move the needle forward? What's needed now? What's needed in the next 18 months?
			What skills or experiences would you like to develop to help you grow in this role or in the future?
			What is your plan for development and how can I support you in getting there?
			Based on our conversation, what will you start/stop/ continue doing as a result?
20 minutes	Tactical conversation with a *current focus* used to assess and support what tasks and projects they are involved with that are making progress toward their goals and development plans.	Monthly	What opportunities exist right now on this project/ task to move the needle?
			What one or two things are you focusing on to grow?
			What opportunities are available to develop the skills we discussed?
			How can I best support you?
			Based on our conversation, what will you start/stop/ continue as a result?
10 minutes or less	Feedback conversation with a *just-in-time focus* used to provide immediate feedback, coaching, and support.	Weekly	Can I sit in on this call with you?
			How about we brainstorm your approach with this customer, vendor, teammate, and so on?
			Would you like to role-play how you will handle this conversation?
			Tell me how *xyz* went? What was challenging? How did you handle it?
			What feedback do you need from me?
			Based on our conversation, what will you start/stop/ continue as a result?

Focusing On a Healthy Lifestyle

Health and wellness are an integral part of your workday whether you work in an office or your home. In fact, engaging remote teams in wellness is even more important because of the isolation of working from home and the sedentary nature of working on a computer for most of your day.

I can speak from personal experience. Some days I get so focused on work that I forget to take breaks and take care of myself. Even if I don't have time for a full workout, I always come back to my laptop refreshed and focused after a simple walk around the block with my 10-month-old Catahoula puppy, Houston.

Many remote workers report that one of the top advantages of remote work is the flexibility to find time to run to the gym or take a yoga class. I agree; however, running and yoga aren't for everyone, and wellness overall refers to a holistic approach to health that includes the full spectrum of wellness (exercise and nutrition) as well as mental health, financial health, emotional wellness, social wellness, intellectual wellness, and environmental wellness. Having a menu of options and support systems in place goes a long way toward creating inclusion amongst your team and encouraging holistic health and wellness at work.

Workplace health and wellness is a broad category, so in this section I provide some helpful information and several options for keeping your virtual team healthy in mind, body, and spirit.

Staying healthy when working virtually

Due to the digital revolution, virtual teams have some great wellness options. And because virtual teams connect everyday via various collaboration tools, intranets, or work-based social media, the stage is already set to connect your virtual team to a comprehensive menu of wellness options.

Here are a few best practices to consider:

>> **Look at what's already in place.** You may not need to re-invent the wheel. Larger organizations may already have wellness options available to you and your team. Team leaders should explore the resources available.

>> **Lead by example.** Team leaders, in addition to introducing your wellness program and encouraging full participation, should also be an active user of the program. Your participation will be a motivator for you to stay healthy as well.

>> **Be inclusive.** Unlike teams who are located in the same building, virtual teams connect people from around the United States and the world. When compiling your wellness program, be aware of time differences, ability levels,

and cultural nuances of your team so that everyone feels welcome and can participate in their own time.

>> **Share and celebrate successes.** Nothing encourages success like recognition. Your wellness program should include opportunities for teammates to post their progress — or frustration, for that matter — and receive the encouragement and support they need.

>> **Keep it fun.** Don't make it heavy handed; design the program so people *want* to participate, but don't feel pressured to do so. Have a low barrier for trial. Make it easy — and fun — to get involved.

Starting your team wellness

Looking for some ideas for your health and wellness program? Here are a few ideas I've collected to kick-start your brainstorming:

>> **Host a virtual team retreat.** If you're fortunate enough to have the opportunity to get together face-to-face, include an active activity on the agenda. Bring in a yoga instructor, go for a team hike, bring in a stress reduction expert. You get the idea.

>> **Create a healthy workspace.** Gather a series of guidelines and helpful tips for creating a safe and productive workspace at home. Include guidance on choosing an ergonomic desk and chair, finding good lighting, maintaining an organized, clutter-free space, reducing eye strain from too much screen time, and so on.

>> **Set up a one-stop wellness shop.** Create a wellness webpage on your intranet or social media that includes a series of helpful links and resources. Include videos for meditation, yoga, stretching, and stress reduction, and a wellness message board where team members can post their own content.

>> **Start a virtual team fitness challenge.** Team goals can be a great motivator. Get the team together to run or bike (virtually, of course) and teammates log miles on their own. Or create a training plan for an actual team event, like a 5K, a triathlon relay race, or an adventure race. Create roles for every team member, athletes, fundraisers, and logistics support team, and then meet up in the designated city for the event. Accomplishing a team goal that uses different muscles other than your brain is an extraordinary motivator.

>> **Get cookin'.** Compile a healthy recipe cookbook full of teammates' favorites, cook, and then share a meal together for a virtual lunch or dinner once a month.

>> **Create healthy reminders.** Use an app or create calendar reminders throughout the day prompting the team to do healthy things like stretching at your desk, doing 10 push-ups, practicing a gratitude break, doing a few jumping jacks, drinking a glass of water, and so on.

>> **Manage money wisely.** Research and post TED Talks on financial planning, preparing for retirement, saving for college, and prepping taxes, which is especially valuable for independent contractors.

Maintaining boundaries

For many people, the idea of working from home sounds heavenly. No commute, no cubicle, no annoying coworkers, no more expensive dry cleaning, no more office politics — the list goes on.

To others, banishment from the office doesn't sound ideal. The concern of social isolation, boredom, career limitations, and fear that they won't be productive working on their own.

TIP

When you work from home, it's your responsibility to set up your space, your schedule, and your boundaries to create a healthy work–life balance. Here is a great list of best practices to help you and your team have healthy boundaries:

>> **Have a dedicated workspace.** Create your space and make it work for you. Don't try to reproduce a corporate office. Make it your own by filling it with things that make you happy (family pictures, diplomas, awards), safe (ergonomic desk and chair), and productive (good lighting, efficient filing system, stable internet connection). Don't bring your work into the rest of the house and try to never bring it into the bedroom.

>> **Set hours.** Working on a virtual team is all about flexibility, but to maintain boundaries and to be transparent with your colleagues, you must establish set working hours. You can (and should) still block time for picking up kids from school or taking your favorite spin class at the gym, but the consistency of set hours can ground you.

>> **Schedule lunch and breaks.** Just like you would in an office, you need to eat and take breaks. Make sure you book them throughout your day.

>> **Get dressed.** I know, I know. Working in your PJs and sweats is tempting, but you need to maintain some professionalism. That doesn't mean you have to put on a power suit and a full face of makeup, but no one needs to see your bed head on video calls, so take a shower and make yourself presentable. More than likely, you'll also feel productive.

>> **Go walking . . . outside preferably.** Get some real-world time every day, even if it's just to stand out on your porch for 15 minutes. Walk, get some sun, smell the fresh air. There's no better way to quickly get some perspective and clear your head.

>> **Set clear boundaries with nonwork friends.** Just because you don't work in an office doesn't mean you're available for unannounced visits from friends. A quick reminder usually does the trick.

>> **Don't do chores.** Setting parameters is key. If you've scheduled an hour in your day to run personal errands, that's fine. You just don't want to get in the habit of haphazardly jumping back and forth between work projects and home projects. You won't do either one well.

>> **Drink water.** In the absence of an office watering hole, keep a large water bottle on your desk and sip it throughout the day.

>> **Stop working when the workday is done.** Although being connected with your virtual team is important, it's equally important to shut off when the workday ends. If you're available all hours of the day, people will expect you at all hours; your work-life balance will be nonexistent.

Discovering Your Legacy

Your *legacy* represents your body of work and the culmination of all your life lessons, leading, experiences, wins, losses, and impacts. Unfortunately, most leaders don't think much about leaving a legacy and are quickly forgotten when they leave a team or company. Some leaders leave a negative legacy and impact the team's morale or the company's culture for months and even years after they're gone. Still, a few noble leaders rise to the top, creating powerful legacies that live on. These leaders make an indelible mark on culture, process, relationships, and even the future of the company. *Remember:* Legacies live on through people and not financial results.

Today's world needs more legacy leaders to ensure a sustainable, just world. Consider what you want to be known for and how you can lead today with the future in mind. What decisions and actions can you take in each moment that will leave everything you impact better off than how you found it? These sections help you figure out what you want your legacy to be and how to start creating it.

Figuring out your legacy

How you're remembered is a deep, personal thought to ponder, and I may be asking you to consider something unfamiliar when talking about your legacy. Thinking about what you want to be known for can be both exhilarating and daunting.

Here are a few questions that I use with my coaching clients when helping them to consider their legacy:

>> Are you clear on your personal values and what you stand for? Do you lead from this place everyday so that others are clear on your values too?

>> What do people experience with you? What are they left with after spending time with you?

>> What do you want others to say about you when you're gone?

>> How do you define ultimate success, other than financial?

>> If I were to ask 20 people you worked with over the past ten years to describe your three greatest strengths, what would they say?

>> Do you actively seek out feedback and mentoring to guide you in life and work?

>> Based on your story so far, what do you want to change or do different over the next ten years? What behaviors do you need to focus on?

Take time to think about this topic. More than likely you'll begin to think about them during the most trying moments of your career, because they're the ones that define you the most. Journal on these questions without judgment to see where the answers take you.

Leading authentically: The how-to

Leaving a legacy is about being authentically you in every interaction Your legacy is influenced by the collective moments of triumph and losses over your career and how you treated people along the way. Here are my top four tips on how to lead authentically:

>> **Practice a learning mindset.** You don't know all the answers, and you can always discover more from everyone around you. Admit mistakes. Ask for help.

>> **Lead from the heart.** Practice humility and empathy. Recognize that leadership is a gift you've been given and practice gratitude every day. Create a daily list of five things that you're grateful for in a journal. Find out how your team likes to be shown gratitude. Some people prefer a one-on-one thank you whereas others enjoy the public recognition. Whatever you do, make your gratitude genuine and heartfelt.

>> **Put people first.** Don't always make leading about results. Gauge what your team members need from you and meet them where they are. Connect with and appreciate your team before getting straight down to business.

>> **Be a role model.** Demonstrate the behaviors you want to see in others.

member

» **Building a passionate team**

» **Applying positive psychology principles to everyday tasks**

» **Having a pulse on how your virtual team members feel about their work**

Chapter **19**

Understanding What Drives Motivation

After working with companies for close to 20 years to increase team member engagement, I've seen firsthand the benefits of helping team members and organizations create environments where they can both give their best each day and where both parties are committed to the organization's goals, values, and success, while ensuring a sense of personal well-being.

Motivation is the desire to take action and drive forward even in the face of adversity. It's a crucial factor in setting and achieving goals. However, motivation is complex because it differs for every person. What motivates one team member may not work for another. To be sure, true desire and motivation comes from within. However, leaders can create a working environment that encourages intrinsic motivation and helps to drive teams to achieve their best.

This chapter helps you understand the difference between an engaged team member and a passionate one and then examines how to use a tool called the Passion Pyramid to drive motivation. I discuss principles of positive psychology and how to use recognition effectively. I also explain the importance of being in the know regarding how your team members are feeling about their work. You can get ideas on what you can do to immediately start building a more motivational environment where your team members flourish and are happy.

Differentiating between Engaged and Passionate Team Members

The idea of team member passion is extremely compelling. Does passion transcend the idea of engagement? Is one more important than the other? In my experience, passion doesn't diminish the idea of engagement, but rather elevates it. To have a clearer understanding of what motivates team members, you need to be clear about one distinction:

>> *Engaged team members* are conscientious about their work, do everything that is expected of them, and comply with policies and procedures to the letter.

>> *Passionate team members* don't just stick to the rulebook, they do whatever it takes to help their team achieve success and delight your customers. These emotionally committed team members are passionate about their work and the organization they work for. They love challenges, they aren't afraid to take risks, they're extremely agile, and they're constantly driven to develop new professional skills.

REMEMBER

Based on these descriptions, team member engagement is just the starting point, and passionate team members take your organization to another level.

But regardless if it's engagement or passion, the research shows that much work is needed. A recent Gallup survey found that just 30 percent of the U.S. workforce is "inspired" by work. In addition, a new study by Deloitte Consulting's Center for the Edge indicates that even fewer — only 11 percent of the workforce — is truly passionate team members. This is costing companies more than $363 billion every year, and the statistics haven't changed since 2013. Here's why:

>> Team members consistently are asked to put on superhuman capes and do the jobs of three people, whether because of superfast company growth or a team member's departure, where finding a replacement is difficult.

>> Managers aren't adequately removing or addressing obstacles that can help team members be successful in their roles, including

- Lack of resources or the right resources

- Lack of training or skill building on a new product or procedure

- Lack of time to do the task successfully

- Lack of prioritization and making everything important

>> Team leaders and managers don't know how to lead in a way that improves engagement and they're getting little to no support and coaching on how to become a leader that others will follow.

As a result, what's left is a gargantuan pool of untapped motivation and a massive opportunity that could literally change the landscape of today's workplace. But the question is are passionate team members born or made? It's really a combination of both. You can seek out and hire team members who exhibit passionate behaviors. But more importantly, as a leader you can create an environment that encourages passion and ignites a fire within your team.

Creating a Passionate Team

Because passionate team members are focused, engaged, and committed and because they'll do whatever it takes to delight your customers, they have an emotional connection and conviction for their work and also a devotion to your company. Make no mistake about it, passionate team members will truly elevate your company.

Understandably, passion doesn't just happen for no reason. Rather, it happens when team members are doing work and tasks that they find both emotionally satisfying and worthwhile or meaningful. And that's the foundation of a model I use as an affiliate of the Intégro Leadership Institute (ILI), called The Passion Pyramid. The Passion Pyramid (see Figure 19-1) was created by ILI founder Keith E. Ayers and identifies five human needs that ignite passion and more importantly the leadership skills to create the environment to satisfy each need. These sections explain the Passion Pyramid in greater detail and offer some examples for each need. Consider where you need to focus on creating more passion with your virtual team and use this simple road map and strategies to get you there.

The need to be respected

Everyone deserves to be treated with dignity and respect. In fact, treating others with dignity and respect is a baseline requirement of a healthy work environment. Imagine trying to be motivated to do your job while dodging daily shouting, insults, and intimidating and sarcastic comments? Respect at work looks like this: showing consideration for others in words, tone of voice, and body language; listening without interruption; and treating people the same regardless of race, religion, gender, sexual orientation, age, gender identity, or country of origin. Respect is especially important on virtual teams where you're connected to coworkers via screens and much of your communication is written, so choose your words, punctuation, and emoji carefully.

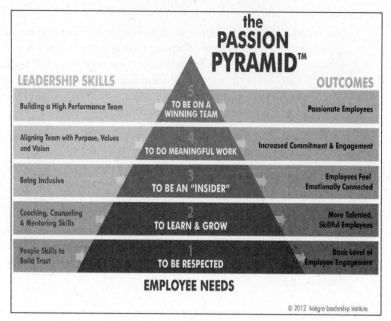

FIGURE 19-1:
The Passion
Pyramid.

Printed with permission from the Intégro Leadership Institute

WARNING

Humans need to be respected as much as they need oxygen. Yet many leaders unintentionally treat their team members with disrespect by not listening, not involving them, or dismissing their personal values. Be sure to create time and space to allow team members to be heard and find out what is personally important to them.

Here are additional tips to let your team members know you respect them:

>> Ask for their advice in areas where they are an expert.

>> Validate why their skill set is important.

>> Share what you know.

>> Support them in achieving balance and a healthy lifestyle.

>> Appreciate the difference in others.

>> Invite different viewpoints and healthy debate.

The need to learn and grow

This need of learning and growing, which has its roots in the classroom, is as natural as it is for a baby to get up and walk. Remember the feeling you had the first time you forgot about taking notes and simply enjoyed learning something new. You were like a sponge, taking in as much new data as you could. You asked deeper level questions, and there was no reward beyond the knowing. Learning and growth are intrinsic motivators. Having a growth mindset is the idea that your intelligence and personal traits, skills, and character are all abilities that can be cultivated through your own efforts, especially by hard work, a love of learning, and sheer determination.

Enthusiasm for learning is the primary motivating force. Human beings are innately curious and want to learn. As a manager, if you're skillful at coaching, mentoring, and counseling, you can satisfy your team members' thirst for knowledge.

Here are some additional tips for this need:

>> Know your team members' career aspirations and work with them to develop a plan to achieve them.

>> Collaborate with your team members to identify their greatest learning opportunities. Partner them with training resources or mentors to help them grow.

>> Secure the budget each year to develop your team members.

The need to be an insider

The concept of being an insider is powerfully seductive. It says you have the respect of your colleagues and leaders, but more so you are highly valued and admired. It says your achievements at work have gotten you noticed and made you *relevant*. You're invited to the inner circle. You're considered a thought leader. People seek your counsel about strategy and tough decisions, and you're often privy to information before the larger organization. And perhaps most importantly, you had to *earn* this insider position through your performance. If you want your remote team members to be devoted to your company, include and involve them as much as possible in decision-making, goal setting, and change.

Other tips include:

>> Discuss how each role has an impact on the entire team's success.

>> Delegate decisions to the team as often as possible.

>> Keep your team in the know anytime you receive new information or insight from the company.

The need to do meaningful work

A leader's job is to create a motivating environment where the work of every team member is meaningful. People work for more than a paycheck. Consider the story of the two bricklayers — one of them saw his job as stacking bricks, the other saw his mission as building a magnificent cathedral. Same job, different worldview. The morale is that you can find meaning in any job.

Many factors can make work meaningful: recognition, goals that are achievable, a clear path to success, the ability to master new skills and improve, and company values aligned with personal values. Here are some additional tips to helping the work be meaningful to your team:

>> Align team goals to personal aspirations.

>> Let people know how they make a difference.

>> Discuss the meaning and purpose behind their work as often as possible.

>> Encourage team members to share the personal satisfaction and fulfillment they get from doing their work.

>> Celebrate and recognize personal milestones and impactful accomplishments.

The need to be on a winning team

A cohesive team that is built on trust and strong relationships ignites passion and exceeds expectations. Your company and every company in the world wants team members to love what they do and more importantly to love the team and company they work for. Check out Chapter 12 for a variety of ways you can build trust and rapport on your team. Here are a few ideas to create a winning team:

>> Clarify each team member's contribution and interconnectivity to the team goal.

>> Do virtual team huddles before any major event, like a project launch, a presentation, or a conference.

>> Celebrate successes with post-project parties, either in person or virtually. Recognize all stars and MVPs. Create awards to ensure that all team members are recognized for their contributions.

BUILDING A PASSIONATE WORK CULTURE HOLISTICALLY

With 100 percent of its workforce remote, Zapier has honed several cultural customs that focus on creating an environment where people flourish and where nurturing team member passion is just part of the job. I talked with Jenny Bloom, CFO of Zapier, to find out how the company has created a culture of engaging, happy remote team members.

After joining Zapier two years ago in her first-time role as a virtual leader, Bloom said that it has made her a better manager. She quickly realized that by excelling at extreme clarity when communicating expectations and goals (in both verbal and written form) and creating various connection moments, Zapier team members stay engaged and build strong personal relationships with one another even though the team is all remote.

In addition to being more intentional about getting to know each team member, Bloom also focuses on what she calls "human writing" and communicates with her team taking the time to be polite, thoughtful, and fun, occasionally using emoji to highlight the emotion associated with the content.

Building a connected virtual work culture is a focus at Zapier, and the company is leading the way in demonstrating what works as it continues to grow at a rapid pace with approximately 160 current team members. Here are examples on how Zapier builds a connected culture:

- Onboarding new team members happens in person where the company flies the team members to meet with the founders and their manager.

- Teams use Zoom or other collaborative software to meet over video once a week.

- The entire company gets together twice a year for a retreat for one week where the focus for several days is on *hack-a-thons* (a sprint-like event for programmers, developers, designers, project managers, and others to collaborate intensively on chosen projects). The team members spend a few days with their own team getting to know one another, working on team strategy, and solving team problems. They spend another fun day with the whole company, taking in a local attraction.

- Team members are randomly paired up weekly with a "donut buddy" who they establish a personal connection and frequently share a virtual breakfast or a donut. Bloom was recently paired up with a colleague in India.

- All-hands meeting happens every Thursday and one person in the company gives a presentation.

- The Friday update happens on the internal blog, and all employees can go there to find out important information to prepare for the following week.

(continued)

(continued)

- Team members pay attention to when others in the company are living the Zapier values (Default to Action, Default to Transparency, Grow Through Feedback, Empathy, No Ego, Don't be a Robot, Build the Robot), and provide recognition as an opportunity to call out when someone "defaults to action" – language used by Zapier to encourage growth through feedback.

- Leaders pay attention to work-life balance issues and check in when they believe a team member isn't shutting work off.

- Leaders are asked to "default to transparency" where they live out the mantra that everything you do, everyone needs to see.

Zapier is a compelling example of a fully remote company that gets it. It understands that without passion and engagement, failure is inevitable. Zapier commits to building passionate teams and enhancing team member motivation every day.

Using Positive Psychology to Create a Motivational Team Environment

The field of *positive psychology* looks at what enables people to flourish and achieve inner happiness, making life worth living. Martin Seligman, American psychologist and founder of positive psychology, points to five key principles that lead to well-being, including positive emotion, engagement, relationships, meaning and purpose, and accomplishment.

These principles draws on some of what is already known regarding human desires and needs, and new research continues to confirm that when people have levels of autonomy over aspects of their work, have the opportunity to make daily progress toward important goals, and believe they're contributing to the greater good, people will accomplish more and live richer lives.

Understanding what really motivates people

Natural motivation takes place when human desires are fulfilled. This comes from the famous hierarchy of needs, created by American psychologist Abraham Maslow in 1943. The theory states that people are motivated to achieve certain needs and that some needs take precedence over others. People's most basic need is for physical survival (food, shelter, safety), which is the first thing that motivates behavior. After that level is fulfilled, the next level is psychological needs (love, esteem, and belongingness) followed by self-fulfillment needs (self-actualization and achieving one's full potential). I simplify this hierarchy in my own words in Figure 19-2.

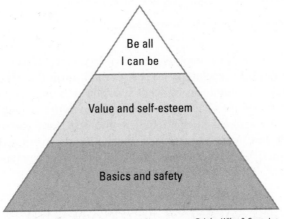

FIGURE 19-2:
Human needs
and desires.

After the basic needs are met of having a roof over your head, being able to put food on your table, and ensuring safety, you look to fulfill higher level needs of belonging, feeling valued, and realizing accomplishments. However, it's difficult, if not impossible, for people to recognize their full potential when they don't feel valued by their team members or never receive any validation that what they're doing matters. And most people look to others for this type of feedback and recognition. Consider how often you and your team:

>> Openly provide recognition and gratitude to one another

>> Engage in one-on-one meetings where team members provide feedback on what's working and what they need

>> Practice inclusion activities in your virtual meeting

>> Discuss regular progress toward important and exciting goals

As soon as these needs are met, then and only then will you notice that people will bring their best selves to the party. When I look at the latest research on what motivates people, a few key factors stand out. People are motivated when they:

>> Understand the purpose behind their work and why their team and role exists

>> Have clarity about what they're responsible for and why

>> Have a level of autonomy over their work and the ability to choose how, when, and for how long they do their work

>> Make regular and consistent progress on work that they care about

>> Get the necessary support and resources to achieve their goals including emotional support

>> Become experts at something that interests them

>> Receive encouragement and recognition

REMEMBER

In this book the tools I recommend are focused on creating an environment where people can do their absolute best. That doesn't mean that you only ever discuss positive things or only focus on what's working. Commit to memory that transparent and honest feedback is necessary for growth. As long as you've done a decent job at creating a motivational environment, your corrective feedback will be heartfelt and in the spirit of continuous improvement. Team members will welcome and desire your feedback and easily spot that you have their best interests at heart.

Using recognition as a powerful motivational technique

Reward and recognition programs are an essential component of every successful department, team, and organization. Numerous studies indicate that praise, recognition, and rewards can motivate team members to put forth their best efforts and perform at higher levels. Recognition can also improve retention and team member satisfaction, which can result in less turnover, reduced team member stress, and burnout.

Simple praise and recognition such as "Thank you", "I appreciate all you do", or "Great job" can many times motivate people more than money. Meaningful, thoughtful rewards and recognition can have a valuable impact on both individuals and the team and don't have to bust the budget. The good news is that if you get creative, you can come up with recognition ideas that don't cost a dime and can have a lasting positive impact on team members for months.

Perhaps the greatest mistake that leaders make when recognizing and rewarding team members is thinking that money is the most important factor. Many other factors are as important, or more important, than money and most likely, what matters to you is closely aligned with what your team members want. Answer the following questions to get an idea of how your team members want to be recognized and rewarded:

>> Think of a job that you loved, what did you love about it and why did you stay in that job?

>> Think of a job that you didn't enjoy, what was missing? What did you want that wasn't offered?

>> Picture your favorite manager during your career. How did that person reward you or recognize your accomplishments?

>> What did that outstanding manager say to you to recognize your efforts and how did she say it?

This exercise is great for zeroing in on what motivates your individual team members. Ask these questions, be patient, and keep listening. Always remember that even if you miss the mark slightly, as long as the appreciation and recognition you express is heartfelt and sincere, you're on the right track. Here are some guidelines to help you.

Providing worthwhile recognition

Recognizing team members is something that doesn't happen often enough. Out of the thousands of team members I've worked with, 80 percent or more say they only hear from their manager when things go wrong. I, for one, would like to change that. Keep in mind that how you give recognition is as important as the recognition itself. Here are six guidelines for giving effective recognition to your team members:

>> **Timely:** Make sure that recognition happens as close to the event or behavior as possible. When you hear a good word about a team member from a customer or colleague, make sure you thank him for his good work as soon as possible. Waiting too long to recognize someone loses all of its value and motivational effect.

>> **Specific:** Explain to a team member why you're recognizing him by giving detailed examples of his behavior. For example, you could say, "John, I want to let you know that three customers have personally commented to me about your pleasant and professional manner on the phone. I want to thank you for providing outstanding service to our customers and helping make this department stand out." This helps the team member understand exactly what behavior or action deserved recognition and what should be continued.

>> **Genuine:** Be sincere in your praise or recognition for a team member. When you're happy or excited with someone's performance, show it with your body language, actions, and words. Smile, shake his hands, and be genuinely excited for him. If at all possible, always give recognition face-to-face because doing so makes the recognition more personal and he can clearly see your reaction. Remember, if someone on your team is doing a great job, it will have a reflection on the rest of the team and the entire organization.

>> **Equivalent:** If you're offering a team member a reward for reaching a milestone or making an extra effort, make sure that it matches the level of the achievement or performance goal. For example, reward a team member who completes a two-year project in a more substantial way than someone who filled in for a sick team member at the last minute. The more important the achievement, the larger the recognition or reward should be.

>> **Meaningful:** Find out what is important to team members, including what hobbies they enjoy so that you can recognize them in a way that is special and meaningful to them. For example, some team members may want personal recognition done in private, some may enjoy gifts or other tangible items, whereas others may view advanced training for their career development rewarding.

>> **Motivational:** Make sure that team members are feeling motivated by your recognition and reward efforts. One way to ensure that recognition is going to motivate team members is to involve the team in determining the types of recognition and rewards offered. If team members aren't excited when they receive a reward and good performance doesn't continue, then it may be time to rethink the program and come up with some new ideas.

Recognizing team members

Here are some recommendations for recognizing your virtual team members when they deserve it:

>> **At the completion of a successful project, schedule a debrief and recognition call.** The purpose of the call is for all team members to review specific actions and behaviors that each team member noticed that contributed to the team's success.

>> **Detail the recognition for the team or individual in a company newsletter.** Be sure to include the team's or individual's picture.

>> **Ask an executive to join a monthly videoconference.** Kick off the meeting talking about the specifics of how the entire team or individuals demonstrated important company and team values. Be sure to prep the executive ahead of time so he knows the whole story.

>> **Send the team member a link to purchase company swag or email it to him in time for your next virtual meeting.** Ask him to wait to open it until you're on the call.

>> **Invite the team to a virtual happy hour.** This is a fun after-work, social event. As team members enjoy their favorite cocktail on the videoconference, you share the good news.

- » **Gamify it.** Create a bingo board of your values, and when team members get recognized for a value, they mark off the board. When they get bingo, they get points to use online to purchase products they love.

- » **Send a handwritten thank you.** This old-school recognition is still one of the best. Put pen to paper and send a handwritten note to whomever deserves it.

Recognizing peers one-on-one

Although recognizing a team member one-on-one is appreciated, sometimes a team member goes above and beyond and you want to do something more publicly. Consider recognizing a team member in front of others in a fun way to make for an unforgettable experience. Better yet, recognize the team member to others when he isn't around and let your words of praise get back to him through the grapevine.

Peer-to-peer recognition is also a powerful motivational tool. Here are a few ideas you can use to encourage team members to recognize one another:

- » **Encourage team members to recognize outstanding effort as part of your weekly staff meetings.** Focus on examples where someone has gone above and beyond what was expected. As the team leader, you can kick it off and model the recognition you want to encourage going forward.

- » **Recognize outstanding skill or expertise by allowing a team member to mentor another.** Everyone has strengths and areas of expertise. Create some cross-team learning by pairing up mentors with interested mentees on topics of interest or opportunities for skill building.

- » **Start a traveling trophy award.** You can send this original award via UPS after someone develops a creative idea or a process improvement.

- » **Develop an electronic "Pay it Forward" card.** Each month a team member sends it to another team member who has made a difference.

- » **Play work bingo together online.** The team gets to fill in a square every time a team member hits a deliverable. As soon as the team gets bingo, they get to share in a reward.

Chapter **20**

Managing Workflow and Execution

Managing workflow on projects with your virtual team requires a different approach then when your team is located in the same office. How you communicate, what online collaboration tools you use, and how you hold people accountable is modified when you have people located all over the world.

In this chapter I share with you how to effectively set up the workflow process on a project, how to choose the right tools to track and manage your project, and how to delegate effectively to team members get the work done. I also discuss the importance of sharing progress and obstacles with other teams and stakeholders that are impacted by your work.

Starting Off on the Right Foot

For every new project hold a virtual kickoff session. Doing so gives the team a chance to bond and builds excitement and connection around the project. If you thoughtfully plan and execute the kickoff session with clear goals and outcomes, you set up your team and the project for success.

You may cover the following in your kickoff session:

>> Clarify project goals, deadlines, and success measures.

>> Talk about the project's purpose and impact and provide an opportunity for team members to share thoughts and feelings about the project.

>> Agree on how decisions are made and the authority levels for decisions.

>> Discuss how the team will address conflict or project issues and who needs to be involved.

>> Define clear accountability and responsibility for the various aspects of the project.

>> Confirm communication guidelines and discuss expectations on how to use tracking tools.

>> Agree on how often the team will meet to discuss progress and follow-up.

>> Review behavioral norms.

REMEMBER

As the team leader, consider yourself a champion of execution. Your role is to make sure that your team members have the resources they need to hit their goals on every project, which may include making sure they has enough time to finish the project and that you've also defined effective processes and procedures, clear communication guidelines, and responsibilities. You have tremendous influence over how work gets executed based on how you set up expectations, team culture, and support from the start.

Clarifying How Work Flows through the Team

Micromanagement doesn't work on a virtual team, so if you operate as a micro-manager, your ship will sink before you ever leave the harbor. To avoid it, invest time up front, gathering as much information on project deliverables and objectives so that you can confidently pass all this relevant, practical information along to the team. Clarify top priorities that your team is responsible for over the next 90 days and consider who on the team has the skill and bandwidth to assign tasks and ensure they're done. Then, let go and allow team members to self-direct their work.

I find it helpful to visually depict the workflow process, including who's involved and who's responsible in a collaborative team meeting. Using a flowchart or online workflow map tool like Creately (https://creately.com/) can quickly clear up any confusion or misunderstandings of what's required and who's involved.

TIP

When assigning tasks to global team members, take into account availability, time zones, vacation time, and holidays. Using global shared calendars are an absolute must on a virtual team. These calendars inform all team members when deliverables and handoffs are due to avoid frustration or conflict because of a time delay or communication gap in workflow.

Team meetings are the foundation of virtual teams. They're how the team connects, makes decisions and gets work done. In these sections I talk about how to set the ground rules for team meetings.

Deciding on meeting formats to stay up-to-date

Agreeing on regular status update meetings and progress reporting is the key way that virtual teams provide maximum visibility and accountability on a project. Make sure that your team comes to an agreement to a plan for progress updates that includes the following:

>> What tool to use to provide updates or keep track of progress

>> What to share and how much detail to share

>> How to track deliverables completed, time spent, and so on

>> How frequently to provide updates

>> How to communicate updates and in what format

>> How to provide feedback to each other on progress and what team members need from one another

WARNING

Keep in mind that having the progress update meetings live every week may difficult, if not impossible, with a global team, which is why a more formal update process is needed. You could have Monday morning email updates that include each team member's focus for the week or forecast deliverables or share statuses using Slack. Some teams may opt to use a shared internal dashboard, blog, or discussion forum that the team updates daily or weekly so that anyone can check progress at any time and provide feedback. Bear in mind, these types of asynchronous methods usually need to be monitored and facilitated.

As a team, be sure to agree on when live virtual meetings are necessary to discuss workflow, progress, or execution. I recommend that certainly the team comes together to kick off a project, commemorate a major milestone, and celebrate the completion of a project. Bringing the team together is important when you notice that communication is going off the rails, deadlines are being missed, or you need to discuss a complex issue.

Establishing communication guidelines

In terms of managing workflow, set clear guidelines of how the team will communicate, update, and share progress from the kickoff. I recommend discussing the following:

>> How the team refers to the project, the client, the issue, and so on

>> How to name project documents

>> How to maintain email threads on one topic and why doing so is important

>> When to plan necessary meetings or calls (certain time when everyone is available)

>> What tools and apps the team will use to communicate and what's appropriate when

For more in depth ideas and information about adopting best practices of communication, read Chapter 13.

Choosing the right collaborative tracking tools for your team

Deciding on the right tools up front will make or break your ability to execute. Because you can't be working together in the same room, your online tools need to keep your team connected, updated, and on track.

Tracking tools that you use should enable you to track time spent on certain task; manage tasks, assignments, and deliverables; provide a document repository for easy access; allow for collaborative feedback and editing; and map out the workflow and responsibilities on the team. For more information on tracking the progress of your virtual teams and knowing what tools work best, check out Chapter 14, which focuses on measuring virtual team and team member success, and Chapter 16 on choosing the right technology tools.

Delegating Effectively to Your Virtual Team

The secret to getting things done on a virtual team is delegation. *Delegation* is about leaders empowering their team members and inspiring trust. Delegation involves the effective assignment of tasks to other staff members while still maintaining responsibility for ultimate results. All the while, leaders are considering each team member's skill level and offering support to complete the assignment.

In these sections you discover the benefits of delegation, why it fails, and how to delegate effectively.

Eyeing the benefits to letting go

One of the most difficult challenges that leaders face is their own inability to let go and delegate tasks and projects. They mistakenly hold on to the idea that no one else can do the job as well as they can. This line of thinking ultimately becomes counterproductive, and the leader misses out on several key benefits to delegation, including the following:

>> Team members discover how to effectively complete responsibilities that you, as the leader, don't have the time to do. In the process, team members build their skill set.

>> Lower priority tasks may be more cost effective for others to complete so you can concentrate on high priority items like strategy, continuous improvement, and business development.

>> Other team members may have skills that are better than yours in certain areas and can complete the task in less time than if you did it.

>> Delegation is an important way to develop your team and improve overall morale.

Understanding why delegation fails: Leaders don't let go

Delegating is a powerful way to produce results on your virtual team and at the same time develop employee skills. Most leaders I work with believe they already delegate really well, but what I find is that they don't actually let go. I've seen delegation fail for several reasons including the following:

>> Lack of planning on the leader's part

>> Taking back the project or task because it appears easier for leaders to do it themselves

>> Concluding that they don't have time to delegate

If you often say, "There just isn't anyone I can delegate to on the team" or you have a fear that tasks won't be done correctly, on time, or under the processes that you use, then you should face the facts — you're just not that into delegating. And you're just not letting go. If you want to take advantage of the benefits of delegation and be a successful virtual team leader, you need to change your game plan.

These reasons don't outweigh the potential benefit you'll receive from effective delegation. Don't let these excuses hold you back from getting the support that you need to reduce your stress, increase your effectiveness, and improve overall team morale. Just be sure to choose the right tasks to delegate, the right people to delegate to, and the right way to delegate.

Trusting in the process

Anyone can delegate effectively if she knows how, can let go, and trust in the process. Follow this ten-step process to become a successful delegator in no time.

1. **Decide on what to delegate and what only you can do.**

   There may be things that only you can work on. However, 75 percent of the time, there are tasks you do on a daily basis that you could delegate.

2. **Communicate a clear vision of the desired end result and what success looks for the delegated task.**

3. **Select the right people for the job.**

   Analyze the skill and willingness of your team to determine who to delegate to. You may find that some people need more direction up front than others, but with your coaching they may improve their ability to carry out future delegated tasks unassisted.

4. **Delegate the whole enchilada.**

   Don't just hand out pieces of a project. People get pleasure from seeing a task to completion, and the final result will likely end up being of consistent quality if one person completes it.

5. **Explain why the task is important and what results you expect, including deadlines, progress reports, resources to use, and so on.**

6. **Check for clarity and understanding.**

   Ask your team member to describe in her own words what exactly you are asking her to take over.

7. **Be available during agreed-upon times to provide feedback and assess progress.**

   Provide support and coaching as needed.

8. **Hold people accountable to the agreed-upon results.**

9. **Give recognition for a job well done so that your staff will feel confident being delegated to in the future.**

10. **Trust in the process that you've established.**

Don't be afraid of mistakes; they're learning opportunities for the future.

Holding team members accountable for deliverables

If you take the time to set up tasks appropriately, assign them to the right people with the right skill set, and use the right level of clarity and right technology, I promise that maintaining accountability will be easy.

REMEMBER

The key is setting up the project systematically from the beginning and then providing frequent opportunities to check on the progress and giving constructive feedback to one another. Letting team members drive those accountability discussions creates stronger pressure to perform. Furthermore, people know what other team members are thinking and don't waste time and energy wondering. Accountability also establishes high standards of performance and teamwork.

You can help your team get more comfortable talking about accountability by:

>> Practicing giving both positive and corrective feedback as a team

>> Asking team members what behaviors were productive and unproductive on a recent project

>> Discussing and agreeing on what behaviors are integral to the success of your upcoming project

>> Sharing examples of appropriate and respectful ways to hold each other accountable

>> Using open collaboration tools to visibly track daily progress

Knowing How to Communicate Externally Regarding Team Progress

Cascading conversations take place in an organization downward, upward, and horizontally. These conversations ensure that the right information is getting to the right people at the right time. For each project, your virtual team members need to consider with whom to communicate and what information they need on your team's progress. You'll also want to consider what stakeholders can impact resolving problems or issues on the project, can help to improve processes or timelines on the project, or may have insight into trends or customer feedback that could effect the project.

A best practice is to establish these communication channels up front and clarify what information they need from you and what you need from them. You can invite stakeholders from each group to your kickoff meeting so they're clear on the project objectives and where they play a role. Figure 20-1 highlights all the people who may be critical to your project and will need communication from you and your team.

FIGURE 20-1: Potential stakeholders critical to team projects.

© John Wiley & Sons, Inc.

6

The Part of Tens

Chapter **21**

Ten Predictors of Virtual Team Success

Virtual teams have different needs than teams who are located in the same office. If you're not careful, the literal distance between team members can create figurative distances. From there you can expect communication breakdown, reduced productivity, disengagement, confusion, mistrust, and ultimately, failure. And when virtual teams fail, usually the virtual part gets the blame — not the lack of planning for their specific needs.

This chapter can safeguard you from virtual team failure. Through my research, I can see the issues that arise if these 10 things aren't managed effectively. Here are the top predictors of success for your virtual team. Think of it as a checklist to guarantee your virtual team success.

Having the Right Technology

Virtual teams rely heavily on technology to connect team members. Technology is essential for virtual teams, but remember that although it exists to enable team communication and collaboration, it can't replace good management.

REMEMBER

Make sure your technology choices support exactly what your team needs. Think about functionality when making your technology decisions. Consider using platforms that integrate all types of communication and include these key components: collaboration, project management, document sharing and creation, video and audio conferencing, instant messaging, scheduling/shared calendar, and social networking. Most highly effective virtual teams have tools that support these functions. Check out Chapter 16 for more discussion on technology.

Hiring the Right Team Leader

If you're the person responsible for finding the virtual team leader for your organization, make sure you do your research and hire the leader who best meets your team's needs. When searching for a team leader, remember the following:

>> They need to have strong management skills, but they also need a healthy dose of additional skills to successfully lead a virtual team, such as communication skills, collaboration skills, and the ability to establish clear roles and expectations — and then get out of the way.

>> They must trust their team and instill that culture of trust throughout the team.

>> They must be intuitive, flexible, comfortable with hands-off management, and experienced with the technology that connects the team.

>> They require strong interpersonal and team-building skills.

See Chapter 5 for more information about hiring strong team leaders.

WARNING

Not all managers are cut out for leading a team they don't see face-to-face every day. Leaders who excel at managing co-located teams may not necessarily be great leaders of virtual teams. A management style that favors a top-down, hierarchical structure, a heavy supervisory role, and a strong clock-watching philosophy isn't going to be successful in a virtual team environment.

Hiring the Right Team Members

Virtual team members also need a special skill set. In fact, a virtual team's success is based in large part on the strength of its members. Virtual team members need to have a few common characteristics, including independence, resilience, and excellent communication and organization skills. They must have self-motivation, the ability to focus, and the ability of using a variety of technology tools.

Job skills are great, but even more important are soft skills, such as problem solving, empathy, conscientiousness, and emotional intelligence. Courtesy and respect become more important when workers are remote and nonverbal communication is limited. Check out Chapter 5 for considerations when hiring virtual team members.

Establishing Clear Team Vision and Values

Your team's vision statement drives behaviors, creativity, commitment, engagement, and determination.

TIP

The best vision statements are aligned with company values, are visible and achievable, are inspirational, and define a future state. Make sure that they're clear, memorable, and ambitious, and developed by consensus. One of the important things in the vision and values in inclusion. Everyone needs to have a say and a sense of ownership. Chapter 4 and 7 discuss how you and your team can establish clear team values and a vision statement.

The vision of virtual teams is no different, but the values of virtual teams should include the following factors: accountability, trust, respect, and emotional intelligence. These values are critical to virtual team success.

Aligning Team Goals with Company Goals

One of the most important responsibilities of a leader is to show his team how to align behaviors, activities, and priorities with the company's strategic goals. These are no different for virtual team leaders. In fact, they may be even more important because the team is dispersed.

WARNING

Don't create team goals in a vacuum. Ensure they're in-line with the company's overall goals, which ensures that a team's work — big or small — is impacting the business. Aligning team goals with company goals also makes the work more meaningful and dramatically increases employee engagement. If your team members know how their work impacts the business, they care more about achieving the team's goals and improving the company's performance.

Having a Solid Team Agreement in Place

Every team needs a written working agreement, which is the first step to good team building. In addition to minimizing friction between teammates, an agreement is great for introducing new team members to the group culture. Most of all, the agreement gives all team members a template for what is expected during their day-to-day work. Chapter 11 discusses what to include in your team agreement.

REMEMBER

Creating team agreements must be an inclusive process, not dictated by upper management. Only your team truly knows what it needs. The team working agreement is a contract between all members. Treat it as a living document by revisiting it periodically and making updates as needed.

Using a Communication Strategy

I read recently that communication is the oxygen of a distributed company. I couldn't agree more. Virtual teams need solid communication strategies to survive. When team members are spread across multiple cities and countries, creating and then utilizing policies and practices to ensure connectivity across multiple communication channels is critical. Flip to Chapter 13 where I discuss how to develop and use a communication strategy.

REMEMBER

The first general rule is to give each communication method you use a designated purpose. Every team member needs to have a game plan for how to best get in touch with teammates for different situations. This clarity will help avoid wasted time, frustration, and missed connections.

Your virtual team communication strategy needs to include a variety of scheduled and unscheduled communication methods. Scheduled events like regular team video calls, one-on-one meetings with each team member and the leader, and regular milestone and project update meetings ensure that your team is managing workflow, hitting targets and goals, and getting the support it needs to be successful. With unscheduled or less structured communication methods such as live chats, instant messaging, and social networking, team members can use less formal written communication styles and can (and should!) connect to discuss nonwork topics like getting a quick answer to a question or to recap Sunday's football game. These informal communication tools keep teams connected and engaged but aren't the most effective way to track progress or manage tasks.

Agreeing on a Process for Team Workflow

Having a team workflow process is another success factor for virtual teams. It's basically the road map for how things get done on your team. You want to create an environment for people to do their best work.

Great workflows keep everyone on the same page, reduce confusion, eliminate bottlenecks, and create efficiency. Although many tools and systems are available to help, keep it simple. Project management tools can get detailed, which is often required, but fight the urge to overcomplicate things. Evaluate processes regularly and eliminate steps that are unnecessary. Check out Chapter 20 for more information on team workflow.

Using an Onboarding Strategy for New Team Members

Gone are the days when new hires are welcomed in person and introduced around the office. Virtual employee onboarding occurs through phone calls or video chat, where new hires rarely meet their team members face-to-face. Hence, that's where having your team vision, goals, agreements, communication strategy, and workflow already in place really pays off.

Those policies and practices guide your onboarding process. Don't make successful onboarding for a new virtual team building all business; include introductions, discussions about team culture, and time to get to know coworkers and their after-hours interests. For more information on onboarding strategies check out Chapter 7 and 15.

Actively Managing Executive Perceptions

Is a virtual team like the proverbial tree falling in a forest? If you can't see the team at work, is work happening? My research confirms that a productivity perception gap does exist. When team members and team leaders report that virtual team productivity is strong, executives overseeing them often don't share that same opinion.

The answer to solving the perception gap is detailed planning and communication with results and data. Virtual teams are measured in large part by metrics so you already have the milestones and progress to report. Formalize the communication process with executives to make sure they're receiving regular communications on your team's contribution.

» **Assessing if the leader is right for the job**

» **Having clarity and process and why it's important**

Chapter **22**

Ten Signs Your Organization Is Ready for Virtual Teams

Virtual teams aren't a good fit for all organizations. Your company may be willing, but not ready — or perhaps it's the other way around. You may not have the technology to support virtual team adoption. Or your organization has the technology in place and employees are asking for it, but your co-located executive team is hesitant to agree to it.

The bottom line is that the decision to have virtual teams must be strategic, not tactical. It can't be driven by just one department, like the facilities department interested in space saving, IT interested in cost savings, or HR interested in better employee recruitment and retention. It must be intentional and thoughtful, endorsed from the top.

Whatever the situation, understand all the factors involved to see if your organization is ready to support having virtual teams. This chapter guides you through the top factors to consider so that you can determine your level of readiness. When you have all the pieces in place, virtual teams can be one of the greatest assets to your company.

Having Champions on the Executive Team

Deploying virtual teams throughout an organization can't be an ad hoc decision. It must have full executive support, and it must be supported with documented policies and practices so that each virtual team in each department in each location follows the same guidelines and receives the same level of support. If you've sold the benefits of virtual teams to your business leaders and they're positive and enthusiastic about launching virtual teams, you've secured support from the most integral group of champions that will help to ensure your teams get what they need to be set up for success.

WARNING

Even a few leaders not fully supporting the use of virtual teams in their organizations can derail the launch of other successful virtual teams. The lack of support or the disregard of your company policy on remote work, whether it's discrete or overt, can grow like a cancer in an organization and call into question the effectiveness of virtual teams.

Having Empowered Leaders

If you already have leaders who excel at managing their co-located team and are poised for a new adventure and team members are excited about the possibility to work remotely, you have a good chance of building a highly functional, high-performing virtual team. Virtual teams need managers who are both enthusiastic supporters and have the skills to effectively manage virtual teams. Be sure to get them the resources and training they need to hit the ground running and definitely have them read this book to put together their virtual team leadership strategy.

Leveraging a Supportive Culture

If you work at a company where it's not necessary for every decision to be run up the organizational hierarchy to get upper management's blessing and you encourage collaborative decision-making and trust employees to get the job done, then you most likely have the right culture to make virtual teams work. Company cultures where leveraging technology and providing flexibility are the norm, where people are rewarded on the quality of their work rather than the amount of time spent, where a healthy balance between work and home life is encouraged, are ready for virtual teams.

Willing to Invest in Technology

Moving teams to a virtual environment without providing the appropriate technology tools to ensure their collaboration and connectivity is like hiring a contractor for a kitchen renovation, but forbidding her to use power tools. Virtual teams don't thrive on conference calls alone. They need videoconferencing, shared calendars, collaboration tools, and project management tools to do their jobs. Virtual teams thrive in companies that enthusiastically support their virtual teams' technology needs. If you're ready to take the leap and make the investment, you're a good candidate for virtual teams. Chapter 16 examines your technology needs in greater detail.

Addressing Issues Early

In a virtual team environment, communication and engagement are critical to success. The isolation of working remotely creates its own literal separation, so figurative separation and disengagement can't be tolerated.

If you're in an organization that is quick to notice communication breakdowns or disengagement on a team and address it quickly, you'll be able to overcome two of the greatest challenges that virtual teams face. Chapter 2 addresses other challenges that you may face as a virtual team leader.

Being Prepared for the Logistical Set Up

Understanding that you'll need a comprehensive logistics plan to ensure your virtual team success is a first step in the right direction to move toward offering remote work options. The plan needs to include space planning and space scheduling if you have a hoteling option or space-sharing option, technology support for when hardware or software breaks down or needs updating, and HR support for benefits, payroll, and training. Other issues need to be included in the logistics plan, such as how to keep employees engaged with the larger organization and how to track expenses around travel, mobile phones, landlines, and office supplies.

Keeping the Team Focused

Companies often have to make decisions around shifting priorities when crises erupt. The all-hands-on-deck mentality is what can drive innovation and allow a company to resolve challenges efficiently. But that kind of urgent response is usually short term and designed to respond to a critical need. Companies that operate in fire-fighting mode all day everyday may not do well in a virtual environment. Conversely, if you work in an organization where leadership excels at keeping their team focused on top priorities by setting clear expectations, goals, and roles and is comfortable holding team members accountable, then the decision to deploy virtual teams will be strategic, thoughtful, and comprehensive.

Using an Onboarding Process

You never get a second chance to make a first impression. The old adage is never truer than with onboarding a new employee. Consider that nearly 70 percent of employees are more likely to stay with a company for three years if they experienced great onboarding. Those early days with a company are when employers need to win the hearts and minds of new employees. Onboarding is a critical process, both in a traditional office environment and on virtual teams. If your company and your leaders are prepared to provide a robust and comprehensive onboarding process to your virtual team members, then you are ready for virtual teams. Chapter 7 discusses the importance of onboarding new team members.

Training Virtual Team Leaders

Some of the top business schools in the country still teach a management philosophy that prioritizes heavy supervision, top-down, carrot-and-stick, competitive, out-of-sight, out-of-mind mentality, so it's not surprising that many traditional managers struggle with supervising virtual teams. Leaders of virtual teams need the requisite skills to lead a distributed workforce. These skills include being an excellent communicator, having a high degree of emotional intelligence, and being an expert collaborator. Virtual team leaders also need to establish clear roles and expectations — and then get out of the way.

REMEMBER

They must trust their team and instill that culture of trust throughout the team. It's important that the leader is intuitive, flexible, comfortable with hands-off management, and knowledgeable on the technology that connects the team. If your organization's leadership training has a focus on developing these key qualities in leaders, then your organization is preparing management to lead effectively in a virtual world.

Having a Clear Idea of Roles and Responsibilities

Recent research has shown that collaboration improves when the roles of individual team members are clearly defined and well understood. Without this clarity, team members waste energy negotiating roles or protecting turf, rather than focusing on the task. This role clarity, in fact, has been shown as *more important* to collaboration than having a clearly defined approach for achieving goals. And because collaboration is so critical to virtual teams, it follows that role clarity is essential. If you're clear on what roles and responsibilities each virtual team member will have and how work will flow through the team, then you're ready to launch virtual teams in your organization.

Index

A

absenteeism, 32
abusive behavior, 148
acceptance, 282
accountability
  culture of, creating, 138–140
  discussing with members, 325
  observable measures, 251–252
  personal disengagement,
    addressing, 193
  team versus individual, 234
acquisitions, 200–201
adjourning stage, 215
advocacy, 50
agendas for meetings, 202–203
agreements, team, 198–200, 332
alignment
  Alignment Funnel, 76–77
  with company vision and
    values, 76–78
  of culture with values, 153
  of goals, 86–87, 331
  personal disengagement,
    addressing, 193
all-hands meetings, 42
analytical culture, 152
applications of independent
    contractors, keeping, 118
assembling virtual teams, 18–19
assumptions, considering in
    communication, 226–227
asynchronous training, 259
augmented reality, training with,
    259–260
authentic leadership, 304
Ayers, Keith E., 307

B

baby boomers, 11, 166
background checks, 117
balance, maintaining, 16
Basecamp, 33
behavioral competencies,
    identifying needed,
    98–100
behavioral strengths, 104
bench strength, 140
benefits, 27, 111
Better Business Bureau, 117
Bloom, Jenny, 311
body language, 227
boundary management, 49–50,
    302–303
Boyer, Wendy, 251
brain drain, 47
brainstorming process, 239
brainstorming tools, 274
brand
  online presence, establishing,
    68–69
  portfolio, building, 67–68
  resume, rebuilding, 66–67
  technology, keeping up to date
    on, 69–70
briefing meeting, before
    interviews, 105
buddy system, 42, 128–130
bullying, 148
business insurance, 117
business strategy, alignment
    with, 27–28
business structures, 70

C

candidate interviews
  communication skills,
    assessing, 102–103
  cultural fit, assessing, 100–101
  engagement, assessing, 102
  expectations, discussing,
    107–108
  overview, 105
  preparing for, 105
  responses, evaluating,
    108–109
  self-direction, assessing, 102
  STAR interviewing method,
    105–107
cause and effect diagram, 239
cell phones, 61
champions, culture, 157–158
changes, adjusting to
  emotional resilience, boosting,
    282–283
  guiding principles, 289–291
  new leaders, 284–286
  new team goals, 286–287
  overview, 281
  reorganization, 287–289
  stages of change, 288
  in team membership, 281–284
character traits, 50–52
charters, team, 200–201
chat tools, 276
checking references, 109–110
check-ins, 43, 130
Chessler, Michelle Greene, 205
clarity, lack of, 186

C-level executives. *See* executives

cliques, discouraging, 217–218

cloud collaboration, 275

coaching, 127, 208, 211, 248

cohesiveness, building
expectations, discussing, 137–138
feedback and accountability, 138–140
overview, 137, 212
rotating leadership, 140–141
Tuckman Team Development model, 213–215

collaboration tools, 17, 272, 322

co-located team, 75

commanding culture, 151–152

commitment, 28–29

communication. *See also* communication agreements; feedback
after member leaves, 283–284
Communication Intelligence Model, 243
communication method matrix, 230
DISC assessment tool, 242
expectations, establishing, 39–40, 137–138
in global virtual team, 218–219
importance of, 225–226
issues with, 186
leadership skills, 177
outside of team, 325–326
priorities, clarity in, 80–81
projects, creating guidelines for, 322
proposal, addressing in, 59
purpose of team, sharing, 78–79
strategy for, 28, 332
with team, 19
techniques for, 226–227
text-only, 228–231
transition plan, 37–38

communication agreements
areas to focus on, 240–241
conflicts, handling, 238
meeting participation standards, 241–242
modes of communication, choosing, 235, 236–238
outside-of-team communication, 239–240
overview, 231, 235
problem-solving model, choosing, 238–239
response times, agreeing on, 235, 238

Communication Intelligence Model, 243

communication plan, 240–241

communication skills, 102–103

communication tools, training with, 255–256

community, sense of, 16

commuter savings, 32

company retreats, 42

companywide training on technology, 279

compensation, 111, 119–120

computer desk, 61

computers, 61

concentration, 48–49, 50

confidentiality, 115, 121–122

conflicts, addressing, 92, 238

connection culture
connection activities, 296–297
isolationism, fighting, 43–44
members, connecting, 42–43, 217
organization, connecting with, 41–44
rapport, building, 298
reach-out strategy, 298–299
role of leaders, 295–296
trust, building, 211, 223–224
at Zapier, 311–312

contracts
deciding on need for, 114–116
for independent contractors, 118–119, 120–121
overview, 27

control-based versus trust-based leadership, 181–183

core values, 132

cost savings, 14, 31, 57, 63

CQ. *See* cultural intelligence

Creately, 320

credentials of independent contractors, checking, 117

cross-cultural teams
benefits of, 159
challenges of, 160
cultural appreciation, practicing, 218–219
cultural intelligence, building, 168–174
miscommunication in, 188
overview, 158–159
predictors of team success, 172–173
training programs, 173–174

cross-functional relationships, building, 64

cultural appreciation, practicing, 218–219

cultural bias, 39

cultural diversity. *See also* cross-cultural teams
connection, creating, 217
cultural appreciation, practicing, 218–219
cultural intelligence, building, 168–174
miscommunication due to, 188

cultural fit, hiring for, 100–101

cultural intelligence (CQ)
cross-cultural training, 173–174
cultural norms, sharing, 170
cultural sensitivity, 171–172
overview, 168–169

predictors of team success, 172–173

team members, getting to know, 169–170

cultural sensitivity, 171–172, 259

culture, team. *See* team culture

CYA culture, 147

D

data protection, 115

decision-making process, 212

delegating, 322–325

Deloitte Consulting's Center for the Edge, 306

desks, 61

development, stages of, 213–215

direct managers, working with, 184–185

direction, lack of, 186

directive style, 179–180

disbelief phase, 251

DISC assessment tool, 242

discipline, 16

disengagement, addressing, 192–193

dispersed teams, 11

distraction management, 48–49, 50

distributed teams, 11

diversity

appreciation by leaders, 177

cross-cultural teams, 158–160

cultural intelligence, building, 168–174

gender differences, 162–164

generational, 165–168

miscommunication due to, 188

overview, 161–162

predictors of team success, 172–173

downward communication, 239, 240

dream team traits, 136

E

early adopters, 277

earnings, 47

Eckhart, Alex, 65

email, 236–237

emotional intelligence, 18, 209

emotional reflective listening, 288–289

emotional resilience, boosting, 282–283

emotions, observing, 251–252

empathetic listening, 288–289

empathy, 282

employee resource groups, 42

employees

benefits of virtual teams, 9

full-time, offering remote work options to, 30

independent contractors versus, 114–116

skill gap analysis, 36–37

willingness to switch to virtual team, 26

employers, benefits of virtual teams for, 9

employment contract, 114, 115, 118–119, 120–121

employment negotiations, 111

encouragement, 43

energizing culture, 152

engagement

of candidates, assessing, 103–105

challenge of, 191–192

culture of, 26–27, 150

goals and expectations, building with, 197

incentives, 43

new employees, discussing with, 131

observable measures, 248, 251–252

passion versus, 306–307

personal disengagement, addressing, 192–193

proposal, addressing in, 58–59

purpose of team, defining, 193–196

recognition, 196

team agreements, 198–200

team charters, 200–201

team values, building with, 195–196

virtual meetings, conducting, 201–204

virtual meetings, etiquette of, 205–206

environmental benefits, 33–34

executives

changing perspective on virtual teams, 183–184

data valued by, 249

managing perceptions of, 333–334

support for virtual teams, 336

expectations, establishing, 137–138, 197, 231–232

F

Facebook, 71

face-to-face meetings, 193, 219–223

facilitative style, 180–181

family, distractions from, 49

feedback

accountability culture, creating, 138–140, 234

expectations, establishing, 231–232

five-step model, 233–234

frequency of, 231

old-school style management, 178

performance discussions, 232–233

trust, building, 209

two-way, 232–233

feedback loop, 227

file sharing, 275

filing cabinets, 62

Fired, Jason, 33

first 90 days

  focusing on, 130–131

  training during, 254–257

fishbone diagram, 239

Five Behaviors of Cohesive Team, 83

Five whys model, 239

five-step feedback model, 233–234

flash polling tools, 274

flat structure, 125

flex jobs, 12

flexibility, of leaders, 19, 176

FlexJobs, 30, 59–60, 70, 97

flowchart, 239

focus, maintaining, 16, 48–49, 50

Form 1096, 118

forming stage, 213–214

foundational best practices

  alignment, 76–78

  framework, choosing, 82–85

  goals, establishing, 85–89

  member roles, determining, 89–92

  overview, 75–76

  priorities, clarity in, 80–81

  purpose of team, communicating, 78–79

  purpose of team, defining, 76

  reputation of team, 81–82

frameworks, 82–85, 125

freelancing. *See also* virtual work

  business structures, 70

  skills, assessing, 50–51

  world travel opportunities, 48, 65

future focused feedback, 139

G

Gain the Edge, 104–105

gender diversity, 162–164

generational bias, 39

generational shift

  communication strategies, 28

  connecting with generations, 165–168

  flexible job trend, 60

  Generation X, 11, 166–167

  Generation Y, 167

  Generation Z, 11, 165, 168

  Millennials, 11, 167

  overview, 11

geographically dispersed team, 11, 217, 218–219

Gilbert, Scott, 200–201

global outsourcing, 12

global virtual team, 11

Global Workplace Analytics, 31, 34

globalization, 9–11

goals

  alignment of, 86–87, 331

  changes in, adjusting to, 286–287

  defining, 27–28, 34–35, 85

  engagement, building with, 197

  motivating, 87

  resources, determining needs, 88–89

  SMART, 88

  systems thinking, 91

Goldilocks effect, 40–41

Google, 136

growth, need for, 308–309

H

hands-off style, 181

Hansson, David, 33

happiness, 47

health insurance, 120

healthy cultures, 149–150

healthy lifestyle, focusing on, 300–303

hierarchical structure, 124

hierarchy of needs, fulfilling, 314–317

hiring. *See* recruiting

historical perspective, 10

holacracy, 125

home office

  boundary management, 302–303

  essential items, 61–62

  setup, 39

  visiting members in, 44

horizontal communication, 239, 240

hoteling, 12, 62–64

HR policies, alignment with culture, 156–157

humor, 283

I

icebreakers, 202

icons, used in book, 4

ICs. *See* independent contractors

important versus urgent tasks, 80–81

in real life (IRL) meetings, 220–223

incentives, engagement, 43

income, 47, 111

independent contractors (ICs)

  compensation, 119–120

  contracts, deciding on need for, 114–116

  contracts, what to include in, 118–119, 120–121

  credentials, checking, 117

  employees versus, 114–116

  insurance, 120

  noncompete agreements, 122

  nondisclosure agreements, 121–122

overview, 113–114

record-keeping, 117–118

innovation zone, 252

in-person meetings, 127, 187, 219–220

inquiry and solutions phase, 252

insider, need to be, 309

instant messaging, 236, 276

insurance, 27, 117, 120

Integro Leadership, 83

Intel Corporation, 17

intent of communication, considering, 226

interactive huddles, virtual, 44

internal control, 282

Internet connection, 29, 61

interviewing candidates

communication skills, assessing, 102–103

cultural fit, assessing, 100–101

engagement, assessing, 102

expectations, discussing, 107–108

overview, 105

preparing for, 105

responses, evaluating, 108–109

self-direction, assessing, 102

STAR interviewing method, 105–107

investment phase, 252

IRL (in real life) meetings, 220–223

IRS website, 116

Ishikawa diagram, 239

isolationism, fighting, 43, 223

IT department, including in decision about technology, 269–271

J

job ads, creating, 95–96

job description, 97–98

job satisfaction, 47

K

keywords, including in resume, 66

kickoff session, 319–320

Kubler-Ross, Elizabeth, 288

L

language, effect of texting on, 229

language differences, 206, 218

laptops, 61

large teams, 40–41

leadership

authentic, 304

choosing right leaders, 330

common virtual team issues, dealing with, 185–188

connection culture, creating, 295–299

control-based versus trust-based, 181–183

cultural boundaries, pushing, 183–184

data valued by, 249–250

delegating, 322–325

directive style, 179–180

executive expectations, working with, 183–184

facilitative style, 180–181

flawed, 27

hands-off style, 181

healthy lifestyle, focusing on, 300–303

legacy, discovering, 303–304

management versus, 179

managing up, 184–185

new leaders, building relationships as, 284–286

old-school style, 175–176, 178

qualities of successful, 176–177

rotating, 140–141, 208

support for virtual teams, 336

training on management of virtual teams, 26

transitioning to virtual, 183–185

Leadership Trust Scorecard, 210–211

learning, need for, 308–309

learning labs, 278

legacy, discovering, 303–304

legal issues, 39

Lencioni, Patrick, 83

liability insurance, 120

lighting in office, 62

limited liability company (LLC), 70

Lino, 200

listening skills, 177, 288–289

local virtual team, 11

logistics plan, 337

lunches, virtual, 92

M

managers. *See* leadership

Manifesto for Agile Software Development, 25

matrix structure, 124

meaningful work, need to do, 310

measures. *See* tracking progress

meeting team members, 127

meetings

all-hands, 42

briefing, before interviews, 105

conducting, 201–204

efficiency of, 32

etiquette of, 205–206

in-person, 127, 187, 219–220

interactive huddles, 44

participation, standards for, 241–242

personal disengagement, addressing, 193

in real life, 220–223

status update, 321

tools for, 274

values, identifying in, 196

members, team. *See* team members

men, benefits brought to team by, 162–163

mentoring, 208, 211, 255, 277

mergers, 200–201

micromanaging, 19, 26

milestone accomplishments, 196

Millennials, 11, 167

mind map, 35–36

mindfulness, 282

mistakes, learning from, 209, 218

mobile options, 276

modes of communication, agreeing on, 230, 235, 236–238

money management, 52

morale, loss of, 187

Morgan, Nozomi, 172–173

motivation
engaged versus passionate team members, 306–307
hierarchy of needs, fulfilling, 314–317
overview, 305
Passion Pyramid, 314–317
passionate teams, creating, 307–312
positive psychology, using, 312–317
recognition, as tool for, 314–317

N

NDAs (nondisclosure agreements), 121–122

new hire training schedule, 254–257

new product launch, 30

Niles, Jack, 10

90 days, first. *See* first 90 days

noncompete agreements, 115, 122

nondisclosure agreements (NDAs), 121–122

norming stage, 214–215

O

observable data, 251–252

office chairs, 62

old-school style management, 175–176, 178

onboarding process
buddy system, 42, 128–130
creating, 126–128
first 90 days, focusing on, 130–131
at Gain the Edge, 104
general discussion, 125–126
in healthy culture, 150
for new leaders, 285
readiness for virtual teams, 338
sharing with candidates, 95
strategy for, 333
training during first 90 days, 254–257

one-on-one meetings, 196

one-on-one recognition, 317

online job sites, 96–97

online presence, 68–69, 71, 117

online training, 258–259

opposition phase, 251

optimism, 282

organizational skills, 62

organizations
alignment with, 76–78
connecting teams to, 42
hoteling, 62–63
inclusion of virtual teams, 50
readiness for virtual teams, 335–339

outsourcing, global, 12

P

Padilla, Jim, 104–105

Pareto chart, 239

parking expenses, reduction in, 32

participation in meetings, standards for, 241–242

passionate teams
engaged versus passionate members, 306–307
Passion Pyramid, 307–310
passionate culture, creating, 311–312

patience, in leaders, 177

pay, 111, 119–120

peer-to-peer recognition, 317

performance discussions, 232–233

performance-related metrics, 247

performing stage, 215

personal life, impact on, 48–50

personal relationships, building, 42–43

personal websites, 68

personalization, team, 43

phone calls, 237–238

phones, 61

pilot, 56

portfolio, building, 67–68

positive psychology
hierarchy of needs, fulfilling, 312–314
overview, 312
recognition, as motivational technique, 314–317

printers, 62

priorities, 80–81, 91, 186

problem-solving model, choosing, 238–239

productivity, 31

progress, tracking. *See* tracking progress

progress update meetings, 321

project management tools, 247–248, 272–273

project workflow. *See* workflow

proposing arrangement to employer
  concerns, addressing, 58–59
  focusing on benefits, 56–58
  overview, 52
  preparing proposal, 52–56
  proposal form, 53–55

psychological safety, 136

purpose of communication, considering, 226

purpose of team
  alignment, 76–78
  communicating to team, 78–79
  defining, 34–35, 76, 79, 193–196
  priorities, clarity in, 80–81
  reputation, building, 81–82

PXT Select, 100

Q

qualities
  needed in remote workers, 101–105
  of successful leaders, 176–177

R

Raindance Communications, 206

rapport, building, 298

reach-out strategy, 298–299

readiness for virtual teams, 335–339

real estate savings, 31

recognition, 43, 196, 314–317

records of independent contractors, keeping, 117–118

recruiting
  behavioral competencies, identifying, 98–100

benefits of virtual teams, 9

candidate interviews, 105–109

cultural fit, hiring for, 100–101

finding right people, importance of, 93–94

job ads, creating, 95–96

job offers, 110–111

online job sites, 96–97

overview, 32–33

qualities needed in remote workers, 101–105

reference checks, 109–110

remote workers, for special projects, 30

selection tools, using, 100

skills, identifying needed, 97–98

skills needed in virtual teams, 330–331

talent, attracting, 94–97

training during first 90 days, 254–257

values of candidates, assessing, 154

work samples, reviewing, 109

reference checks, 109–110, 117

relationships, building personal, 42–43

Remember icon, 4

remote office
  boundary management, 302–303
  essential items, 61–62
  overview, 16
  setup, 39
  visiting, 44

remote work. *See* virtual work

Remotive website, 97

reorganization, adjusting to, 287–289

reputation, building, 81–82

resilience, boosting, 282–283

resource groups, employee, 42

resource needs, determining, 88–89

respect, 217–218, 307–308

response times, agreeing on, 235, 238

restructuring, adjusting to, 287–289

result-orientation, 177

resumes, 66–67, 118

retention, 32–33

retirement, phasing into, 47–48

retreats, company, 42

reviewing work samples, 109, 117

rewards, 91

Reynolds, Brie Weiler, 59–60

risk taking, encouraging, 212

role clarity, 89–92, 194–195, 339

rotating leadership, 140–141, 208

S

safety, psychological, 136

samples of work, reviewing, 109, 117

scanners, 62

schedule, control of, 46–47

seasonal staffing, 30

selection tools, using, 100

self-analysis, 50–51

self-care, 283

self-direction, 47, 102

self-discipline, 16

sense of community, 16

sense of humor, 283

seven-step method for prioritization, 80–81

shared calendar tools, 273

SHRM (Society for Human Resource Management), 100, 126

sick time savings, 32

size of teams, 40–41

skills
  assessing, 50–52
  communication, 102–103
  listening, 177, 288–289
  needed in virtual teams, 330–331
  organizational, 62
  recruitment process, identifying in, 97–98
  skill gap analysis, 36–37
Skipthedrive website, 97
small teams, 40–41
SMART goals, 88
social capital, 208
social interaction of team, 187
social learning, 264
social loafing, 41
social media
  choosing platforms, 275
  employee use of, 115
  independent contractors, checking out on, 117
  online presence, establishing, 68–69
Society for Human Resource Management (SHRM), 100, 126
sole proprietorship, 70
special projects, hiring remote workers for, 30
Staff website, 97
stages of change, 288
Stages of Team Development, 83
stakeholders, 325–326
STAR interviewing method, 105–107
status update meetings, 321
storming stage, 214
strategic alignment, 27–28
strengths of members, leveraging, 215–216
strengths-based assessment, 216
stress, reduced levels of, 47

structure, team. *See* team structure
success measures, 119
support from others, importance of, 283
supportive culture, 152
survey study, 20–21
systems thinking, 91–92, 140

T

tasks, assigning, 320–321
teach-back method, 260
team agreements, 198–200, 332
Team Alignment Survey, 83
team charters, 200–201
team culture
  analytical, 152
  assessing, 150–151
  building, 153–155
  commanding, 151–152
  cross-cultural teams, 158–160
  culture champions, 157–158
  discussing with candidates, 95
  diversity in, 47
  energizing, 152
  general discussion, 18, 37–38
  guiding principles, establishing, 155–156
  healthy, 149–150
  HR policies, alignment with, 156–157
  importance of, 145–146
  new employees, discussing with, 131
  new leaders, adjusting to, 285–286
  supportive, 152
  toxic, 147–148
team frameworks, 82–85, 125
team members
  changes, adjusting to, 281–284
  characteristics of successful, 50–51

connection activities, 298–299
  cultural intelligence, building, 169–170
  data valued by, 250–251
  diversity among, 47
  face-to-face meetings with, 219–223
  framework of team, choosing, 85
  personal disengagement, addressing, 192–193
  recognition of, 314–317
  role clarity, 89–92, 194–195, 339
  skills needed, 330–331
  social interaction between, 187
  strengths of, leveraging, 215–216
  systems thinking, 91–92
Team Performance Model, 83
team personalization, 43
team purpose. *See* purpose of team
team spirit, loss of, 187
team structure
  common structures, 124–125
  frameworks, 125
  overview, 40–41, 123–124
team values
  culture, alignment with, 153
  defining, 132–135, 331
  dream team traits, 136
  engagement, building with, 195–196
  living, 135–136
  overview, 132
technology
  assessing needs before choosing, 266–267
  brainstorming tools, 274
  challenges related to, 29
  chat tools, 276
  checklist of features, creating, 268–269
  choosing, 41

cloud collaboration, 275

collaboration tools, 17, 272

companywide training on, 279

face-to-face interaction through, 25

file sharing, 275

flash polling tools, 274

growth in virtual teams due to, 9

importance of choosing correct, 266, 329–330

instant messaging, 276

investing in, 26, 337

IT department, including in decision about, 269–271

keeping up to date on, 69–70

leadership skills, 20, 177

learning to use, 188

meeting tools, 274

mobile options, 276

opinion of team members, listening to, 269

overview, 265–266

project management tools, 272–273

shared calendar tools, 273

social media, 275

time-tracking tools, 273

training programs, 263, 276–279

trends in, 267–268

videoconferencing, 276

virtual meetings, problems during, 203–204

workflow management tools, 273

TEEM, 290–291

telecommuting, 10, 12. *See also* virtual work

telehealth, 25

telephones, 61

telework. *See* virtual work

temporary assignments, testing good fit through, 19

1099-MISC form, 118

text-only communication, 228–231

Thomas, Trish, 290–291

360 process, 216

Time magazine, 228

time management, 46, 48–49

time-tracking tools, 247–248, 273

Tip icon, 4

tone of voice, loss in texting, 229

toxic cultures, 147–148

tracking progress
coaching with data, 248

collaborative tools, 322

engagement levels, observing, 251–252

executives, data important to, 249

importance of, 245–246

leaders, data important to, 249–250

performance-related metrics, 247

project management tools, importance of, 247–248

team members, data important to, 250–251

training
augmented reality, using for, 259–260

evaluating effectiveness of, 260–262

during first 90 days, 254–257

importance of, 253–254

ongoing, 257–258

online, 258–259

readiness for virtual teams, 338–339

supporting struggling members, 262–263

teach-back method, 260

on technology, 276–279

technology issues, 263

veteran team members, 263–264

virtual reality, using for, 259–260

training plan, 127

transition plan
communicating about adoption of virtual teams, 37–38

considerations for, 26

purpose and goals, defining, 34–35

roles, establishing, 35–37

skill gap analysis, 36–37

transition routine, work-to-home, 49

transparency, 28

travel, 48, 65

Trello, 17

trust
building and repairing, 208–209

cohesiveness, behaviors that build, 212–215

connection culture, creating, 223–224

cultural appreciation, practicing, 218–219

face time, giving members, 219–223

foundation for, setting, 211–212

lack of, 187

Leadership Trust Scorecard, 210–211

new leaders, building relationships as, 284–286

overview, 136, 207–208

respect, encouraging, 217–218

role of leaders, 27

strengths of members, leveraging, 215–216

trust-based versus control-based leadership, 181–183

Tuckman Team Development model, 213–215

in virtual employees, 14, 19, 176

Tuckman, Bruce, 83
Tuckman Team Development model, 213–215
turnover costs, reduction in, 32
two-way feedback, 232–233

U

Uber, 147
unified communications (UC), 95
upward communication, 239, 240
Upwork.com, 30
urgent versus important tasks, 80–81

V

values, team. *See* team values
veteran team members, training, 263–264
video communication, 17, 202, 223, 276. *See also* virtual meetings
virtual lunches, 92
virtual meetings
  conducting, 201–204
  etiquette of, 205–206
  participation and engagement, ensuring, 202–203
  technological issues, 203–204
virtual reality, training with, 259–260
virtual teams
  assembling, 18–19
  benefits of, 13–14
  common issues, dealing with, 185–188
  concepts related to, 11–12
  disadvantages of, 14–15

flaws of, 27–29
globalization effect, 9–11
growth in, 7–9
historical perspective, 10
incorporating, 29–34
key considerations, 16–18, 25–27
planning for, 34–38
readiness for, 335–339
setting up, 38–40
statistics supporting, 20–21
virtual work
  benefits of, 46–48
  business structures, 70
  flexible jobs, state of, 59–60
  freelancing, 50–51
  home offices, 61–62
  hoteling, 62–64
  online presence, establishing, 68–69
  overview, 45–46
  personal life, impact on, 48–50
  portfolio, building, 67–68
  proposal form, 53–55
  proposing arrangement to employer, 52, 55–59
  resume, rebuilding, 66–67
  self-analysis, 50–51
  technology, keeping up to date on, 69–70
  travel opportunities, 65
  work-life balance, focusing on, 71–72
Virtualvocations website, 97
vision statement, 331
voice mail, 237–238
voluntary participation, 212
volunteer groups for technology, 70

W

W-9 Form, 118
Warning icon, 4
websites, personal, 68
welcome care package, 126–127
wellness, focusing on, 300–303
Wells Fargo, 147
Weworkremotely website, 97
winning team, need to be on, 310
women, benefits brought to team by, 162–163
work desk, 61
work environment, 16
work samples, reviewing, 109, 117
workflow
  agreeing on process, 333
  assigning tasks, 320–321
  collaborative tracking tools, 322
  communication guidelines, 322
  delegating, 322–325
  external communication, 325–326
  kickoff session, 319–320
  overview, 319
  progress update meetings, 321
workflow management tools, 273
working from home. *See* virtual work
Workingnomads website, 97
work-life balance, 71–72, 178
workload, reassesing, 193
workspace, 16, 61–62, 65
world travel, 48, 65

Z

Zapier, 17, 311

About the Author

Tara Powers, team builder, leadership champion, strategic advisor, and speaker, is on a mission to help fast-growing companies and socially responsible organizations to lead innovatively and authentically and in alignment with their values.

As a 20-year talent development professional, Tara has worked with more than 200 companies and 15,000 leaders around the globe, building custom programs and launching coaching and training initiatives that deliver high touch and high impact. She is the founder of Powers Resource Center (http://www.Powers ResourceCenter.com) and is a sought-after speaker at leadership conferences, executive strategy meetings, and corporate team building events.

For the past four years in a row, Tara's leadership programs have earned the prestigious recognition as a Top 10 Leadership 500 Award winner by HR.com, with more than 4,500 companies applying and 600,000 people voting on the programs. Tara has consistently served as a judge for the well-known Brandon Hall Group Excellence Awards that focuses on talent development programs and attracts entrants from leading corporations around the world.

In addition to *Virtual Teams For Dummies*, Tara is the co-author of *Success University for Women™ in Business*, an international best seller. She's also a Five Behaviors of a Cohesive Team Authorized facilitator and Everything DISC Solutions provider.

Tara's commitment to her clients is to serve as a catalyst for change, to be a business partner that takes your team collaboration, employee engagement and leadership credibility to the next level, and to deliver results that make you want to do that happy dance. Tara resides in Colorado, with her husband, two beautiful daughters, and a Catahoula rescue puppy named Houston.

Dedication

To my husband Dan and my two "sweet peanuts" Kyla and Fallon. I've spent close to 20 years working virtually, and I've been involved in all sorts of extraordinary and innovative projects. Nevertheless, writing this book took a lot of my time and dedicated focus and required your ongoing support daily. I could never adequately express the love and gratitude I have for your understanding and care and how you cheered me on and lifted me up when I didn't think I could write one more page. Every single day you make this journey called life more amazing than I could have ever hoped for.

Author's Acknowledgments

Thanks to Tracy Boggier, Executive Editor at John Wiley & Sons for reaching out to me, convincing me I could write this book, and getting as excited about this title as I was. To Chad Sievers my project editor who kept me on track when I didn't think it was possible, and to the rest of the Wiley team who helped make this book a reality.

This book would still be on my bucket list if it weren't for the amazing work of Kelly Doyle Duncan, principal at Doyle Duncan Communications LLC. Kelly supported me as my content strategist, sanity checker, and cheerleader. I was able to leverage her 25 years of experience as a corporate writer, editor, and master's degree holder in journalism to help get this book across the finish line.

I want to acknowledge my personal and professional support system that encouraged me throughout this journey. My mom, Sheila Murray, my closest friends Stacy Strayer and Tanya Gardner, and my rock-star team Ashley Winby, Jessica Granish, Jessica Gorrell, Alex Eckhardt, Amy Heinzman, and Brenda Abdilla. Your thoughtfulness, coaching, and support kept me moving in the direction of my goal. Special thanks to my valued clients and colleagues who agreed to be interviewed and featured as a case study in this book. You made the concepts and strategies in this book come to life, and you inspire me to continue to do my work every day.

Publisher's Acknowledgments

Senior Acquisitions Editor: Tracy Boggier

Project Editor: Chad R. Sievers

Technical Editor: Hassan Osman

Production Editor: Siddique Shaik

Cover Image: R_Lan/Shutterstock